Science, Technology,
and American Foreign Policy

Science, Technology, and American Foreign Policy

Eugene B. Skolnikoff

The M.I.T. Press
Massachusetts Institute of Technology
Cambridge, Massachusetts, and London, England

To my Mother and Father

the Office of Science and Technology) are presented in the pages following, but that is only an incidental purpose of this book.

For the nearly five years I served on the staff, working within the White House structure, with government departments and agencies, and with the scientific community at large, my major responsibility was a concern for many of the interactions between science and the nation's foreign affairs. During that period, which proved to be an exhilarating learning experience, it became apparent that the role of science in foreign affairs was both more significant and more subtle than was generally appreciated at the time either among scientists or among those in the foreign affairs community. Scientists tended to focus primarily on international scientific activities, to the neglect of the many other more direct interactions between science and foreign policy. Or else they became heavily involved in specific issues in military, disarmament, or similar areas and had little opportunity to generalize to other foreign policy interests. Nonscientists with foreign policy responsibility were all too often unaware of the relevance of scientific elements to their major concerns or thought of the role of the scientist or engineer as that of an expert to be called in from time to time to advise on narrowly defined questions.

These attitudes seemed to me to be deficient for what I believed to be the growing relevance of science and technology to many of the central areas of foreign policy; this deficiency could have serious consequences in the future. The idea of a book to lay out my conception of the relationship of science to foreign affairs and to evaluate existing policy machinery formed at

that time. The need for such an analysis was emphasized when I realized that there was astonishingly little in print that seemed to me to have the proper focus
or the requisite quality. When M.I.T. offered an opportunity to come to Cambridge to write such a book
and, at the same time, present some experimental
courses in the subject, I decided to make the attempt.

M.I.T.'s science and public policy program in its
Political Science Department offered a natural and,
in fact, unsurpassed home for the necessary research
and writing and also for experimenting with new
courses. Professor Robert C. Wood, now on leave as
Under Secretary of the Department of Housing and
Urban Development in Washington but at that time
engaged in launching the science and public policy
program, invited me to the Institute and offered creative help, criticism, and encouragement throughout
the work; quite clearly it would not have been accomplished, perhaps not even undertaken, without his
support.

The Rockefeller Foundation, and especially Dr.
George Harrar, provided the means to make my early
stay possible. Dr. Harrar's personal interest was also
instrumental in convincing me at the beginning that
the task should be undertaken. In the later stages of
the work, the Center for Space Research at M.I.T.,
funded by NASA, provided the necessary unfettered
support. The willingness, and even enthusiasm, of the
Space Agency and the M.I.T. Center to encourage
social scientists to examine objectively relevant social
and political issues is a hopeful sign for our future
ability to cope with the implications of a rapidly advancing technology.

For my early exposure to the subject, and for continuing personal advice and inspiration, I have three remarkable men to thank: Dr. James R. Killian, Professor George Kistiakowsky, and M.I.T. Provost Jerome Wiesner, the first three of the President's Special Assistants for Science and Technology. I worked under all three in Washington and with them subsequently in Cambridge, and have enormous respect for their very different but unique competences. Their friendship is highly valued.

Many others, particularly on the President's Science Advisory Committee and in the Department of State, have contributed to this work—some knowingly, some unwittingly—some who will be in agreement with the ideas expressed, and some opposed. Not all can be credited, but I cannot fail to mention Dr. Detlev W. Bronk, who was chairman of the first PSAC Panel on Science and Foreign Affairs, and Dr. Jerrold Zacharias, with both of whom I worked on many different problems, not always in perfect agreement, but always with a high measure of excitement and originality. Also, several of my colleagues on the staff in the White House were instrumental in helping to develop my ideas, most notably David Z. Beckler, Spurgeon M. Keeny, David Z. Robinson, George W. Rathjens, and Robert N. Kreidler.

I want also to thank Mr. Howard J. Lewis of the National Academy of Sciences and my colleagues at M.I.T., William Kaufmann, Ithiel de Sola Pool, and Norman Padelford, who read and criticized early drafts of the manuscript. Judith Lang was responsible with high skill and good humor for the extensive typing and related work involved, and my wife and family suffered without complaint the long hours at various stages of the work. But, of course, I am alone responsible for what is contained within.

Eugene B. Skolnikoff

Cambridge, Massachusetts
September 1966

Contents

PART I

The New Relationship

1

The Changing Ingredients of Foreign Policy

It is a common observation that the progress of science and technology is the predominant force causing today's unprecedented rate of change in man's physical and social environment. Nowhere are the changes more evident than in international affairs, where the scientific and technological developments during and since World War II have sharply altered former relationships among nations, overturned traditional measures of power and influence, and made the future a hostage to the scientific discoveries that are uncertain in form but sure to come.

It was the atomic bomb that in the public mind swept away the elegant but fading separation of science and international affairs. But developments in many other areas — jet aircraft, nuclear submarines, missiles, space technology, and high-speed communications — were equally responsible.

Science and technology affect the international scene not only as the causes of change, however. They also have entered into the substance of international relations and thus into the heart of the foreign policy process in all nations, and particularly in technologically advanced nations such as the United States. With increasing momentum, the subject matter in international relations, the execution of foreign policies, and even the conduct of diplomacy directly involve, or are heavily influenced by, science and technology. The foreign policy process today must face issues, facts, and relationships that are entirely new or startlingly altered from the past. Moreover, the resolution of many of these issues is highly sensitive to a rapidly changing technological environment — an environment changing either by design or, more often, in unplanned and uncertain ways.

There has been little systematic effort to probe the character of the relationship of science and technology to the substance of foreign policy, although there have been intensive studies in depth of some of the new issues of foreign policy, such as atomic energy or space exploration. Broader studies that attempt to examine the actual interactions of science and technology with foreign affairs are sadly lacking.

The absence of such systematic study is of concern in its own right, for the pervasiveness of the relationship indicates that it ought in principle to be developed and more widely understood. A more immediate practical motive for mounting such a study is the need to evaluate the effectiveness of the mechanisms in the U.S. Government designed to cope with relevant aspects of science and technology in the formulation of foreign policy. Are these mechanisms adequate to the task? Has there been real recognition of the opportunities science and technology offer as new instruments of policy? How well is the government able to recognize and plan for the uncertain technological future?

There is, in fact, ample justification for concern that the foreign policy organs of the American government, and particularly the Department of State, are not adequately organized to deal with science and technology in the formulation and execution of foreign policy. Several important innovations in the government have been made in recent years for the purpose of coupling science to policy making more effectively, but the results of these innovations are uneven. In particular, the Secretary of State's role as chief foreign policy adviser to the President is in increasing jeopardy because the Department has been unable to find ways to develop the necessary scientific/political competence. As many of the issues that face the Department come to include highly sophisticated scientific or technological elements, its ability to keep itself free of domination by the more technical agencies of government depends directly on its understanding of the interaction of science and foreign policy, and its own ability to deal with that interaction. President Johnson's directive early in 1966 for a broader role for the Secretary of State will have a hollow ring if that understanding and ability are not better achieved.[1]

The objective of this study will therefore be twofold: first, to provide that systematic analysis of the relationship of science and technology to foreign affairs that

[1] *The New York Times,* March 5, 1966, p. 1.

is a necessary prerequisite to understanding; and second, to explain and evaluate the organization, within selected government agencies, designed to reflect that relationship in the policy process.

A PATTERN OF INTERACTION

Many of the central issues of foreign policy, such as military affairs, arms control, international influence and prestige, and foreign economic assistance, have important, occasionally dominating, scientific or technological elements. Other areas of foreign policy concern may also have significant scientific or technological elements, even though the relevance of those elements may not be as obvious or as persuasive.

As a way of ordering the discussion, it is useful to make a gross classification of foreign policy issues according to their technical content. In effect, such a classification is a guide to the probability that the scientific or technological aspects will be relevant in specific kinds of issues, and thus a guide to those areas that call for extensive analysis.

Five categories of foreign policy issues can be enumerated:

1. *Issues associated with dominant technical objectives:* Those issues in which the *technical* objectives, even if established to achieve basic political goals, set the framework for policy making. Space and the peaceful exploitation of atomic energy are good examples. So, too, is the advancement of science in programs such as those of the International Geophysical Year.
2. *Issues of a political nature heavily dependent*

on scientific considerations: Those issues that arise because of, or have been significantly altered by, advances in science and technology and that continue to be sensitive to scientific considerations. In distinction from the first category, the political objectives here more dominantly set the framework. National security policy is a good example, as are issues associated with international organizations or exploitation of ocean resources. Included as well would be the issues that arise from the emergence of scientists as an influential pressure group concerned with international political problems.

3. *Issues of a political nature not sensitive to technical factors:* Those issues that may have been altered in a general way by advances in science and technology, or that may even have arisen because of advances in science and technology, but that in the short run are not heavily dependent on technical variables. The problem of disposing of surplus agricultural products in other countries is a good example.

4. *Issues associated with the application of scientific methods to the policy process:* Those issues and opportunities that grow out of the application of the techniques and analytical tools of the sciences to foreign policy problems. These are essentially issues in the social sciences: the validity and limitations of simulation techniques, war games, and survey analysis.

5. *Issues associated with the implications of future developments in science and technology:*

Issues arising from possible or probable developments in science and technology. The international implications of control of the weather or control over man's genetic patterns are examples, as are more far-reaching queries about national freedom of action, control of territory and decentralized decision making on the international scene in an era in which the developments of science and technology may have altered traditional concepts.

There are no hard and fast separations between these categories for they are designed to be useful for analysis rather than absolute. In most cases, it is the perspective from which the issue is viewed that determines the category in which it should be considered. If broken down far enough, every technical program of the government could be seen as complete unto itself, with its technical objectives dominating associated political issues. Carried to the other extreme, every government program is ultimately carried out for a political purpose, even the support of basic research, in which case it could be said that technical objectives never set the framework within which policy must be considered.

Neither extreme is useful as a point of departure. The classification presented here proves workable and meaningful for purposes of analysis and to obtain a rough structuring of the subject. Parts II and III of this study will be devoted to the development of the first two categories, although many of the ideas presented will also bear on the last category — that most elusive and speculative subject of the implications for world affairs of future developments in science and technology. The concluding chapter of this study will also be concerned with that last category.

One consideration that must be borne in mind when assigning issues to specific categories is the uncertainty associated with initial judgments as to the relevance of science and technology. The seemingly technical nature of an issue, say international atomic energy policy, is not always a good indicator of the actual importance or relevance of technical considerations of specific facets of the subject. Policy issues with respect to the International Atomic Energy Agency, for example, are often concerned with administrative, budgetary or political matters in which the scientific aspects of the exploitation of atomic energy are of minor relevance.

The reverse is also true. That is, the seeming lack of relevance of scientific considerations is not a sure proof that they are not important. A good example is the planning of policy for international trade negotiations such as the "Kennedy-round" of tariff talks. On the surface, scientific aspects would appear to be of minor importance. Yet such negotiations are planning for trade patterns for many years in the future. It is entirely possible, even likely, that scientific developments now in process will have a profound effect on the export or import interests of quite a few countries, and within a very few years.

And, what is of greater importance, it may be possible consciously to direct R & D resources toward a particular objective that would affect trade patterns in desirable ways. An example would be the acceleration of oceanographic research off a nation's coast in an effort to make that country self-sufficient in (or even an exporter of) fish and protein resources. Another example would be a domestic R & D program aimed at finding a substitute for a necessary but politically costly import.

Thus, scientific and technological factors may be highly relevant to some part of an issue, even when a first look would not have indicated the need for inclusion of technical elements. It is not an easy matter in the policy process to protect against the neglect of scientific and technological factors, when their relevance is not initially obvious. And the difficulty of this situation puts a premium on an effective mechanism for broad integration of science and technology in the nation's foreign policy agencies. Part IV will be concerned with that mechanism.

POLICY MAKING IN FOREIGN AFFAIRS

The literature analyzing the policy-making process in foreign affairs in the United States is extensive and growing.[2] Though there is little point in a general summary of the excellent studies that have been done, there are several particular aspects of the present situation in the Federal government that have an important bearing on how well scientific and technological elements can be coupled to the other elements of foreign policy issues in the policy process.

One important observation is the uncertain power of the State Department in the formulation and execution of American foreign policy. The responsibility for foreign policy is, of course, centered constitutionally in

[2] One of the best sources that relates directly to the changes in international relations induced by postwar advances in science and technology is John H. Herz, *International Politics in the Atomic Age*, (New York & London: Columbia University Press, 1959).

the President; traditionally, the Secretary of State and his Department are expected to be the President's chief foreign policy advisers and pre-eminent in government councils on foreign policy matters.

Today, the scale and scope of American overseas activities, and the direct relationship between domestic and foreign affairs, have tended to dilute the State Department's role. The situation at any time varies markedly with the relationship between the President and the Secretary of State. Even when the relationship is close, there are now many more actors in the scene, with inevitable effects on the State Department's influence.

The most prominent of these new actors are in the White House and Executive Office of the President, for recent Presidents have found it necessary to establish sizable staff arms to help them maintain their influence in the Federal bureaucracy. The National Security Council, of course, but also the Bureau of the Budget, the Office of Science and Technology, as well as individual Presidential assistants are involved in issues stemming from or affecting America's foreign relations. Conflicts of power and influence between these staffs and the State Department cannot be avoided; they may also be encouraged by the President as a means of surfacing alternative policy choices or policy innovations.

Beyond the Presidential staffs, many departments and agencies of government have a legitimate say in the making of foreign policy, and some of them have enormous financial and political resources with which to exert influence on the course of events overseas, on the Congress, and on the public at large.

Moreover, these other departments and agencies can be thought of as technical agencies in the sense that they are fully cognizant of detailed technical matters within their responsibilities that may influence foreign affairs. They are more cognizant, certainly, than any other agency not directly concerned with the same subject matter, and therefore in a position to influence policy by their near-monopoly of technical information.

Largely for these reasons, the Department of State is not in the dominant position it often enjoyed in the past. It must fight constantly to make its views heard, and on issues that depend on specialized knowledge in the hands of the technical agencies it is at a great disadvantage unless able to understand how that specialized knowledge affects political choices. How President Johnson's call for greater control by the Secretary of State over international operations of the government will affect the Department's position, if at all, is not clear.

The President, too, must face this problem of gaining ascendancy over the technical agencies. He also must have independent sources of information and analysis if he is to be able to evaluate and supplement the choices presented to him and keep the agencies "honest." The creation of the post of Special Assistant to the President for Science and Technology in 1957, discussed in detail in Chapter 11, stemmed directly from this need as perceived by President Eisenhower.

The role of the Congress in foreign affairs is also quite different than in the past, especially on those issues with high technical content. The Congress has a major responsibility, of course, in foreign policy formulation not only as a result of its treaty ratification, appointment, and war-making functions, but also by virtue of its appropriation and investigatory powers.

But this responsibility is increasingly difficult to exercise except in relatively minor emendations of the wishes of the Executive Branch. The enormously increased pace of events, the drastically altered meaning of power, and the greatly increased scale of American worldwide involvement, all of which are in some measure the result of the scientific revolution, have worked to reduce the Congress' ability to carry out its responsibilities. The Executive Branch has the responsibility for action and control of the information. The information problem is particularly serious when issues depend heavily on technical variables, for the Congress until now has had only marginal internal capability for understanding the scientific and technological elements of foreign policy issues and relating them to the political choices open to the nation.

A few Congressional committees have worked to overcome the information problem, notably the Joint Committee on Atomic Energy. But the record is spotty and results more often in frustration and ex post facto criticism than in positive influence on policy formulation.

One other aspect of the foreign (or any) policy process deserves mention to dispel any lingering notions that it is inherently an orderly process. It might seem to be desirable to have policy made in a theoretically rational manner, with goals clearly defined, all relevant information taken into account by policy officials selected for their objectivity, and decisions clearly taken and executed. The actual process, fortunately, bears only a distant relationship to such a model.

Rather, national goals are very rarely explicit or, if they are, almost always prove to be too general to apply to specific cases. Decision makers recognize that information gathering to reduce uncertainty, as Herbert Simon notes, is costly.[3] The decision makers themselves approach issues with limited information, with prior biases and with external pressures that are in turn based on partial information and special interests.

The policy process is better characterized as a series of partial decisions; in fact, there often may not even be discrete events that could be called decisions.[4] Instead, the set of premises with which a decision maker approaches a problem may dictate a policy choice without his conscious realization that a choice was involved.

[3] Herbert A. Simon, "Theories of Decision-Making in Economics and Behavioral Science," *American Economic Review*, Vol. XLIX (June 1959), p. 272.

[4] Bauer, Pool, and Dexter showed this well in their exhaustive study of the politics of foreign trade. Their conclusions about decision making included:

> It often seemed to us that the term "decision-making" was a misnomer. What we saw did not often warrant so intellectual-sounding a label. . . . Not only may the formulation of a problem not have taken place deliberately, but the decision, also, may not have been deliberate. Under the pressure of circumstances a man does something that seems small, and suddenly he finds himself committed to something much larger than he envisioned . . .
>
> In any study such as ours, the question of whether a decision has been made at all should be regarded as a moot point. It is an issue that should be settled on empirical grounds in each instance. The label "decision-making" probably cannot be abandoned entirely, but it is necessary to call attention to how far this phrase fails to describe what happens in a social group between the time that an issue is recognized and the time that one or more persons are committed to a course of action.

Raymond A. Bauer, Ithiel de Sola Pool, and Lewis Anthony Dexter, *American Business and Public Policy* (New York: Atherton Press, 1964), p. 482.

Or, actions taken on apparently minor aspects of a problem or for short-term purposes may lead to seemingly inevitable or "obvious" policies at a later time on bigger issues. It is a common occurrence to have a program or policy established to meet a particular isolated need develop a life of its own that conditions future policies in other issues.

It is also a common occurrence to have major policies made in the context of preparing a speech. The Point Four Program under President Truman resulted from just such a situation, as did the Atoms for Peace proposal of President Eisenhower and the joint lunar program proposed by President Kennedy at the United Nations in 1963.[5] As Dean Acheson has noted, "The despised speech, often agreed to be made months beforehand without thought of subject, a nuisance to prepare and an annoyance to deliver, has proved the vehicle for statements of far-reaching effect for good or ill."[6]

Thus, the policy- or decision-making process is complex and seemingly disorderly, and further complicates the problem of relating scientific considerations to policy making. Decision makers in foreign affairs normally will have only very limited information available on the technical aspects of the issues they face, and often inadequate appreciation of the character of the interaction between those technical aspects and the political choices open to them. Often, the time available to ex-

[5] See discussion of these space and atomic energy initiatives in Chapter 2.
[6] Dean Acheson, "The President and the Secretary of State," in Don K. Price (ed.), *The Secretary of State*, The American Assembly, Columbia University (Englewood Cliffs, N.J.: Prentice-Hall, Inc., 1960), p. 44.

plore the technical aspects, even if their relevance is realized, is short. And when technical information is sought, the tendency is to seek "expert" testimony— specific answers to specific questions — when in fact the significance of the technical elements may be their uncertainty and their dependence on the political alternatives.

These problems of injecting science and technology effectively into the foreign policy process in the face of the complexity of that process in the United States, emphasize the importance of understanding the nature and character of the relationship between science and foreign affairs. In turn, such understanding is a prerequisite to designing policy machinery that, if adequately manned, can make possible that necessary integration.

SOME DEFINITIONS

Semantic debates about the terms "science" and "technology" can plague any analysis of a subject concerned with their social and political implications. Attempting to provide precise definitions can also be a source of debate, however. The distinctions between basic and applied research are typical of the problem in that there is no objectively observable boundary between them; the difference, in fact, depends on the purpose for which the distinction is to be made. Definitions of a few basic terms are necessary, but they will be presented arbitrarily with a view to avoiding irrelevant argument while making the analysis of maximum usefulness.

This procedure does not deny that the very real distinctions between science and technology are of great importance in the fields themselves and in the formulation of government policy for research and development; the distinctions occasionally are also pertinent to the analysis of foreign policy issues. But that pertinence is usually of a descriptive kind not fundamental to the analysis. For example, describing the technical aspects of the Atoms for Peace Program as technological or scientific is of little consequence in analysis of the political effects of the program.

Moreover, to attempt constantly to maintain a distinction between what is basic research and what is development inevitably raises difficult questions of definition that are, in fact, not relevant to the major argument.

Hence, science as used here will be treated as a generic term intended to encompass the entire research and development enterprise. This usage avoids the constant repetition of the phrase science and technology and conforms to common practice, at least among nonscientists. To most laymen, the term science includes the development of equipment and the application of the methods of science as well as the systematic study of phenomena to discover general truths. It is recognized that use of the term science in this way will offend some, for it is quite true that technology is often slighted or misunderstood by being subsumed under science. But because the distinction has little substantive importance for this particular analysis, there is more to be gained by using a term that corresponds to general public understanding than there is by continuing an awkward and possibly distracting distinction.

Occasionally it is necessary to be more precise, as in

discussions of the role of various kinds of research and development in foreign assistance programs. At those times, analytical distinctions between research and development will be carefully observed. Often the description of some components of an issue as scientific or technological means simply that they are of a technical nature in a field of science or technology (as opposed to finance or economics or law). "Technical" can also serve, therefore, as equivalent to "scientific" when the meaning is clear, and will be used in that way.

A different and more substantive problem is whether to include the social sciences in the analysis. There is no question of the importance of the interaction between the social sciences and foreign affairs; the very study of foreign affairs in a systematic way is, of course, part of the discipline of political science. However, the focus of interest in this analysis is the interaction of the physical and life sciences with foreign affairs. It would be a mistake to blur that focus, without doing justice to the broader subject, by including the social sciences as an appendage to the "hard" sciences. Accordingly, the term science is not intended to include the social sciences. Where in the course of analysis there are relevant points to be made about the social sciences, they will be referred to explicitly.

The terms "scientists" and "engineers" warrant somewhat different treatment because they involve somewhat less semantic debate, and the distinctions can be easily maintained. Moreover, there are important differences in the characteristics of the science community as opposed to the engineering community which bear on the analysis. Most often, the individual himself determines the community with which he identifies. For this analysis, scientists are considered to be those individuals engaged in basic or applied research, in the systematic search for new knowledge whether or not specific applications are in mind.[7] The term will be meant to encompass not only scientists in physical and life science fields, but also those in the social sciences.

The term engineers will refer to those primarily engaged in the application of knowledge to the development of specific technological end items such as equipment, processes or products. Many engineers, particularly in universities, are engaged in what has come to be called the engineering sciences. Here the work is heavily research oriented, for it is devoted to advancing the techniques, knowledge, and tools required in engineering. Still, most of those engaged in this work consider themselves engineers notwithstanding the indistinct boundary between their field and the sciences. They, too, will be considered engineers, for it is their own view of their affiliation that is most important.

[7] Whether a scientist is engaged in basic or applied research is often simply a difference in point of view: The administrator with an application in mind may see it as applied research; the scientist interested in the subject without reference to possible application may see it as basic research. Dr. Walsh McDermott of Cornell University offers the best definition: "The work you or your immediate colleagues are doing is clearly basic research; all other research is applied."

PART II

Foreign Policy Issues Arising from the Scientific Enterprise

2

New Technologies:
Space and Atomic Energy

On September 20, 1963, President John F. Kennedy in a speech before the United Nations General Assembly said:

Why, therefore, should man's first flight to the moon be a matter of national competition? Why should the U.S. and the Soviet Union, in preparing for such expeditions, become involved in immense duplications of research construction and expenditure? Surely we should explore whether the scientists and astronauts of our two countries — indeed of all the world — cannot work together in the conquest of space, sending someday in this decade to the moon, not the representatives of a single nation, but the representatives of all our countries.[1]

The proposal to join with the Soviet Union in a lunar program took the public, the Congress, almost surely

[1] *The New York Times,* Sept. 21, 1963, p. 1.

the Russians, and even the National Aeronautics and Space Administration (NASA), by surprise. Nothing came of the proposal, except to create difficulty in the Congress over the appropriation for Project Apollo — the manned lunar program — as the Congress reasoned, not irrationally, that if the United States wanted to cooperate with the Soviet Union, there was little justification for a race.[2] The fact that nothing came of the proposal, however, does not mean that the President was not prepared to follow through had the Russians responded favorably. In fact, there is no doubt that President Kennedy was deadly serious, while at the same time not averse to reaping any propaganda or prestige gain the proposal might bring.[3]

President Kennedy's initiative in 1963 was remarkably similar in tone, structure, and even in motivation to one on the subject of the peaceful use of atomic energy made by President Eisenhower almost exactly ten years earlier at the United Nations. The major difference lay in the less harrowing military potential of space than the already proven military uses of the atom.

In his speech on December 8, 1953, President Eisenhower also decried the need for competition, this time more deadly competition: he refused to accept the

hopeless finality of a belief that two atomic colossi are doomed malevolently to eye each other indefinitely across a trembling world.

He, too, held out the vision of cooperation:

[2] John Walsh, "NASA: Talk of Togetherness with Soviets Further Complicates Space Politics for the Agency," *Science*, Vol. 142 (Oct. 4, 1963), p. 35.

[3] See discussion later in this chapter for elaboration of the motives behind this proposal.

I therefore make the following proposals:

The Governments principally involved, to the extent permitted by elementary prudence, to begin now and to continue to make joint contributions from their stockpiles of normal uranium and fissionable materials to an international atomic energy agency . . . to be allocated to serve peaceful pursuits of mankind. . . . A special purpose would be to provide abundant electrical energy in the power-starved areas of the world.[4]

This proposal did not sink into oblivion as did President Kennedy's space initiative in 1963. From it came the Atoms for Peace Program and the International Atomic Energy Agency (IAEA), the latter established three years later with the grudging and reluctant participation of the Soviet Union.[5] Unfortunately, the premise put forth by the President, that "the U.S. knows that peaceful power from atomic energy is no dream of the future," proved to be technically correct but economically optimistic. Only now, in 1966, does atomic power appear to be on the threshold of becoming economically competitive in substantial areas of the world.

These initiatives illustrate two of the dramatic attempts to use technically based programs as instruments of international political gain. Of course, the U.S. space program is itself in large part an instrument for achieving international political objectives. A program of exploration of space would have been a natural scientific and technological step forward once large rockets had been developed, but the size of the exist-

[4] *The New York Times*, Dec. 9, 1953, p. 2.
[5] Harlan Cleveland, "Role of International Atomic Energy Agency in U.S. Foreign Policy," *Department of State Bulletin*, XLVII, Dec. 24, 1962, p. 966.

ing space program is an implicit recognition of the hypothesis that a nation's power and vitality are measured in part by its technological achievements. Once challenged by the Soviet Union in space, the United States concluded it could not afford to remain in second place. There are other motivations for mounting and maintaining a large-scale program, but national prestige was certainly the most important at first and is now still the determining motivation for most Congressmen and for decision makers in the Executive Branch.[6]

At a less dramatic level, there are many other examples of the use, or attempted use, of space and atomic energy for political purposes. The National Aeronautics and Space Act, for example, calls for NASA to conduct its programs in cooperation with other nations and groups of nations.

Accordingly, by mid-1965, NASA was involved in cooperative space projects with sixty-nine nations.[7] These included ground-based cooperative projects, joint flight experiments, cooperative sounding rocket launchings, personnel exchanges, and other activities. Beyond that, the U.S. Government has taken an active role in promoting U.N. interest in space, has worked closely and creatively with *nongovernment* international scientific organizations, and, of course, has actively advanced the first important practical applica-

[6] Vernon Van Dyke in *Pride and Power, the Rationale of the Space Program*, (Urbana: University of Illinois Press, 1964) presents an excellent evaluation of the variety of motives behind the U.S. space program.
[7] Arnold W. Frutkin, *Space and the International Cooperation Year, A National Challenge*, U.S. GPO, 1965, p. 6.

tions of space — communications and meteorology —
necessarily in cooperation with other countries.

Some of the international activities were essential
for the successful prosecution of the U.S. space program: tracking stations at strategic points around the
earth, for example. They were thus dictated by the
technical objectives of the program. Most of the others
had broader motivations, however, stemming directly
from the desire to realize political results from the
space program.

Similarly, in the atomic field, the revised Atomic
Energy Act of 1954 calls for

a program of international cooperation to promote the common defense and security and to make available to co-
operating nations the benefits of peaceful applications of
atomic energy as widely as expanding technology and considerations of the common defense and security will permit.[8]

Accordingly, aside from participation in the IAEA,
the United States mounted a bilateral, and in many
ways competitive (to the IAEA), Atoms for Peace Program in which it supplied nuclear research reactors or
atomic materials to more than forty countries.[9] In addition, the United States has cooperative research programs with other countries, especially the United Kingdom, and with groups of countries, such as those
represented in Euratom.

Thus, both the space and atomic energy programs
pose many policy issues with scientific content for the

[8] *Atomic Energy Legislation Through 88th Congress, 2nd Session,*
Joint Committee on Atomic Energy, Congress of the United States,
December 1964, p. 6.
[9] Personal communication from John A. Hall, Assistant General
Manager for International Activities, AEC, Apr. 1, 1965.

foreign policy apparatus of the U.S. Government. Some of these issues are largely operational or service in nature. Others, however, are more significant, for example, fallout from atomic tests, disposal of atomic wastes in international waters, allocation of the radio frequency spectrum, and development of international space law, to say nothing of the national security issues involved in the possible military uses of space or in the attempts to advance arms control measures involving the control of the atom.

Clearly, the technical aspects of these issues take many different forms. Physical data about a known technology, about recent research, or about the expected results of R & D, are necessary elements in issues as widely varying in their consequences as estimating the possibility of clandestine diversion of nuclear material from peaceful to military applications and determining sites for space tracking stations. Information pertaining to the scientific and technological communities is involved as well, for example, in planning international scientific programs in space or atomic energy fields, or in coping with the public activities of scientists on major issues such as fallout or the test ban.

Many of these technical inputs are not difficult to obtain. Most can be provided directly by NASA or the Atomic Energy Commission (AEC) or other technical agencies involved. Alternatively, the entire question can be handled by the specific agency, under general policy guidance of the State Department or the President. Such delegation of responsibility for some international operations is entirely appropriate, for once the objectives of a program have been established and some basic decisions taken, most of the issues then depend heavily on detailed technical considerations best handled by those closest to the problem. Delegation of responsibility, of course, does not do away with the need for good political judgment on the part of the technical agencies or for knowledgeable oversight on the part of the State Department.

But for many issues, and always for issues with significant political meaning, the technical aspects cannot be isolated from the foreign policy maker in this way. The technical aspects may not be simple matters of fact; more important, there will be a degree of interaction between the technical alternatives and the related policy alternatives that the foreign policy maker can ignore at great cost to his prerogatives in the determination of foreign policy.

The validity of this judgment can be seen best in an examination of a few selected cases in the space and atomic energy field. The cases can also illustrate the special problems faced by a foreign policy maker when dealing with highly technical programs: the classic difficulty of even knowing that there is a technological alternative possible; the problem of planning political initiatives in the face of opposition by a technical agency; and the difficulty of controlling well-defined technical activities when concern arises over their ill-defined political implications.

U.N. SPACE CONFERENCE

On October 6, 1959, early in the U.N. General Assembly meeting of that year, the U.S.S.R. announced that it would propose "the calling of an international conference of scientists under U.N. auspices, on the question of exchange of experience in the study of outer space."[10] The announcement, just two years after Sputnik I, was made by Soviet delegate Kuznetsov. The initial response by the United States in the United Nations was noncommittal. In Washington, the response was decidedly cool.

Not surprisingly, the State Department assumed that the lead the Soviet Union held in space exploration would enable the Russians to score a propaganda coup in any such conference, hence that must be their motive in making the proposal. Comparisons were made with the earlier U.N. Atoms for Peace Conferences where the shoe was on the other foot and the United States was able to make substantial propaganda gains. Thus, the initial reaction in the Department of State was that a space conference would not be in the U.S. interest.

In fact, the issues were rather more complicated. Better appreciation for the U.S. space program (as opposed to the view then current in the press and public of an ineffectual effort) and greater realization of the desirability of obtaining technical information about the Russian program, might have produced a different reaction. For, although it was true that the Soviet Union held a substantial lead in technological spectaculars, by the time a conference could have been mounted (1961 or late 1960 at the earliest) the United States would almost surely have had important accomplishments to its credit. And U.S. successes would have been completely open in contrast to the secrecy that surrounded the Soviet program.

Moreover, if the conference had the effect of the

[10] General debate, United Nations General Assembly 823rd Plenary Meeting, Oct. 6, 1959.

Atoms for Peace Conferences of pressuring the Soviet Union to release previously secret information, it could have been justified on intelligence grounds alone. The United States was quite anxious to learn more about Soviet booster technology, for it was all but identical with Russian ballistic missile technology.

Therefore, the United States stood to gain one way or the other from the conference. If the Russians remained secretive, the United States had a good chance of scoring a propaganda coup — the more effective because it would be unexpected. If the Russians opened up, the propaganda balance might well go to them, but valuable information would have been obtained.

It is not known if the Russians were serious about the conference when they first made the proposal, or whether credit for making the proposal is all they were after. In any case, they were capable of the same reasoning and no doubt soon realized they had created something of a box for themselves. The only U.S. response that had a chance of taking advantage of the Soviet offer would have been an immediately favorable reaction that resulted in firm action on the conference before interest and attention cooled in the United Nations.

This immediate response was not forthcoming because of lack of appreciation of the technical situation and of the political implications of that technical situation. NASA was not enthusiastic, for it was concerned about diversion of resources from its primary task. Because the State Department had to rely heavily on NASA for its technical evaluations, NASA's original lack of enthusiasm reinforced the Department's own initial political judgment.

Pressure for a positive response came from the Presidential level in the person of the President's Special Assistant for Science and Technology, Dr. George Kistiakowsky. First on an informal basis, and then by letter to the Secretary of State, Dr. Kistiakowsky forced the discussion to higher levels. Meanwhile, interest in the idea began to pick up at NASA and within the State Department.

Eventually, after wide government consultations, the U.S. position was fixed in favor of holding such a conference, but by that time the opportunity was lost. The Russians apparently became suspicious of the sudden American enthusiasm, or had second thoughts in any case, and soon the matter was bogged down in political arguments over the selection of officers for a conference and the political makeup of the U.N. Committee on the Peaceful Uses of Outer Space. A quick, well-publicized response to the Russian proposal might have called their bluff and avoided some of the ancillary political issues. The General Assembly eventually authorized such a conference but it was left as the responsibility of the Outer Space Committee.[11] The Conference has not yet been held, though the U.N. Committee has now formally agreed to call a conference in 1967.[12]

U.S./U.S.S.R. SPACE COOPERATION

A different example, with different lessons for policy formulation when science and technology figure prominently, stemmed from President Kennedy's interest in

[11] Resolution 1472 (XIV), International Cooperation in the Peaceful Uses of Outer Space, Dec. 17, 1959.
[12] "Report of the Working Group of the Whole," U.N. Committee on the Peaceful Uses of Outer Space, A/AC.105/30, 26 Jan. 1966.

the possibility of using science and technology directly as foreign policy instruments. Kennedy came to the office of President with a good feeling for science and technology and with a determination to develop and exploit new avenues for advancing America's foreign policy interests. He was therefore not only sympathetic to the requirements for maintaining a strong and creative science in the United States but also intrigued with how science could be used in other ways to support political objectives.

In his inaugural address, the new President expressed this interest in a way that he carried through his entire time in office: "Let both sides seek to invoke the wonders of science instead of its terrors. Together let us explore the stars, conquer the deserts, eradicate disease, tap the ocean depths, and encourage the arts and commerce."[13] This philosophy pervaded the science establishment in Washington during the succeeding years and was responsible directly or indirectly for many initiatives relating science to foreign policy.

One of the President's first acts after assuming office was to ask his Special Assistant for Science and Technology, Dr. Jerome B. Wiesner, to follow up the inaugural address and develop specific proposals for scientific cooperation with the Soviet Union.

The President's motivation was complex, but figuring prominently was his desire for a détente with the Soviet Union, which he believed could be helped by (1) the demonstration and enlargement of areas of common interest with the Soviet Union that could be gradually expanded as time went by, and (2) the development of a habit of cooperation between the United States and

[13] *The New York Times,* Jan. 21, 1961, p. 8.

Russia that could be directed to more central issues as it became accepted by both countries. In the inaugural itself he said, "And if a beachhead of cooperation may push back the jungles of suspicion, let both sides join in creating a new endeavor. . . ."[14]

With this and other subsidary objectives in mind, a large package of tentative projects in a variety of fields was prepared by Dr. Wiesner's office through the use of outside consultants and active participation of Federal departments and agencies. The Department of State took part in this effort but assumed only a minor role.

The coolness in relations between the United States and the Soviet Union in 1961, emphasized by the Vienna meeting and the erection of the Berlin Wall, prevented any progress with the proposals that year. They were filed in their tentative state for possible future use.

In 1962 the opportunity came when Premier Khrushchev responded to the successful orbital flight of Colonel John Glenn with a congratulatory telegram that said: "If our countries pooled their efforts — scientific, technical and material — to explore outer space, this would be very beneficial to the advance of science and would be acclaimed by all people who would like to see scientific achievements benefit man. . . ."[15]

President Kennedy responded the same day, most likely to Khrushchev's great surprise, saying, ". . . I welcome your statement that our countries should cooperate in the exploration of space. . . . I am instructing the appropriate officers of this government to prepare new and concrete proposals for immediate projects of

[14] *Loc. cit.*
[15] *Ibid.*, Feb. 22, 1962, p. 10.

common action and I hope that at a very early date our representatives may meet. . . ."[16]

The space projects had already been separated from the previously prepared package, and elaborated and winnowed out further by NASA. Now, they were brought forward for final selection. Because State had not participated actively in the preparation of the original or the shortened list and was not in a position to formulate technical possibilities independently of NASA, it was greatly circumscribed in its ability to know what was, in fact, the full range of possibilities. In essence, NASA was determining the boundary conditions within which the State Department was to exercise its political judgment as to which proposals should be submitted to the President for approval.

In this particular case, the President's Special Assistant for Science and Technology was able to provide a broader range of technical/political alternatives for consideration than NASA brought forward. This late intervention was necessary, for NASA had selected only those projects that *it* thought would be technically *and politically* desirable. NASA's selections emphasized collaboration on information exchange rather than more extensive and intimate cooperation that would have involved joint research and development programs. Their judgment was not necessarily wrong, but that judgment should have been the President's, not the Space Agency's.

The State Department, responsible for making the final political recommendations to the President, then had to make its evaluation of the political advisability

[16] *Loc. cit.*

of the various possibilities without study in an open interagency meeting. The Department chose information exchange over more extensive cooperation, the course NASA favored, although vague possibilities for future, more intimate cooperation were half-heartedly included. Would the Department's judgment have been different if it could have considered a wider range of alternatives in the privacy of its own offices? Perhaps not, but in effect it abrogated its own responsibilities by not having the capability for such consideration.

The specific proposals went to Premier Khrushchev on March 7, 1962, and he responded favorably to President Kennedy on March 21, 1962.[17] Official negotiators met periodically after that, and by mid-1963 agreements had been worked out for collaboration on space experiments in meteorology, communications, and magnetic field measurements.[18]

The high hopes for meaningful cooperation engendered by the original exchange of telegrams between Kennedy and Khrushchev gradually faded as the specific projects developed into interesting but minor efforts. It is worth noting that even on these limited projects Russian participation has not been equal to what was promised.[19] Whether Soviet participation would have been greater, or absent altogether, if the projects suggested had been of a scale that required attention by the Soviet leadership directly, is a moot point. The only evidence of likely Russian response is the silence of the Soviet Union when President Ken-

[17] *Ibid.*, March 22, 1962, p. 18.
[18] Press briefing by Dr. Hugh Dryden, *NASA News Release*, Mar. 25, 1963.
[19] *The New York Times*, Feb. 18, 1965, p. 13.

nedy offered in 1963 to mount a joint lunar program, although that was a much less specific offer. Quite clearly, the minor character of the proposals in 1962 meant that neither Kennedy nor Khrushchev had to be involved directly.

Several years later, in 1966, the Russians reopened the issue of cooperation in space endeavors in a letter from Foreign Minister Gromyko to U.N. Secretary General U Thant in which they proposed an international agreement that would include a call for international cooperation. Exactly what the Russians have in mind, or what will come of the proposal is not clear at the time of writing.[20]

President Kennedy's lunar proposal of 1963, in distinction to the 1962 package, was quite apparently not staffed through the Space Agency but originated in the White House.[21] Without question, some of the earlier experience of caution and reserve by both NASA and State figured in the President's decision not to ask for detailed elaboration by the Agency or by the State Department before making the lunar proposal publicly. One effect of this treatment was to cause consternation in the Space Agency because it had not been consulted on a matter so vital to its objectives and timetable.

The lunar proposal may have been ill advised in the light of its probable rejection by the Soviet Union and of the domestic problems it would create within NASA and before the Congress. But it is a testimonial to the frustration a President faces when attempting a sharp innovation in highly technical areas in which the tech-

[20] *Ibid.*, June 1, 1966, p. 27.
[21] *Ibid.*, Sept. 21, 1963, p. 1.

nical bureaucracy does not, and cannot, have the perspective of the President and in which his foreign policy advisers outside the White House are not able to challenge the technical judgments of the agencies.

The joint lunar proposal can be questioned on other, more speculative but highly pertinent, grounds. If the United States was willing in 1963 to contemplate using its space program as a tool for major cooperation with the Soviet Union, why was it not willing to use the program, with a higher probability of acceptance, for major cooperation with its allies in Western Europe? What would have been the political results if the 1963 lunar proposal had been made to Western Europe in 1961, or even in 1959? It is worth while to explore that possibility for a moment.

On the negative side, there might have been several unfavorable consequences: the proposal of a joint program with Western Europe could have been interpreted as an admission of American inability to match Russian space progress; it would have carried the danger of supplying information on missile delivery systems to the French at a time when it was American policy to attempt to delay the achievement of an independent French nuclear weapon system; there was always the possibility that de Gaulle or European countries in general would have refused to cooperate, or that once having agreed, the Europeans would not make the necessary commitment of resources and would become a drag on the whole program; and the domestic reaction in the United States might not have been sufficiently enthusiastic to allow the necessary sharing of information and tasks.

These are all valid points, but on the positive side are

the potentially enormous gains possible if the United States had made a major proposal to Western Europe and meant it seriously. By building on a sense of common enterprise in the exploration of man's newest frontier and by proposing a program truly massive in size, it is possible that one or more major political objectives could have been materially advanced, depending on how the cooperative efforts were designed. For example, by encouraging the development of European institutions as a prerequisite for extensive U.S./European cooperation, a new and important economic and political link between the Common Market countries and Great Britain might have been established. Subsequently it might have had effect on other British policies toward Europe and ultimately on de Gaulle's policies toward England. It must be remembered that a major commitment to space exploration can have large effects on a country's resource allocation problems (as the United States has learned), could quite conceivably cause significant realignments of traditional patterns of economic policy within European countries, and, if the program were truly cooperative, could bring about a degree of interlocking of the economies and the policies of Western Europe that was not achievable through coal and steel or atomic energy.

Alternatively, a joint space program could have been used as a lever for bringing about much greater technical integration, and to some extent political integration, of U.S. and Western European economies. In the early years of the U.S. space program, scientific and technical assistance from Western Europe could have provided a valuable boost, and Western Europe would have gained at the same time. There would have been spilloff into NATO because of the relationship between space and military hardware, and at least some of the present difficulties in the North Atlantic Alliance might have been avoided.

Less ambitiously, the cooperative space effort could have been used to strengthen the Organization for Economic Cooperation and Development (OECD), the major vehicle for nonmilitary cooperation among Western countries, by giving that organization a measure of responsibility in carrying out this joint effort.

Certainly the problems and costs of such a proposal would have been great. It was and is hard to evaluate the likelihood of being able to achieve any of the possible political objectives. But the psychological effects of launching a peaceful Atlantic Nations program that truly involved the economies and the technologies of the participating countries on a venture into space are also not easily gauged. The payoff could have been massive. That is why it could not have been a small or marginal proposal. It would have had to have been, simply, on the order of the proposal that President Kennedy made in 1963 to the Soviet Union.

Clearly, originating such a proposal and shaping it to be a politically feasible and profitable endeavor would require the most intimate kind of integration of political and technical factors in policy making. The opposition within the government from the technical agencies and from the Congress would no doubt have been great. Meeting that opposition would have required sophistication and understanding of the technical as well as the political opportunities and problems on the part of foreign policy officers.

It is interesting to observe in passing that strong

leadership did come from within the Department of State a few years earlier on the question of American policy support for the creation of the European Atomic Energy Community (Euratom), and particularly for U.S. action with regard to provision of nuclear fuel and financial support. The individuals responsible at that time saw this technical effort as having potentially great influence in moving toward a united Europe and were anxious to use this technological opportunity to support that goal.[22]

Unfortunately, the technical judgment was overly optimistic, and, in any case, the success of the Common Market overshadowed the political effects of Euratom. The technological situation, as in President Eisenhower's Atoms for Peace proposal, was not as promising as it appeared at the time. Coal and oil were not in as short supply as imagined, and nuclear power was not as attractive economically as had been hoped in comparison with conventional fuels. Euratom may yet have important economic and political significance in Western Europe; at the moment it is useful, but other events have tended to overshadow its political contributions.

PROLIFERATION

In an article in *International Science and Technology* in February 1965, Mr. S. K. Ghaswala of India said quite bluntly: "In this ten years [since the start of the Indian atomic energy program] we have attained a

[22] Testimony of Ambassador C. Douglas Dillon, *Hearings Before the Joint Committee on Atomic Energy*, 85th Congress, 2nd Session, July 22, 1958, p. 22; personal communications from J. Robert Schaetzel, Deputy Assistant Secretary for Atlantic Affairs, Department of State, Mar. 25, 1965.

position from which it would be relatively easy to leap to making bombs, should we ever want to."[23] As long ago as 1958, the late Dr. H. S. Bhabha, Chairman of the Indian Atomic Energy Commission claimed that his scientists could produce a bomb in eighteen months from the time a decision was made.[24]

Whether Dr. Bhabha was optimistic or not in 1958, there is little question today that India has the scientific knowledge, the practical experience of working with nuclear material, and available plutonium from existing nuclear power reactors to produce an atomic bomb. The exact time it would take is uncertain, but the successful outcome is not. The explosion of Chinese nuclear devices, coupled with Chinese belligerency has of course made the question of whether or not India should follow suit a major issue of Indian politics.

India is perhaps the best example, but not the only one, of countries that have been aided — sometimes pushed — along the road to nuclear capability by accepting the peaceful atom. Others are also acquiring power reactors that produce plutonium as a by-product, plutonium that can be used to fabricate atomic weapons after separation from the spent fuel. A larger number of countries have gained experience and knowledge about atomic energy, but not weapons material by acquiring research reactors. These latter nations are far from any immediate nuclear capability, but the problem for them now becomes primarily economic rather than technical.

[23] S. K. Ghaswala, "India's Peaceful Atomic Program Reacts to Chinese Bomb," *International Science and Technology*, No. 38 (Feb. 1965), p. 78.

[24] *The New York Times*, Oct. 5, 1964, p. 30.

The Atoms for Peace Program, whatever its motives and safeguards, has unquestionably speeded up the proliferation process. The dissemination of knowledge may have been inevitable in any case. As many have pointed out, the most important information the United States provided was the knowledge that a man-made atomic explosion was possible. Therefore, the issue is not whether the knowledge and capability to produce atomic weapons could have been contained altogether but whether its dissemination should have been accelerated.

Here is a clear, though complex, example of the longer-range issues that can accompany attempts to use science and technology for political purposes. President Eisenhower's motives for initiating the Atoms for Peace Program were to advance a variety of political objectives, most notably to draw national and world attention away from excessive concentration on the destructive aspects of atomic energy and to find ways for the world to use the atom cooperatively for constructive purposes.[25] Presumably, the Administration also wanted to demonstrate on an international stage the peaceful constructive intentions and the scientific leadership of the United States.

As already noted, the proposal had at least one important flaw: the economic prospects for nuclear power were overstated. But it had another flaw as well: the effect of the program on an equally or more important political objective — that of preventing or delaying the proliferation of atomic weapons — was not adequately appreciated.

[25] Robert J. Donovan, *Eisenhower, the Inside Story* (New York: Harper & Bros., 1956), p. 185.

It is easy to make damning judgments by hindsight. Still, the measure of the effectiveness of the policy-making process can only be sought in the results of the policies that are chosen. And in this case, the results of the Atoms for Peace Program look less desirable as each year passes.

In defense of the program, the argument is made that, because the dissemination of knowledge about atomic technology was inevitable in any case, a policy that served to create an international safeguards system and at least had a chance of bringing the atom under control in the future was a wise policy.[26] But the safeguards system has no teeth in it as yet, and the question must be asked as to whether an alternative, less enthusiastic policy that attacked the proliferation problem more directly would not have been much more successful in controlling the spread of atomic technology.

This is not just an issue from the past. It has remained current because, at least until recently, the Atomic Energy Commission has actively pursued its goal of encouraging international peaceful applications of atomic energy by all interested countries. On November 1, 1964, President Johnson appointed a special group under Roswell L. Gilpatric to study the question of nuclear proliferation.[27] Quite clearly, the President had in mind the new impetus to proliferation that could result from the explosion of the Chinese A-bomb. The concern was reinforced by the likely future abundance of fissionable material as the brighter economic pros-

[26] J. Hall, "Atoms for Peace, or War," *Foreign Affairs*, Vol. 43, No. 4 (July 1965), p. 602.
[27] *The New York Times*, Nov. 2, 1964, p. 1.

pects of atomic power induced more countries to invest in power reactors.

The report of the Gilpatric committee has not been made public, but according to press reports it has recommended a much more restrictive approach in providing atomic assistance to other nations than has prevailed in the past.[28]

Policy making in this area requires a formidable level of appreciation of the technical situation in reactor and weapons technologies and of how that situation may develop in the future. It requires an appreciation of the relationship between reactor and weapons technologies and the ability to relate these technical matters to the pertinent national political objectives. And it requires that most important ability: competence to weigh the various policy alternatives with their certain and uncertain technical variables.

This problem area of nuclear proliferation is current for yet another reason. Atomic energy is not the only technology involved. Nuclear weapons are not useful without delivery systems, and even though planes can qualify, missiles are more attractive because of their greater ability to penetrate defenses.

Is the United States repeating its error in the Atoms for Peace Program by making available, through international cooperation in space activities, a technology that can be used for military as well as peaceful pursuits?

Once again, the question is whether the United States is artificially and undesirably increasing the pace of technological advance by other countries. A lid cannot

[28] *Ibid.*, Feb. 12, 1965, p. 3.

be put on the gradual spread of scientific and technological knowledge but there *is* a policy choice between retardation and encouragement.

Undoubtedly, the United States *is* speeding up the spread of scientific knowledge about space; however, it is at the same time consciously attempting to slow down the acquisition by others of that knowledge about booster technology which would have the most direct relevance to weapons. NASA cooperates extensively with other countries on scientific experiments in space but does not provide boosters to other countries except under strict agreement as to their use. Such an agreement is quite easy to police by comparison with agreements in the atomic field.

But does encouraging other nations to become involved at all in space exploration increase their ability to find military uses for space or their ability to develop missile systems? Even if the United States restricts the sale of boosters abroad, nations with some familiarity with space technology can easily obtain information on booster technology in international scientific and engineering forums.[29]

That the issue of proliferation is receiving renewed attention in the U.S. Government beyond the basic atomic reactor problem is attested to by other developments. On December 18, 1964, the AEC disclosed that it had cautioned manufacturers against selling to other

[29] At the Fifth International Symposium on Space Technology and Science in Tokyo, an American firm, Cubic Corporation of San Diego, presented information on a complete space launch and support facility they were offering *for sale*. The system could place up to 125 lbs in an earth orbit with a perigee of 300 nautical miles. The cost, if bought in quantities of ten, would be under $600,000 per launch, exclusive of launch pads.

countries equipment that could be used in the development or testing of atomic weapons.[30] And the Administration has refused to grant an export license for advanced computers ordered by the French, computers clearly destined for the French nuclear program.[31]

These are startling developments in many ways, for computers and much of the equipment used for atomic testing are not classified on security grounds. The knowledge and production capability they represent are for all intents and purposes freely available in the literature, and such equipment is reproducible, in time, by competent scientists and engineers. In fact, there is no indication that the United States would not be willing to sell similar equipment or computers to other countries so long as their intended use is not to assist a military nuclear program.

The proliferation issue therefore begins to pose a much larger problem for policy in the future. Any technology has the potential for military as well as peaceful application. This was always true, but as the technology available to man increases in power and in the range of its effects, the danger of its misuse becomes correspondingly greater. Has the stage been reached at which a technologically advanced country must begin to explore ways of preventing or controlling the diffusion of many technologies, not just the ones obviously and immediately related to military power?

Clearly, this is a complex issue with implications reaching to the very heart of the traditional mores and

[30] *The New York Times*, Dec. 19, 1964, p. 1.
[31] Howard Simons, "American Newsletter," *New Scientist*, No. 426 (Jan. 14, 1965), p. 97; *The New York Times*, May 22, 1966, p. 43.

procedures of the American scientific and industrial effort. It is also closely related to the old, and, to scientists, dismaying issue of the suppression of science and technology. These implications will be taken up again in the concluding chapter, where some of the broader and more philosophical effects of science and technology on international relations will be considered.

But the shorter-term implications of these questions of proliferation, of feasible policy alternatives, and of the cost to American science and technology are urgent matters. They can be considered adequately only with full integration of their technical and political elements. The scientific genie cannot be put back in the bottle, but there may be possibilities for greater leverage and control of the dangerous aspects of the dissemination of technology. The implications of the present situation must be well understood, and so, too, must be the relevant considerations — scientific, economic, and political — that condition the policy choices.

These examples illustrate something of the interaction between foreign policy and the new technologies of space and atomic energy. Many additional examples could be adduced that would show other facets. But they all tend to emphasize the inseparability of the technical and the political variables in important issues. And they also demonstrate the inadequacy of relying solely on the technical agencies to represent the scientific elements in the foreign policy process of the Federal Government.

The reason for this latter situation is neither mysterious nor shocking. It stems simply from the different viewpoints and objectives of the various departments and agencies of the American government. Each has its own primary objectives; to the extent that a technical agency is concerned with foreign relations, it is bound to have a somewhat parochial viewpoint. Operating agencies cannot be expected to see the totality of American foreign relations or to be highly sophisticated about foreign policy. In fact, the agencies are expected to champion their own causes, for only in that way can the decision-making process proceed with reasonable expectation that all the relevant arguments in a particular isue will be brought to the surface. But the functioning of this "confrontation of protagonists" process depends for its success on approximately equal knowledgeability of all the protagonists. This is where the difficulty lies for the foreign policy maker, from the President on down, when dealing with issues with high scientific content.

For the policy maker must be cognizant of the technical aspects of these issues and must have, or be able to obtain, technical information that will enable him to see the policy alternatives and possibilities from *his* vantage point. This means working closely with the technical agencies involved. It also means having alternative mechanisms for obtaining information; it means knowing how to ask the right questions; and it means being aware at an early stage of the interactions between the technical variables and the political issues.

The ways of accomplishing this integration are not easy to achieve. American foreign policy will adequately reflect the problems and opportunities of space and atomic energy, however, only to the extent that the foreign policy process is able to achieve that integration.

3

International Scientific and Technological Activities of the U.S. Government

Space and atomic energy are the most visible of the international scientific and technological activities of the U.S. Government, both because they are large in size and bear an obvious relation to the nation's political goals. But they are by no means the only international technical activities sponsored or supported by the government.

Every major U.S. Government department and agency has international programs of a scientific or technical nature, some of considerable size. Individually, most of these activities cannot be considered to be of major foreign policy concern. Collectively, however, they can have considerable impact on this nation's international relations. Moreover, because they stem from the authorized missions of the departments and agencies, the foreign policy apparatus of the government has a responsibility to maintain a favorable climate in which the activities can be carried on successfully.

The overseas technical activities of the government cannot easily or usefully be listed in terms of dollar costs, though it would be advantageous if such a simple measure were available. The major difficulty is that several "domestic" R & D programs, such as those in oceanography and meteorology, are carried out in part, often primarily, in an international environment. There would be little to be gained by attempting for accounting purposes to apportion the large costs of those programs between domestic and international activities. In addition, a good part of the program of the Agency for International Development (AID) is technical in nature, yet there is no simple criterion for choosing a dollar figure that would meaningfully reflect the actual scale of international scientific and technological activities of that agency. And NASA carries out its international cooperation programs without any exchange of dollars so that many of its international activities would not show up in a listing according to dollar expenditures.

In any case, dollar figures for any international program can be misleading as a measure of political significance, for programs with small dollar costs, such as exchange of persons or international coordination of research, may be of more importance to external relations than those costing many times as much. For all these reasons, the temptation to attempt to add up the total cost of U.S. Government international scientific and technological programs will be eschewed in favor of less satisfactory, but also less misleading, qualitative descriptions of the kinds of programs being conducted.

The international activities supported by U.S. Government agencies range over a wide spectrum. Most agencies support research by American scientists abroad, international travel and meetings of scientists, and training fellowships for foreign nationals. All of them are involved in the activities of one or more international organizations, and in international cooperative research with scientists of other countries. Some of the cooperative programs are of large size: mutual weapons development with NATO allies (North Atlantic Treaty Organization), cooperative oceanographic research, and bilateral desalination development projects are examples.

In addition, some agencies, notably the Departments of Defense (DOD) and Health, Education and Welfare (HEW) support American laboratories abroad or participate actively in international laboratories. Many agencies support research by foreign scientists directly and provide financial and material support for data exchanges and international activities of scientists. All agencies have overseas technical operations, such as mapping activities by the DOD; oceanographic research by Commerce, DOD and others; and ground support activities by NASA. Some are engaged in science education overseas and some in mounting science exhibits in foreign countries.

This is by no means an exhaustive list, but it gives some feeling for the scope of the international scientific and technological activities of Federal agencies. These activities are initiated and carried out in principle to further the missions of the agencies involved. Only the National Science Foundation (NSF), of the major agencies involved with science and technology, has

authority to support basic research without consideration of ultimate application.

The requirement to establish the relevance of a particular project to an agency mission is an essential in-
gredient in the American policy process, for it provides
a chief measure of control by the President and by the
Congress. When considering basic research projects,
establishing relevance may be an academic exercise because the results of the research or the application of
the research results may be so indeterminate. Still, for
the bulk of R & D, the relevance criterion, which figures
as a major element in the budgetary process within the
Executive and before Congress, allows for attention to
questions of resource allocation, relative quality, and
over-all budgetary control that would be much more
difficult or impossible without it.

The requirement for international projects to be
relevant to an authorized agency mission has implications that bear directly on the concerns of the foreign
policy maker as he confronts these extensive overseas
activities.

GUIDANCE, ASSISTANCE, AND OVERSIGHT

The first and most evident implication is the obliga-
tion for the foreign policy apparatus of the government
to assist the agencies in carrying out their approved
international activities. By the nature of the budget and
legislative process, once a project has been approved, it
is, in effect, certified as being in support of an accepted
national objective. As such, it is incumbent on those
responsible for foreign policy and foreign operations to
assist as necessary in carrying the project forward.

Of course, a particular project may have implications that conflict with a quite different policy objective, in which case a choice or modification may have to be made to resolve the conflict. An excellent example is the proposal by the military services in the late 1950's to extend to Japan their foreign scientist research support programs that had been so successful in Europe. The programs themselves would have furthered American scientific interests, but the fact of military sponsorship was thought by the State Department to be a serious political detriment because of the antimilitarism of an influential part of the Japanese scientific community. A compromise was eventually worked out that allowed the American military to support research in Japan but only in fields directly related to the medical sciences.

This kind of policy problem is the exception rather than the rule for individual projects. More often, the embassy abroad or the State Department in Washington finds itself in the position of simply providing useful administrative services for other agencies, or else attempting to keep abreast of the multitude of activities going on.

But there are other aspects of these international activities, especially when seen as a whole, that raise new problems for the foreign policy maker.

The very number of independent agency programs, each justified in terms of its narrow mission, can be of concern to the policy maker. For example, it often happens that several different U.S. agencies are operating simultaneously in the same country with similar programs. Each program may be entirely legitimate in its own right and proceeding without evident stress.

But in sum they may be tying up a substantial portion of the best technical manpower of the country or diverting the domestic scientific institutions to work on problems that the United States, rather than the host country, deems important.

The situation in Israel is a good example, for that country finds itself with excess capacity for basic research and insufficient capacity for applied research on the immediate problems it faces.[1] The availability of support from American agencies primarily for basic research tends to exacerbate the situation and makes it more difficult for the Israeli Government to take effective measures to redirect its scientists.

The conditions under which programs are set up can also cause political problems. For example, U.S. agencies sometimes grant fellowship support for study in the United States without providing for adequate follow-up on the student's return. The result, if the student cannot put his new competence to work, or if the training in the United States bears little relation to his own country's need, can be dislocation and disaffection, or worse.

In some countries, the sheer variety of U.S. agencies and personnel involved in scientific activities, in providing funds for research, in assisting universities or research institutions, and in building research stations, has caused problems. Ambassador Galbraith when he first went to India was appalled at the numbers of Americans in India in an official capacity, carrying out tasks that affected United States/Indian relations but of which he had known nothing. Even when there are close ties between operating agencies and the local

[1] Victor K. McElheny, "Israel Worries About its Applied Research," *Science*, Vol. 147 (Mar. 5, 1965), p. 1123.

embassy, the different objectives of those who have a clear technical task and want to get on with the job, and of those who are concerned with the broader political implications of the activities on the host country, can result in friction.

Even a desire to withdraw from an international program can be a source of political concern. The three military services, the National Institutes of Health, the Department of Agriculture, and, to a lesser extent, several other agencies have all had programs since the early 1950's for the support of research by foreign scientists. These programs had been instituted originally in Europe by the U.S. military to help European scientists over the difficult postwar reconstruction period. They worked so well as a means of enlisting first-class scientists in other countries to work on problems of interest to U.S. agencies that the programs were continued beyond the period of acute financial need in Europe, and expanded to other agencies and other areas of the world. The programs also had other desirable effects, such as providing research support for younger scientists not yet recognized in their own countries, and improving knowledge and information about the United States on the part of influential groups in other countries.

Notwithstanding the positive aspects of the programs, there had been debate in the United States for many years about the advisability of continuing them indefinitely. The concerns were that too many foreign scientists were becoming dependent on U.S. support; that there seemed to be evidence that the availability of dollars was allowing other governments that could afford it to shirk their own responsibility for the support of research; and that there was a real problem of skewing the scientific development of other nations, especially the less-advanced countries, in the direction of America's scientific interests instead of their own.

In 1963, a new issue arose and became controlling: the U.S. balance-of-payments problem. At first, sentiment in budget circles inside the U.S. Government called for complete cessation of the overseas science support programs. Sudden withdrawals would have had serious repercussions, for many foreign scientists had come to depend on the U.S. programs. There would have been charges of bad faith, and undoubtedly great resentment on the part of an important segment of the intellectual community in countries of political importance. Ultimately, a gradual scaling-down was instituted instead of a sudden withdrawal.[2]

Aside from the scale of U.S. activities and the manner of their operation, the subject matter of a particular program can in itself be a problem, especially in the social sciences. The celebrated case of Project Camelot is all too apt an example.

In early 1965, the Department of the Army launched a behavioral science study in Latin America through the Special Operations Research Office (SORO) of American University in Washington, D. C. The study, designated Project Camelot, was designed to "produce a better understanding of the processes of social change and mechanisms for the established order to accommo-

[2] D. S. Greenberg, "Foreign Grants: U.S. Reducing but Not Ending Support Program for Research Activities Abroad," "News and Comment," *Science*, Vol. 145 (Sept. 11, 1964), pp. 1160–1161.

date change in an effective manner."[3] More popularly, it was known as a study of the dynamics of revolution in other countries.

Though some State Department personnel were aware of the project, key embassies were apparently not informed. The project threatened to become an international incident in the summer of 1965 when word of it came to the attention of Communist circles in Chile and a Communist newspaper in Santiago charged that the American military was intruding into Chilean affairs.

It did become a serious domestic incident in the United States as a result of the vehement protests of the American Ambassador in Chile that he had not been informed of the project, and when several Congressmen, notably Senators Fulbright and Morse, strongly attacked the rationale for this kind of overseas behavioral science research. The Army canceled the project.

President Johnson responded more broadly, however, by directing that the State Department establish effective procedures to clear all federally supported foreign aid research that might impinge on American foreign relations. In his letter to the Secretary of State, the President said, "I am determined that no Government sponsorship of foreign area research should be undertaken which in the judgment of the Secretary of State would adversely affect United States foreign relations."[4]

[3] John Walsh, "Social Sciences: Cancellation of Camelot after Row in Chile Brings Research Under Scrutiny," *Science*, Vol. 149 (Sept. 10, 1965), p. 1211.

[4] Address by Thomas L. Hughes, Director of Intelligence and Research, Department of State, "Scholars and Foreign Policy:

These "effective procedures" have been established; their performance in practice remains to be evaluated over time. Although the State Department has always been informed of agency overseas programs whether in the natural or the social sciences, this is the first time a regular, centralized clearance process in advance of project implementation is being tried. Whether or not the Department will be able to resist the temptation to review projects on their merits (the prerogative of the sponsoring agencies) as opposed to reviewing only to assure no adverse effects on foreign relations is uncertain. This is of particular concern because of the Department's own very limited competence in research and a generally negative attitude of many in the Foreign Service toward the value and requirements of behavioral science research.

Undoubtedly, however, the State Department must be cognizant of the variety of scientific and technical activities the U.S. Government carries out overseas, and be in a good position to monitor the activities and raise its voice with regard to the foreign policy implications. If it is not alive to the technical needs and opportunities, able to understand them and to move quickly when necessary, it is likely to become a bottleneck rather than an aid. If the foreign policy machinery simply imposes delays and objections, rather than searches for constructive solutions to problems, it will not be able to fulfill a useful role in molding and supporting these overseas activities that, in sum, touch sensitive and important chords in the totality of U.S. relations with others.

Varieties of Research Experience," Root-Jessup Lecture, Hamilton College, Oct. 21, 1965.

GRAY AREA SUPPORT

There is another implication of the requirement that all international activities conducted by government agencies must be relevant to the mission of that agency, an implication that affects the potential use of those activities for specific foreign political purposes. For the requirement of relevance makes it difficult for an agency to mount a program that has as its primary justification a political rather than a scientific return. In practice, programs are developed first on the basis of how they contribute to an agency mission, and only afterwards are the positive (or negative) political ramifications explored. Especially when dealing with basic science projects, this procedure is proper and safe, for it tends to keep to a minimum the temptation to plan programs on the basis of nebulous and possibly distorting foreign policy considerations. Instead, it emphasizes clearer criteria of quality, need, objective scientific merit, and scientific opportunity.

However, the mission relevance requirement makes it extremely difficult for the foreign policy maker to encourage new programs and activities that he believes will have favorable political benefits. For he may see political value in specific scientific activities, yet the agency that would have to carry them out may be unable to justify those activities in terms of its mission, or may find the proposals of lower quality than competing uses of the funds. Without independent funding available that can be allocated on the basis of political criteria, the State Department and the U.S. Government as a whole are in a poor position to mount programs for political purposes when those programs cannot be fully justified on grounds of mission relevance and scientific merit.

Occasionally, the government has been able to surmount this barrier, but such incidents involve major policy departures in which the President and the Congress were directly involved. As already noted, the space program itself is illustrative of a technical enterprise justified primarily on political and not scientific grounds. The Atoms for Peace Program is another example, and so, too, in a limited way is the U.S./Japan science cooperation program that will be discussed later. In addition, AID's mission to advance economic development is at times, though rarely, usable as a justification for an overseas program in which the primary interest is political.

But there are frequent opportunities that arise for which a legitimate case can be made on grounds of political gain, which do not warrant Presidential intervention, and in which the U.S. Government is essentially powerless to act. For example, research and development on disease problems faced by other countries cannot normally be supported with dollar funds of the National Institutes of Health. To do so involves making the case that U.S. nationals are living in those areas and must be protected against local diseases, or else that the diseases may be imported into the United States, or that the solution of particular health problems is a necessary prerequisite for economic development, in which case very limited AID research funds are eligible. Yet for political reasons there may be excellent justification for mounting an attack on diseases in specific countries.

Agricultural research is in a similar situation. Unless

a project can be justified and supported by AID, the Department of Agriculture is unable to proceed to meet research targets of opportunity overseas that do not bear on American agriculture problems. Even when political interest is high, the legislative authorization of the Department of Agriculture bars action. The problem is made harder by the concern in the farm states that support for agriculture in other countries will reduce export markets for American crops.

President Johnson's proposed new legislation in the health, agriculture, and education fields may sharply alter the situation in these fields. As presently conceived, the legislation will allow those agencies to expend their own appropriated funds on problems relevant to other nations, especially the less-developed countries.[5]

Examples arise from time to time in other fields. When planning was under way for the major cooperative oceanographic exploration of the Indian Ocean, proposals were made within the U.S. Government to help the smaller countries on the Indian Ocean rim to participate as guests of the United States. It was believed that taking part in the work of the expedition, even for countries with no indigenous oceanographic competence, would be of economic importance to them in the future, would give them a sense of participation in a major cooperative scientific endeavor off their shores, and would redound politically in favor of the United States. The proposal foundered largely on the lack of any responsible focus of authority in the U.S. Government that could legitimately put up the money.

[5] "State of the Union Message," *The New York Times*, Jan. 13, 1966, p. 14; John Walsh, "Exporting the Great Society: Funds are a Limiting Factor," *Science*, Vol. 152 (Apr. 1, 1966), p. 45.

Another example arose at the time of the Belgian withdrawal from the Congo, when a research institution outside Leopoldville suddenly found itself without funds.[6] The Institution was doing some work of interest to local Congo problems; more important, it represented a nucleus of highly trained Congolese who might be of considerable importance to education and research in the Congo in the future. The U.S. Government was approached to provide support for some of the specific projects already under way. These, too, had to be rejected, for their quality was not competitive with projects in similar fields within the United States, and there was no formally acceptable justification for providing support.

The situation typified by this latter Congolese example is one of the most common. Quite often there are in other countries the nuclei of scientific research groups, or competent lone investigators, or even larger research institutions doing good work and unable to obtain adequate support for their work. They are unable to obtain support because of lack of local resources, lack of interest of the local government, an inability to compete for scarce funds at home with better known investigators, youth of the individual or institution, or a combination of these and other reasons.

The question is whether it is in the U.S. interest to provide some direct means for support of scientists or institutions abroad when their work does not satisfy the normal U.S. criteria of competitive quality or mission relevance. It is clear why the Bureau of the Budget (BOB) or the Congress would be reluctant to open this particular avenue of expenditure. Once criteria

[6] Institut pour la Recherche Scientifique en Afrique Centrale (IRSAC).

are used that include "political interest" as a primary variable, the problem of choice is made many times more difficult. Where is the cutoff? How can the Department of State determine the degree of political interest?

Moreover, if regular agency funds are used, then in effect American scientists are being denied funds in favor of foreign investigators. And the basis of such a choice would have to be a political judgment that is allowed to override judgments based on scientific merit. Who is to make such judgments? Scientists? Foreign Service Officers?

Yet, for all its dangers, it is unconscionable that the U.S. Government does not have the institutional means to respond to situations in which there appears to be a clear political opportunity but for which the necessary scientific case cannot be made.

There is no easy answer to this problem, but one possible innovation is for a limited fund to be voted, either to the State Department or to an agency such as the NSF, over and above the regular appropriations for domestic scientific support. Quite clearly, if the foreign policy maker is to be able to take advantage of special opportunities abroad, opportunities in science and technology that may not have sufficient political visibility to attract high-level attention, there must be in existence some kind of a regularized mechanism to which he can turn.[7]

[7] The proposed revisions in the National Science Foundation Act would reinforce quite explicitly the authorization for the Foundation to undertake international activities at the request of the Secretary of State or the Secretary of Defense (HR 14838, Sec. 3b, Report No. 1650, House of Representatives, 89th Congress, Second Session, June 23, 1966). In fact, the original NSF Act can be interpreted to

Quite clearly, the foreign policy maker must himself be able to recognize these scientific opportunities and to see their political possibilities. He cannot rely wholly on the technical agencies to identify them for, by definition, most of the opportunities will not fall in an agency's purview because of their subject or their lower relative quality. He is the one who must realize how the technical project can relate to American foreign policy interests, and must be able to follow it through on both technical and political grounds.

mean that the Foundation already had this authority, but the more explicit language will be helpful. However, this authority does not solve the problem of how funds will be made available, as discussed in the text.

4

Strengthening Science
and International Science Policy

After the erection of the Berlin Wall in 1961, the NATO allies retaliated by sharply restricting the access of East Germans to NATO countries. Before long, representatives of the scientific community in Western countries complained to their governments that scientists residing in East Germany were unable to come to NATO countries to meet with them or attend international meetings.

The scientists protested within their respective governments, arguing that the restrictions were demeaning, were a negation of the scientific tradition of free and open intercourse independent of political attitudes, and in the long run would be damaging to science in the West. In April 1964, the travel policy was liberal-ized by the United States, United Kingdom, and France with the concurrence of other NATO governments.[1]

This sequence of events exemplified a new facet of the concerns of the foreign policy maker: the responsibility to support, protect, and strengthen a nation's scientific enterprise, including maintaining the conditions of free scientific intercourse the scientist believes so important.[2]

To many scientists, it is this concern with and responsibility for the international relations of science that is considered to be the essence of the subject of science and foreign policy. As a result, there has been substantial work, largely by scientists, in this area. In particular, the pathbreaking study led by Lloyd Berkner for the Department of State in 1950, *Science and Foreign Relations*, deals with many of the implications of this responsibility for U.S. foreign policy machinery.[3]

The involvement of the government in matters of free scientific exchange is not new. Thomas Jefferson wrote to John Hollins in 1809:

These [scientific] societies are always at peace, however their nations may be at war. Like the republic of letters, they

[1] Announcement by Allied Travel Office, Berlin, April 1964.

[2] Science as used in this section refers to basic science and is not meant to include technology. The assumption underlying this discussion is that it is in the national interest to support maximum scientific advance. This assumption, especially as it relates to technological applications of scientific advances, will be raised for examination in Part IV.

[3] *Science and Foreign Relations*, International Science Policy Survey Group, Department of State, Publication 3860, May 1950; Also see W. Albert Noyes, Jr., "Do We Need a Foreign Policy in Science?" *Bulletin of the Atomic Scientists*, Vol. XIII, No. 7 (Sept. 1957), pp. 234–237; and Dean Rusk, "Building an International Community of Science and Scholarship," *Department of State Bulletin* XLIV, May 1, 1961, pp. 624–628.

form a great fraternity spreading over the whole earth, and their correspondence is never interrupted by any civilized nation.[4]

In a similar and more direct vein, Benjamin Franklin sent an oft-quoted directive to the commanders of all U.S. armed ships in 1779:

> Gentlemen, a ship was fitted out from England . . . to make discoveries in unknown seas under the conduct of . . . Captain Cook. . . . This, then, is to recommend to you that should the said ship fall into your hands, you would not consider her as an enemy, . . . nor obstruct her immediate return to England.[5]

In those times, science had little direct or immediate relation to a nation's power, so that the nation's leaders, in many cases themselves accomplished scientists, saw no problem whatever in allowing international scientific activities to proceed independently of current political disputes. Moreover, only small groups in a population actually identified themselves with the foreign policy of their nation. The policies were those of the rulers or the government, not the collective policies of the nation. Thus "republics," such as those Jefferson refers to, cutting across borders and ignored by rulers, could easily exist and prosper without reference to purely national objectives.

Today, the political situation is different, and the relation of science to the power and influence of states is drastically altered. But the republic of science remains; it is many times larger, beholden to government patronage, highly visible, more bureaucratic, and

[4] As quoted in Hans J. Morgenthau, *Politics Among Nations,* (3rd ed.; New York: Alfred A. Knopf, 1961), p. 104.

[5] As quoted in *Science and Foreign Relations,* p. 87, *op. cit.*

fragmented but still bearing strong resemblance to the republic of 1809. Not only does the republic remain, but it has fostered traditions and mores about science and scientific progress that have become sacrosanct to scientists.

These traditions are founded in part on the fact that scientific research requires that results be reproducible, thus that there be uniform standards and language. An experimenter's research design, experiments, and conclusions from the results must be based on the scientific facts and not be influenced by personal bias, political ideology, or any other nonobjective factor if his work is to have scientific validity.

In practice, scientists will agree that science is rather more subjective and that certain preconceptions may color their perception of worthwhile experiments, their hypotheses and generalizations, or their immediate interpretation of the significance of results obtained.[6] Still, the ideal is complete objectivity, and scientists will vehemently defend against any encroachment of a political or other character that threatens that objectivity.

Therefore, scientists will argue that research must be planned on the basis of scientific criteria alone. A government may want research in certain fields for its own reasons, but what experiments are actually carried out within that field must be planned on scientific grounds. Similarly, on the international scene, scientists believe it is appropriate for governments to indicate a willingness to support research in, say, the atmospheric sciences, but what detailed research is worth doing and

[6] See Thomas S. Kuhn, *The Structure of Scientific Revolutions* (Chicago: University of Chicago Press, 1963), for a discussion of how current scientific theories condition scientific progress.

how should be left to the scientists alone. Clearly, any such flagrant interference in the evaluation of research results and scientific theories as occurred in the Soviet Union in the Lysenko case is improper. It is also unwise, as is amply demonstrated by the present lag in Soviet biology.

Scientists have other traditions, derived in part from their need for objectivity, and in part from the simple requirement that research results must be available to others if they are to be reproduced and used by other scientists. Scientists insist on the importance of being free to publish their results and, as a corollary, free to meet and exchange information with colleagues regardless of their political affiliation. Of course, there frequently have been impediments of one kind or another to the free exchange of information. Much research is still classified on security grounds, and, in fact, there are mechanical impediments that flow from the sheer volume of research being published.

Still, scientists protest vigorously attempts at "artificially" restricting the flow of information or persons across national boundaries. If political motivations enter, then the objectivity nerve is touched once again; a scientist feels he can look down a long road of gradually growing interference until all science is of lower quality and undoubtedly stunted in growth. How important it is then to the scientist to resist the first encroachments, no matter how innocuous they may appear.

For the nation, there is another less idealistic motive at work here as well. It is that science will progress faster if scientists are able to talk to and exchange information with scientists of their own choosing wherever they reside. Thus, a nation that believes that advance of science will be of benefit to itself has a selfish motive in preventing the erection of unnecessary barriers between its scientists and those of other nationalities.

On quite a different plane is the argument based on science as a cultural activity. In this age it is in many ways man's most striking cultural activity. And the United States has a great deal to be proud of in its pre-eminence in this unique intellectual search, a pride that should lead to great concern in maintaining the conditions and freedom that made the pre-eminence possible. Especially is this so because the traditions of an "open" science conform so closely to American traditions of an open society.

Therefore, in a world in which science has come to have great meaning to the power and influence of nations, foreign policies must be formulated in the knowledge that the progress of science and the national benefits derived from science are likely to be affected by those policies. In practice, this means that the policy maker must be conscious of why international activities and organizations of scientists are important to the advancement of science, what those activities and organizations are, what the traditions and mores of the scientific community are, why they developed, and how specific foreign policies can further, or interfere with, the "normal" working of science.

Recognition of the relationship between specific foreign policies and the progress of science does not also imply that political objectives must give way to the objectives of scientists whenever they are in conflict. Sometimes the concerns of scientists are as much politically based as they are scientifically based. For example, some scientists argue for increased contacts with Communist China because of their disagreement with current U.S. policy toward China, not because they are being frustrated in a particular scientific endeavor. (This is not to imply that scientists have no important scientific arguments for contacts with Communist China.) Most often, the policy maker is simply faced with the traditional problem of reconciling conflicting objectives, each of which may be valid but all of which cannot be achieved simultaneously.

An excellent illustration of the latter problem is the issue of admission to the United States, for attendance at scientific meetings of scientists who would normally be excluded (1) because of previous activities that are proscribed by the Immigration and Nationality Act, or (2) because they come from countries whose governments are not recognized by the United States.

The International Council of Scientific Unions (ICSU), the leading international organization of science, approved a policy statement in October 1958 that states well the attitude of most scientists toward restrictions on admission to a country when a scientist is on bona fide scientific business.

INTERNATIONAL COUNCIL OF SCIENTIFIC UNIONS RESOLUTION ON POLITICAL NON-DISCRIMINATION

To ensure the uniform observance of its basic policy of political non-discrimination, the ICSU affirms the right of the scientists of any country or territory to adhere to or to associate with international scientific activity without regard to race, religion or political philosophy.

Such adherence or association has no implications with respect to recognition of the government of the country or the territory concerned.

Subject only to payment of subscriptions and submission of required reports, the ICSU is prepared to recognize the academy, research council, national committee, or other bona fide scientific group representing scientific activity of any country or territory acting under a government de facto or de jure that controls it.

Meetings or assemblies of ICSU or of its dependent organisms such as its special committees and its joint commissions should be held in countries which permit participation of the representatives of every national member of ICSU or of the dependent organism of ICSU concerned, and allow free and prompt dissemination of information related to such meetings.

ICSU and its dependent organisms will take all necessary steps to achieve adherence to these principles.[7]

The problem of admission of scientists from the Chinese mainland came to a head several times during the Eisenhower Administration at a time when the "China Lobby" was particularly influential. American scientists were anxious to be hosts to large international scientific conferences as a reflection of the new leadership of American science and as a natural recognition of the increasing personal role of American scientists in international scientific affairs. The international community of scientists considered it proper and appropriate to hold more of their meetings in the United States. But to do so meant the United States would have to conform to the ICSU resolution just quoted that called for par-

[7] "Policy of Political Non-Discrimination," 8th General Assembly of the International Council of Scientific Unions, *ICSU Review*, Vol. I, No. 3, July 1959, p. 144.

ticipation of representatives of *every* national member of ICSU.

The case of the International Astronomical Union (IAU) which included Communist China as a member was typical. To issue an invitation for the prospective meeting in Berkeley in 1961, American scientists had to assure the Union at the previous full meeting, which happened to be held in Moscow in 1958, that all official representatives of member nation scientific bodies would be able to attend.

The Department of State balked at providing assurance in advance to admit Red Chinese scientists to the United States on the grounds that to do so would have important political repercussions throughout Southeast Asia, presumably as indicating a softening or weakening of American China policy. The scientists retorted that the Department was willing to sacrifice basic traditions of science, which also happened to have their own international political importance, for a rather nebulous and short-term connection between admission of Chinese citizens and recognition of the Chinese regime.

Neither side understood the objectives of the other. At times, members of the Department became highly incensed, arguing in effect that because American China policy was designed in the long run to protect the values the scientists were concerned about, the scientists were stupid, or worse, to object. Feelings ran high.

The situation was at an impasse until Under Secretary Christian Herter evolved a temporary compromise that committed the Department to admit Red Chinese scientists to the United States in 1961 as long as the IAU remained "apolitical." This was to mean that the IAU had to accept the National Chinese as members of the

Union if they applied. Some scurrying about was necessary to encourage a suitable Taiwanese organization to apply, and, of course, Red China withdrew from the IAU when Taiwan was admitted to membership. Thus, the actual problem of allowing Communist Chinese scientists into the United States for the Berkeley meeting never arose.

Since then, however, the Communist Chinese have been invited to other meetings in this country but have never come. In general, the conflicts between the scientific community and the Department of State over these impediments to free movement have greatly lessened. In part the reason has been more liberal policies by the Department; in part it has been because scientists have become more sophisticated about the clashes of objectives that a policy maker must always face and attempt to resolve.

The responsibilities of the foreign policy maker toward science extend beyond avoiding negative actions whenever possible. He also has a positive role in encouraging international scientific contacts, finding ways to make them more fruitful, and supporting the international organizations of science.

Scientists are organization minded, largely because meetings of scientific societies prove to be an effective way to exchange information and to organize and plan needed scientific programs. The important international scientific organizations include in particular the International Scientific Unions and ICSU, their joint policy body. ICSU has as members, in addition to the Unions, the leading scientific societies of individual countries (the National Academy of Sciences/National Research Council for the United States), and the Special Committees that ICSU has established in multidisciplinary fields such as space and oceanography. In addition to the ICSU complex are many ties between literally thousands of scientific organizations such as the American Association for the Advancement of Science, or the Instrument Society of America, and their foreign counterparts.

The major activities of these bodies are designed to aid in the exchange of information and to encourage the advancement of particular scientific fields. In addition, especially within the ICSU framework, there has been increasing activity to plan for future growth in new fields of science that require international cooperation. This is an important development for governments, for it makes it possible to obtain objective plans for international scientific programs that can provide the necessary basis for government planning. Without such a mechanism, divorced from governments, international planning for scientific programs has to be done by governments in a more political environment and therefore with less reliability as a scientific guide to what is needed and useful.

The recent International Geophysical Year (IGY) is the great triumph of this scientific planning process.[8] The plans and concepts were first laid out under the auspices of ICSU. Once their plans were in preliminary shape, the scientists lobbied through their National Academies and related bodies for support by national governments. The detailed planning and coordination necessary throughout the full term of the IGY was conducted almost entirely by scientists at times represent-

[8] J. Tuzo Wilson, *IGY, The Year of the New Moons* (New York: Alfred A. Knopf, 1961).

ing their governments, at times acting as independent individuals.

The successful IGY led to proposals and planning for other international programs such as the IQSY (International Year of the Quiet Sun — a follow-up of the IGY), a Biological Program, a Hydrological Decade, and an international program in the atmospheric sciences. In most cases, the first initiative came from the scientists themselves; in some, notably the international programs planned in the atmospheric sciences, governments took the first step.

In all these cases, the caliber of the programs was greatly aided by enabling scientists to take the first cut at actual programs in an atmosphere in which they were relatively free of political, or even budgetary, restraints. Later, governments could bargain, indicate what resources they were prepared to commit, integrate plans, and so forth. But the basic plan, grounded on objective scientific judgments, was required as a basis for sound negotiation.

International scientific planning need not always be carried out by scientists operating in a nongovernment framework, though that is the preferred pattern. But when governments attempt to plan international scientific programs directly, then it is important that they establish adequate machinery within the country to obtain objective plans based on the actual scientific situation. One way or the other, justification and planning on scientific grounds should be obtained prior to injection of the many other constraints that condition international programs. When the international projects are large in scope and involve many countries, the framework of the international scientific organizations provides a logical place in which to carry out the initial scientific planning.

INTERNATIONAL SCIENCE POLICY

Along with the rapid growth of domestic support for science has been a parallel development on the international scene. Scientists in many fields have looked to the success of the IGY as an inspiration and as a model for their own planning of large-scale international programs. And nations have helped regional and U.N. organizations to launch extensive international scientific programs related to the objectives of each of the organizations. The result has been a great expansion in the scale of international science programs that are supported directly or indirectly by national budgets.

At one time, the funds required for international activities were only a small part of those budgeted for domestic programs; now, some smaller countries find appreciable percentages of their science budgets going to pay their share of international programs.[9] In the United States, the funds going to international programs are still a small percentage of the total available for science, but high enough to raise important issues of scientific choice. How do these international programs compare in scientific interest with alternative domestic science programs? Is there a bandwagon philosophy operating in which programs proposed in an international framework tend to be favored, perhaps for the wrong reasons, over wholly domestic programs? (One result of the IGY's drawing power has been the proposal of large-scale programs in fields that do not necessarily

[9] *International Scientific Organizations*, OECD, 1964, p. 30.

require international cooperation.) Some of the smaller European countries have voiced their concern in the councils of the Organization for Economic Co-operation and Development (OECD) that they have inadequate control over the pace and size of international scientific programs to which they are committed.

Nations often find it difficult to integrate international science programs into their regular science planning. Frequently, different individuals or agencies within a country are responsible for domestic and international programs. Or two or more international agencies will mount projects in the same field, and the national representatives to those international agencies will not be aware of the work of the other agency. Sometimes the international program is dominated by the objective or perspective of a few countries, a situation that may result in a program tangential to work in similar fields within a given country. Sometimes the planning cycles of international programs do not coincide with those of domestic programs, adding to the planning problems. Most bothersome of all, individual nations may find themselves outvoted in international organizations and, as a result, participating in programs that strain their resources or that divert their scarce scientific talent to problems that they consider of low priority. Often, these days, the United States and other scientifically advanced countries find themselves outvoted by the less-developed countries on issues concerning science programs in UNESCO, just as some of the smaller countries in NATO sometimes found it necessary to go along reluctantly with NATO science programs proposed by the United States.

The burgeoning international activities of science are

creating a situation that is becoming steadily more pressing for consideration by the science policy and foreign policy machinery of every nation. The periodic frustrations expressed by governments as a result of the rising scale of international scientific activity over which they seem to have little control typically leads to proposals for an international clearing house for information that will identify and keep track of international programs.[10] The desire for more information catalogued in one placed is laudable. There is, most certainly, an astonishing lack of centralized comparison and collation of information about on-going or proposed international science programs. The tendency of international organizations to keep their own counsel and to consider other international organizations as competitors does not ease the information problem.

However, the need for more centralized information is just one aspect of the problem and far from the most important. What governments really must face is that their international science policy, their participation in international science programs and activities, is not an item separable from their national science policies or from their international political objectives. The desire to package all international programs together and separate them from domestic scientific activities in the planning or budgetary process can lead to misleading conclusions and poor planning criteria.

International science policy must be seen from several different perspectives. One is the perspective of the international organization. That is, what is the total science program of an international organization? How

[10] Emmanuel G. Mesthene, ed., *Ministers Talk About Science*, OECD, 1965, p. 132.

does it relate to that organization's mission? Does the organization have the manpower and the political means to carry out its programs?, and so forth.

A second perspective is that of national objectives in science. International programs must be seen in the context of domestic allocation of resources for science, modified by additional relevant foreign policy considerations. In fact, at times the political considerations may dominate, or the opportunities for international scientific cooperation may feed back and alter domestic programs or domestic objectives.

A third perspective must be the broader one of the general interaction of the science policies and achievements of individual nations. Many issues of international policy arise today because what each country does at home or internationally in science can affect scientific, or political, or economic matters in other nations. A good illustration is provided by the current debate over the international effects — in many spheres of national interest — of the apparent growing technological gap between the United States and Western European countries, a gap that is attributed to the relatively large scale of American investment in R & D.[11]

Thus, formal programs of cooperation, or extensions of domestic programs into international environments, or international industrial activities and agreements of a technical nature, or decisions to "go it alone" in particular scientific fields must be viewed from many different angles and not simply on the basis of the program or activity itself.

Obviously, the foreign policy maker must be a par-

[11] See discussion of this issue in Chapter 7.

ticipant in this process. The relevant issues cannot be represented by scientists or by the interested government agencies alone. It must be a joint process in which the foreign policy maker recognizes the need to relate the choices to national science policy and to international political effects and opportunities. He must also know enough about the scientific aspects to be able to make a case for altering domestic as well as international scientific objectives if the political considerations seem to warrant such a step.

5

The Side Effects of the Scientific Enterprise

One of the striking aspects of the continuing rapid development of science and technology is the increased scale of operations that is required. Many research projects are now carried out on a global basis; even single experiments may involve worldwide effects. Technological systems become larger, more complex, and have global uses and effects. The financial support required for scientific research itself reaches proportions that raise serious allocation of resource problems within nations and have effects that reach beyond national borders.

This greatly expanded and expanding scale of operations of science and technology carries with it some side effects or problems that raise new and novel issues in foreign affairs. Some of these, such as the question of free scientific movement among nations or the political implications of large technological systems that require international cooperation for effective operation, are considered elsewhere in this book. But two of these new issues deserve to be singled out for separate discussion: the problem of environmental alteration through scientific experimentation, and the problem of migration of scientists and engineers, more commonly called the "brain drain."

ENVIRONMENTAL ALTERATION

There are two related but separable parts of the environmental alteration problem. One is the aspect referred to in discussions of pollution: the gradual alteration of the environment that results from man's increasing use of technology in his society. Included here is environmental pollution of air and water, destruction of open land and forest resources, modification of the environment through overpopulation, and so forth.

The other aspect of the environmental alteration problem, the one that receives major attention here because of the nature of the issues it raises for foreign policy, is the potential danger to man's environment of large-scale experimentation that may have discontinuous, as opposed to gradual, environmental effects. Only recently has man acquired the physical power to carry out experiments that can have immediate and perhaps irreversible effects on the entire planet's environmental system; but he has this power in his hands now, and it is sure to grow. Basic issues of national freedom of action and international responsibility are raised by this new capability.

There are many examples from the past that can be cited, and potentials for the future. Fallout from nuclear weapons tests is one. The spread of radioactive material from the tests via the atmosphere to all parts of the world carried with it threats to the health of people who had no connection with the motives for conducting the tests and no say on whether or not the tests should be held. The radioactivity also carried an uncertain, and unknown, genetic threat.

Nuclear tests have been conducted so far by only five nations; fallout from the tests was deplored but was obviously not a controlling consideration in the decision to conduct tests in any of the five countries. The basic decisions have been made on the grounds of national security and have been made unilaterally.

Another example is Project Westford. This was an American military communications experiment intended to inject in a polar orbit a thinly spaced belt of copper filaments that would act as tiny radio reflectors from stations on the ground. If the experiment was successful, it would indicate that a higher-density operational belt could provide highly reliable radio links for secure military communications backup in case of need. The proposed experiment, designed to test only theoretical principles, ran into strong, sometimes violent reactions from the international scientific community on the grounds that such a belt might seriously impair the future of optical and radio astronomy. In distinction from the fallout example, the concern here was permanent interference with science rather than direct harm to people.

The United States argued, with impressive scientific studies as a basis, that the experiment itself would have no long-term effects because the density of filaments would be so low. In any case, it was calculated that the lifetime of the filaments would be short if they were injected into the proper orbit. An operational belt of higher density might be a more serious problem, but the United States agreed not to put a higher-density belt into orbit until the results of the first experiment were evaluated.

The international scientific community, in particular the astronomers, were never wholly reconciled to the experiment. Many felt a successful experiment would inevitably lead to a potentially more damaging dense operational belt. Others had personal or political reasons for protesting publicly, but most were concerned because of the principle that one nation was arrogating to itself a decision that could seriously and perhaps permanently affect an entire scientific field.

The United States went to great pains to release scientific data in advance and to encourage scientific evaluation of the U.S. calculations that indicated there was no danger in the experiment. Without bowing to any demands for formal international approval, the United States eventually proceeded with Project Westford, first in an abortive launch in October 1961 and later, successfully, on May 9, 1963. The technical results were as expected. As far as is known, no decision has yet been made about a follow-on operational system.

Other technical experiments that had environmental effects on an international scale are relevant. For example, the high-altitude nuclear bomb tests, Project Starfish, conducted on July 9, 1962, resulted in new bands of trapped electrons around the earth.[1] Once

[1] Wilmot N. Hess, "Man-Made Radiation Belts," *International Science and Technology* (Sept.) 1963, p. 40.

again, it was the scientists who most vehemently objected to the tests because of the danger to science. Another example was the introduction of a new irrigation system on the Colorado River that resulted in serious economic dislocation on Mexican farms. The effect of the irrigation system, located entirely in the United States, was to increase greatly the salinity content of water reaching Mexico.[2]

Looking to the future, more experimentation on a grand scale is possible: for example, weather modification, creation of artificial ocean currents intended to increase fish resources, and construction of large dams such as the one the Russians have proposed across the Bering Straits.[3] Any of these experiments or projects will undoubtedly have the motive of serving man. Nevertheless, they also have the potential of altering the environment in ways that may be antithetical to man's long-term needs.

In the case of both the high-altitude bomb tests and Project Westford, there were angry demands from abroad, echoed also within the United States, that this nation should not proceed with the experiments without prior study and approval by international bodies. The IAU in 1961 asked all governments launching space experiments that might interfere with astronomy to consult the IAU and refrain from launching until it could be established beyond doubt that no damage would be done to astronomical research.[4] The assumption was that no nation has the moral or ethical right to

[2] *The New York Times*, July 1, 1962, p. 1.
[3] In 1964, the NSF set up a special panel to study the scientific, social, and economic effects of weather modification. *Science*, Vol. 145 (July 3, 1964), p. 34.
[4] John W. Findlay, "West Ford [*sic*] and the Scientists," *Proceedings of the IEEE*, Vol. 52; No. 5, (May 1964), p. 455.

take unilateral actions that will affect others so drastically without first getting their approval.

It is easy to dismiss the demand for international approval as absurd, especially when it pertains to an experiment justified on national security grounds. In fact, it is not absurd; it is simply impractical today for the same reasons that make it impractical to achieve general and complete disarmament quickly. So long as no international mechanism exists for control of armaments, it is folly to expect any nation to submit actions it deems vital to its security to any kind of international veto. But that does not mean that the question of principle involved — the right of a nation to take actions unilaterally that modify the earth's natural environment and significantly affect others — should be dismissed.

The United States, for example, has several political objectives that should influence its current policies with regard to these large-scale programs:

1. This nation is committed to the gradual development of a body of international laws for regulating the international policies and actions of nations. A good part of international law is created by precedent rather than through a legislative or negotiating process. Thus, actions that countries take now in new areas not previously covered tend to set precedents that in time have the force of law. For the United States to continue to carry out actions with global effects on a unilateral basis certainly does not encourage, and may inhibit, the development of international law that eventually

could restrain nations from casual or selfish use of techniques that could cause global damage.

2. The United States, in the absence of international law on the subject, has a need to deter other countries from carrying out actions with wide-ranging undesirable effects. The United States sees itself as a responsible nation, yet it took a risk for all mankind in its unilateral actions with potentially damaging environmental effects. By setting the precedent of unilateral action, it is harder for the United States to protest when other nations decide they want to carry out experiments that also have possibly deleterious effects. It is also a measure of this nation's conceit that it has been willing, on its own responsibility, to tamper in quantum jumps, and perhaps irreversibly, with man's total environment.

3. In a more immediate and positive sense, these problems of large-scale experimentation can be viewed in the context of arms control and disarmament objectives. Some proposed experiments that have international side effects might well be used as subjects for international consultation and approval to establish precedents and machinery that could carry over into arms control negotiations.

4. Last, the sense of responsibility, or lack of it, that the United States shows in its handling of these large-scale and highly visible actions may become an important factor in shaping the image of this country held by others.

It is futile now to advocate submission of all proposed large-scale actions for definitive approval or disapproval by international bodies; the national security issues are too dominant. But the United States could assist in the development of an international mechanism for discussion and study of proposed experiments by competent scientists, a mechanism that might prove useful in years to come when some form of international review and approval will be acceptable. The Committee on Space Research (COSPAR) of the International Council of Scientific Unions has established a consultative group of scientists that could form the basis of such an international mechanism if the United States and other countries made full use of it.

At the very least, the U.S. Government must develop its own procedures so that all proposed major experiments with potentially harmful effects are raised for discussion and analysis early in the planning phase.

The government must know thoroughly the technical justifications for the proposals and must have as complete an evaluation of likely effects as possible, including evaluations that are made by those who are not the advocates of the experiments. Perhaps the experiments can be modified so as to produce lesser side effects and still develop the required information. Perhaps the scientific or political or legal costs are too great to warrant proceeding. Perhaps the scientists are too uncertain about the detrimental effects to take a chance. Perhaps the actions are sufficiently removed from security needs to allow an attempt to develop a "principle of consultation" in which adequate information would be provided publicly beforehand so that other nations may carry out their own calculations of likely effects. Perhaps the projects allow the advice and counsel of responsible international scientific bodies to be formally sought before proceeding.

Aware of the inadequacies of the governmental procedures at the time of the high-altitude tests and of Project Westford, President Kennedy established a formal process, centered on his Special Assistants for National Security Affairs and for Science and Technology designed to "assure expert review before potentially risky experiments are undertaken."[5] The purpose of the new procedures was to ensure that the kind of questions raised here would automatically be considered before an agency received approval to proceed.

Once again, those responsible for foreign policy formulation have a major stake in how these matters are handled but are in a difficult position. In forming judgments, they cannot rely wholly on the technical information provided by the agencies that are the proponents of the project. The foreign policy maker must understand the relationship of the project to broader policy issues, must be able to call for an independent, scientific evaluation if necessary, and must be able to participate in developing a sensible technical/political procedure if the decision is made to carry out a particular program. These responsibilities cannot be delegated for they are intrinsically foreign policy matters, and they cannot be adequately performed alone by part-time experts brought in on single issues. There must be individuals in the foreign policy process who can understand the technical issues and who can un-

[5] J. F. Kennedy, address to the National Academy of Sciences, *The New York Times*, Oct. 23, 1963, p. 24; J. B. Wiesner, *Where Science and Politics Meet* (New York: McGraw-Hill, 1965), p. 53.

derstand the uncertainties of the technical justifications and evaluations. There must be people who can see and articulate the tie to broader areas of foreign policy concern and who can identify and balance the sometimes competing claims of foreign policy and technical objectives. And there must be individuals who can work with the technical agencies and departments of the government, and with the private scientists in the United States and abroad.

BRAIN DRAIN

A recent survey of Iran, Pakistan, and Turkey estimated that 50 per cent of all their scientists trained abroad did not return home. Another study of Argentina indicates that that country lost 5,000 engineers through emigration in recent years. As high as 50 per cent of the honor students in science in New Zealand have been emigrating each year until recently; some 5 per cent of all German graduates in science emigrate each year; and 14 per cent of the total Ph.D.'s in natural sciences in England are now working abroad.[6]

Many science and engineering émigrés, particularly from Europe, have come to the United States. Recent studies show that from 1952 to 1961 the United States gained over 30,000 trained engineers, 9,000 scientists and 14,000 physicians and surgeons.[7] From July 1961 to June 1963, 10,000 more natural scientists, social sci-

[6] S. Dedijer, "Migration of Scientists," in First National Institutes of Health International Symposium, Oct. 31–Nov. 2, 1963, Kelly West, ed., U.S. Public Health Service, Bethesda, Maryland, 1964.

[7] Ibid. Dr. Dedijer also points out that more of the emigrant scientists from less-developed countries and the British Commonwealth have settled in Europe than in the United States.

entists and engineers were admitted to the United States as immigrants.[8]

This flow to the United States of scientifically trained manpower represents the output of several large universities. For other countries, conversely, it represents a cost measured not only in the value of the education these individuals received but also in the loss of the potential contributions to the societies they left behind. This phenomenon has popularly come to be called the "brain drain," a term coined in Britain, from which country many prominent scientists have emigrated.

The brain drain was not planned, nor is it a new phenomenon. Historically, there have been many migrations of individuals and large populations, usually brought about by the belief that conditions of one kind or another will be better in a different country. The present flow of scientists and engineers has become a prominent issue because of the greater public awareness of science and scientists and as a result of the belief that there is a direct relationship between the size and caliber of a country's scientific establishment and that nation's economic and military well-being.

The flow from a few advanced countries to the United States, notably from the United Kingdom and West Germany, has tended to excite the most attention (20 per cent of those emigrating to the United States in 1961-1963 came from England, 8 per cent from Germany).[9] In fact, the issue became important for British domestic politics in the 1964 British election

[8] "Scientists and Engineers From Abroad, Fiscal Years 1962 and 1963," *Reviews of Data on Science Resources, NSF 65–17*, Vol. I, No. 5 (July 1965). p. 1.

[9] *Ibid.*, p. 1.

campaign.[10] The reasons for the movement of scientists and engineers to the United States stem primarily from the greater scale of American scientific activity, which, in turn, means more opportunities for research and engineering positions and support. The more flexible organization of universities in this country that provides more senior faculty positions than in Europe, and hence more permanent openings, also contributes to the relative attraction. European countries, particularly England, tend to make up some of the outflow through emigration from the less-developed countries, though in the words of a report of a Royal Society committee, ". . . the high quality of our losses to the United States stands out."[11]

As important as the problem may be to scientifically advanced countries, it is clearly not catastrophic. In many cases, European governments recognize that they cannot afford the resources necessary to keep scientists in certain fields fully occupied. Limited funds and competing investment possibilities in science or other areas often are of higher national priority, notwithstanding the desire to keep scientific talent at home whenever possible.

The real issue is the importance of the loss of scarce talent by the less-developed countries. From the figures compiled by the National Science Foundation (NSF)

[10] Would that all problems could be dismissed as easily as Mr. Quinton Hogg, former U.K. Secretary of State for Education and Science did in Parliamentary debate, when he exhorted British scientists to stay in England because "It is better to be British than anything else." *The New York Times*, Feb. 12, 1964, p. 9.

[11] "The Emigration of Scientists From the United Kingdom, Report of a Committee Appointed by the Royal Society" (London: The Royal Society, 1963), reprinted in part in *Minerva*, Vol. 1, No. 3 (Spring 1963), p. 361.

for the fiscal years 1962 and 1963, some 19 per cent of those emigrating to the United States were born in Asia, and another 5 per cent were born in Latin America.[12] Vice-President Humphrey pointed out that for one country, Korea, there are "several times as many Korean Ph.D.'s in science living and working in the United States as in their own country."[13] One estimate for Taiwan is that only 5 per cent of the 2,000 per year who leave for graduate study abroad return after completing graduate work.[14] Even though the absolute numbers involved are relatively small compared to emigration from scientifically advanced countries, the loss of even a few highly trained personnel can have more serious effects on a less-developed nation's scientific and industrial activities.

The significance of this loss to a small struggling nation is hard to evaluate. The loss affects not only the research and industrial development in the countries from which the scientists and engineers come but also the competence of the educational system, the ability to introduce technical innovations, and the capability to increase the productivity of industry and agriculture. How much these elements are affected by the loss of scientists and engineers and to what extent the country could or should provide the competitive resources necessary to encourage scientists and engineers to remain at home are open questions. In part, the strictly

[12] NSF 65–17, op. cit., p. 4.
[13] Remarks of Vice President Humphrey at Weizmann Institute dinner, New York, Dec. 6, 1965.
[14] Joseph B. Platt, "Emigration of Scholars and the Development of Taiwan: Chinese-American Cooperation," a paper presented at the Seventh World Conference of the Society for International Development, Washington, D. C., March 12, 1965 and excerpted in Development Digest, Vol. IV, No. 1 (Apr. 1966), p. 43.

economic answer turns on the return to a society of investments in science and technology. Economic theory has not yet provided a means of measuring those returns.[15] In addition, there are other elements beyond the narrowly economic that must also be taken into account. These points are discussed further in Chapter 9.

Whatever the detailed economic and other effects on development may be, as a source of political controversy and concern the issue of scientific emigration is clearly one that must be watched as a natural by-product of the U.S. scientific enterprise. The indications are, in fact, that migration to the United States is increasing, and may be stimulated further by the new immigration law that puts a premium on skills of use in America. One expression of the seriousness of American concern is the legal requirement for all who first enter the United States for study to leave the country for a minimum of two years before being allowed to re-enter on an immigrant visa. But other steps are also necessary, such as more active encouragement of measures in other countries that will lead scientists and engineers to remain at home, or more emphasis on educational programs in the United States that are geared to the needs of the countries from which the students come.

Some portion of the problem is unsolvable, and should be that way. That is, from the point of view of the individual involved, of science in general, and even

[15] Harry G. Johnson, "The Economics of the 'Brain Drain': The Canadian Case," *Minerva*, Vol. III, No. 3 (Spring 1965), pp. 299–311; R. S. Eckaus, "Notes on Invention and Innovation in Less Developed Countries," paper prepared for the American Economic Association, Dec. 30, 1965.

of his native country, a highly talented scientist should be free to move where he will contribute the most. His scientific contribution will not be limited to the country in which he performs his work. In fact, in many cases if he is not allowed to migrate he will not be able to perform useful work at all. However, that applies only to a small number of the ablest scientists. Other scientists and, in particular, engineers can direct their efforts in a variety of directions, and with the right inducements and training can contribute to their country's advancement as well as to their own fields.

Thus the brain drain is another example of a complex political issue that has grown up as a by-product or side issue of science. It is not only a scientific issue but has a range of political and economic overtones which must be adequately reflected in the policy process.

PART III

*Foreign Policy Issues
with Important Scientific
and Technological Elements*

generations of general war weapon systems have been developed and discarded because of obsolescence without ever being used in actual warfare. The measure of a nation's total military power, the measure of its ability to support its major international commitments, must now be based on highly complex estimates of a great variety of technical factors such as the kinds of weapons the nation has, their effectiveness against various defensive systems (also changing rapidly), the ability to command and control the weapons during attack, and the likely developments in both offensive and defensive armaments in the immediate future.

Another order of uncertainty is added by the need to estimate, without good experience or precedents, the effectiveness of other nations' weapons and the probable strategies of their employment. Testing and maneuvers are of course carried out with the aid of intelligence information. Extensive war games and systems analyses are performed so that a nation believes it has a reasonable estimate of the strength and effectiveness of its forces against the probable capability of a potential enemy at a given moment of time. Nevertheless the accuracy of that estimate cannot be certain. A determination made with reasonable confidence one day, such as the estimate of Russian military power in 1949, may be suddenly changed or even overturned by a technical development the next, as by the evidence in 1949 that the Soviet Union had the atomic bomb. Possibilities of scientific "breakthroughs" that might have enormous impact on the effectiveness of a force must be anticipated. Yet breakthroughs cannot be foreseen in any detail simply because their parameters are unknown in advance. John Herz summed up the over-all situation well: ". . . the new weapons developments seem to affect the system of international relations in novel fashion: where formerly innovations, even radical ones, would permit the emergence of more or less stable new systems of some durability, the dynamic of the present is such as to foreclose any kind of stability."[1]

The advent of nuclear weapons has, of course, added an entirely different dimension to the power relationship between states than anything known in the past. The enormous destruction possible with nuclear weapons has forced the great powers to recognize that national objectives can only be achieved if calculations of the real balance of power are never put to the test in general nuclear war.

A great power, therefore, must be quite clear as to the strengths and limitations of its power and clear as well about what are its vital national interests. The opportunities for bluff, the importance of accurate evaluation of another nation's vital interests, the credibility of force structure and of the commitments that a nation enters into, are now matters of life and death to a great power in a literal sense that has no earlier parallel.

These new weapons systems have also contributed to the development of an international system in which there are, so far, only two great powers. Instead of a balance of several approximately equal states as in the nineteenth century, two superpowers have emerged, superpowers whose strength is based on the fact that they had the scientific competence and the economic strength to make and exploit the advances in science

[1] John Herz, *International Politics in the Atomic Age* (New York: Columbia University Press, 1959), p. 19.

and technology. Only two nations have been able to make the race and to remain in contention. More have tried, and more will undoubtedly succeed as other nations deepen and broaden their scientific capability and strengthen their economies (or as new groupings of nations emerge).

And the weapons developments continue. The pace of change may have slowed, for the introduction of a second- or third-generation missile is not as radical a step as the introduction of missiles themselves. In fact, later models of weapons systems tend to make power relationships more stable by reducing vulnerability and by making quick reaction time a less significant factor.[2] Radical and potentially destabilizing innovations resulting in entirely new weapons systems will surely come in time, however.

Science and technology figure prominently in foreign policy dealing with military matters not only on this broad plane of over-all strategic power but also in narrower policy concerns. One example that offers many illustrations of the science/policy interaction was the question of the appropriate American response to the plans of the French Government to develop an independent nuclear capability. Basic to determining American policy at the time was a series of scientific or technological judgments that had to be related to the many other political, diplomatic, and economic considerations relevant to the issue. For example:

1. Was France capable of developing an atomic weapon and associated delivery systems on her

[2] "Thinking Ahead with Harold Brown," *International Science and Technology,* (Sept., 1963), p. 49; Jerome B. Wiesner and Herbert F. York, "National Security and Nuclear-Test Ban," *Scientific American,* Vol. 211, No. 4 (Oct. 1964), pp. 27–35.

own on the basis of her scientific competence? What would be the price that France would have to pay in terms of denial of other objectives toward which her technical resources could have been directed if not for the nuclear effort? Would this opportunity cost be severe enough to give the United States any leverage on French policy? To what extent would France have to depend on American science and technology for the development of the bomb and, more subtly, for the development of the associated weapons systems necessary to make the bomb useful? Was the United States in a position to deny all or some of this help, or was so much of the necessary scientific and technological information in the public domain that the United States had control only of the atomic weapons information?

2. What would be the likely technical capabilities of a French *force de frappe*, and what would be its strategic implications? Would Soviet and American weapons developments during the period necessary for French development be likely to alter the meaning of the force when it is achieved? Are there other technical/military initiatives the United States could take in Europe along the lines of nuclear sharing, or mechanisms for joint control of weapons that might tempt the French once they realize the costs of a nuclear system?

3. What would be the broader significance to American objectives toward Europe and to its relations with France of the French decision to go it alone with nuclear weapons? How

much independence of action will this give France? Are there other areas, outside the nuclear field, in which France is dependent on American information or products? Can this dependence be used to influence French policy?

These questions and many others were, and some still are, relevant in determining U.S. policy toward France. Very few can be answered with simple facts. Most require judgments of varying degrees of certainty. Most require a good understanding of the political situation if relevant judgments of the future technical situation are to be made. (E.g., how quickly France could develop nuclear weapons depended on the willingness of the French Government to allocate scarce resources to the project and forgo programs in other areas such as health, industrial development, alternate military capability, etc. that might also be important objectives.) Vice versa: many of the political judgments of future developments require a good understanding of the technical situation. (E.g., the degree of French dependence on other European countries for scientific information or equipment for the *force de frappe* might be a major determinant of her attitude on other issues toward those countries.)

Policy making, to be reasonably sound on a subject of this kind, must have fully integrated within it these technical factors. Such integration implies, among other characteristics, the ability to ask the right questions so that technical information is relevant, and the ability to express technical information or judgments as functions of the political and other variables. It should be noted that quite similar questions can be asked today with regard to the possibility of an Indian decision to develop nuclear weapons. And current debates about the Multilateral Force and the deployment of antiballistic missile systems involve a similar series of questions in which the technical and the political variables are closely intertwined.

Naturally, for such issues, the Department of State, which must be in a position to formulate the right questions, works closely with and relies heavily on the technical agencies — primarily the Department of Defense and Atomic Energy Commission — for relevant information and answers. But, as noted before, it must be able to develop independent evaluations on its own on important points if it is to maintain its authority in the policy process.

Innumerable other examples in the field of arms policy could be cited to illustrate the new breadth of the relation of science and technology to fundamental security issues. The Skybolt controversy, IRBM emplacement in Europe, Bomarc for Canada, new weapons developments for limited war, and so forth, are all pertinent, as is over-all U.S. military strategy itself. But the relationship is obvious and so frequently referred to in other writing that it does not warrant further development here.

ARMS CONTROL AND DISARMAMENT

On January 12, 1958, President Eisenhower in a letter to Chairman Bulganin of the Soviet Union proposed joint technical studies of the inspection and control measures necessary for possible future disarmament

agreements.[3] In his letter, the President mentioned subjects such as a test ban, prevention of surprise attack,
cessation of production of nuclear material, and ban-
ning of weapons in outer space. The idea of discussions
by technical experts as a prelude to formal negotiations
was not entirely new (such technical talks had been
proposed originally by the British at the 1957 disarmament talks in London), but when the proposal was
later accepted by Khrushchev, who had succeeded Bulganin as Chairman of the Council of Ministers of the
U.S.S.R., a major innovation in arms control negotiations was set in train.[4] The purpose, of course, was to
attempt to separate discussions of technical facts from
political issues in the hopes that agreement on the
former could make negotiations on the latter more fruitful. And, it was implicitly assumed, agreement on the
technical facts should be quite straightforward because
meetings of scientists on technical subjects ought to be
"objective."

The technical negotiations on the test ban — for
they turned out to be negotiations, as discussed later
in more detail — demonstrated vividly the degree of
involvement of science and scientists in arms control
and disarmament issues. Robert Gilpin summarizes this
involvement, especially as related to nuclear weapons,
in sweeping terms:

American scientists, at least in the area of national policy
toward nuclear weapons, have become full partners with
politicians, administrators, and military officers in the formulation of policy. The American scientist has become a man

[3] *The New York Times*, Jan. 13, 1958, p. 6.
[4] Harold K. Jacobson and Eric Stein, *Diplomats, Scientists, and
Politicians* (Ann Arbor: University of Michigan Press, 1966), pp.
17, 50.

of power to perhaps even a greater degree than Snow [C. P. Snow], his audience, or scientists themselves appreciate. Neither in any other nation of the world with the possible exception of contemporary Russia, nor in any other historical period, have scientists had an influence in political life comparable to that presently exercised by American scientists.[5]

There would no doubt be little argument on the subject of arms control — less than on almost any other subject — that the scientific aspects of the issues must be woven into the fabric of the policy process. For it is quite clear today that the components of arms control policies must involve major technical matters.

Many of the same technical questions relevant to issues of military policy are also relevant here: characteristics of existing and possible future weapons systems, effectiveness and vulnerability of weapons systems in a variety of mixes, elements of command and control of forces, and estimates of existing or potential military capabilities of other countries.

But, in addition, a host of other technically based issues arise. What are the capabilities of detection and inspection systems that could be designed on the basis of existing scientific knowledge? What are the costs of such systems in relation to their relative effectiveness? How are these likely to improve in effectiveness with increased knowledge? What R & D programs should be mounted to improve monitoring system capabilities? Note that here the social sciences must also be included. Some of the questions about effectiveness

[5] Robert Gilpin, *American Scientists and Nuclear Weapons Policy*, (Princeton: Princeton University Press, 1962) p. 299. This book offers an excellent detailed discussion of the role of science and scientists in American nuclear policy since 1945.

of inspection systems depend on matters concerning human behavior; for example, how will individuals in particular environments respond to requests for information from foreign observers?

Questions about possible violations must also be understood — not just the obvious question, would cheating be technically possible, but also what would be the significance to military power relationships (or to a weapons development program) of certain patterns of violations? Will R & D be legally possible under a proposed agreement, and, if so, what military significance might it eventually have? If an agreement effectively halts development in one direction, is it likely to reinforce technical efforts in another direction? Is that a serious danger?

Most of the technical aspects of arms control issues are oriented to the future in that they are judgments about what is likely to happen. The degree of uncertainty is very large. Moreover, these predictions are in most cases inseparable from the political parameters of the issue if the judgments are to be of any value for policy making. To give one illustration, it is useless to hypothesize about the weapons that could be developed from a series of clandestine development programs and say no more. What policy makers need are evaluations that include the relative risk of discovery of clandestine development programs given a variety of political environments, the resource allocation problems the potentially offending nation would face, the payoffs of particular programs versus the relative risk of exposure, and so forth.

Therefore, while some of the technical questions may be studied in isolation by scientists and engineers

if the right questions are posed, the technical considerations cannot be separated from the political at the
policy-making levels. This conclusion raises obvious
questions about the soundness of the "conference of
experts" approach to arms control negotiations and
leads to some observations about the nature of the U.S.
Government's policy groundwork for the test ban negotiations.[6]

Curiously, where scientists would argue that in most
foreign policy areas the scientific elements have not
been adequately represented in policy making, in the
case of the test ban issue from 1958 to 1961 many, including many nonscientists, would say that scientific
considerations were given too much weight.

When Dr. James R. Killian became the President's
Special Assistant for Science and Technology in November 1957, President Eisenhower had, for the first
time in his administration, full-time scientific advice
divorced from individual agency positions and objectives. The availability of independent advice to the
President was particularly important on an issue such
as the test ban, for the internal Administration debate
was, by 1957, at dead center.[7]

At the same time, international pressure for a test
ban was increasing as a result of mounting concern
over the dangers of fallout and a desire for at least a
first step toward disarmament. The Russian announcement on March 31, 1958, of unilateral cessation of test-

[6] A detailed history of policy making for the test ban is contained
in the recently released, *Diplomats, Scientists and Politicians* (*op.
cit.*). The brief account and the analysis presented here, however,
are derived from other sources and from the author's personal
experience and evaluation.

[7] Gilpin, *op cit.*, p. 177.

ing, if other countries did the same, added to the pressure.[8] The stage was therefore set when Dr. Killian reported to the President in April 1958 that an interagency panel, which had been set up at the President's request under the chairmanship of Dr. Hans Bethe, had concluded that a test ban would not prejudice the nation's security and could be monitored with acceptable risks.[9]

The President reiterated his proposals for technical studies of a variety of disarmament issues in a new letter on April 28 to Chairman Khrushchev and singled out as examples of suitable issues a test ban and measures to prevent surprise attack.[10] Mr. Khrushchev responded favorably, if grudgingly, on May 9 to the idea of technical talks on the test ban question alone.[11]

So began five years of frustrating, occasionally hopeful, and often depressing negotiations that eventually culminated in the 1963 agreement to ban atmospheric and outer space tests. This is not the place to attempt to trace the history of those negotiations or even to speculate in detail on whether or not the Soviet Union was ever seriously interested in reaching a comprehensive agreement. In retrospect, it seems most probable that the Soviet Union was as uncertain about the issues and the effect on its own security interests as the United States. Undoubtedly, Russian policy fluctuated in response to new information in much the same way that American policy did.

Whatever the Russian situation, one characteristic

[8] The New York Times, Apr. 6, 1958, Section 4, pp. 1, 3.
[9] Gilpin, op. cit., p. 180.
[10] The New York Times, Apr. 29, 1958, p. 10.
[11] Ibid., May 12, 1958, p. 9.

of the early American attempts to cope with the issue was a yearning to discover a new scientific mousetrap. The policy makers were constantly searching for the technical gadget that would make detection and identification of suspected atomic tests foolproof, or so nearly so, that violations would be impossible.

Of course, no gadget could be foolproof. No agreement can provide absolute certainty that evasion or circumvention cannot take place. The policy maker is always faced with a balance of risks, basically a political question, even if that balance depends in important ways on technical matters. Technical improvements in means of detection could only alter, not remove, the question of risk. Improved means for remote detection and identification of underground nuclear explosions would, in fact, ease the political problem by requiring fewer on-site inspections. Nevertheless, the overriding question is still that of the risks entailed in the possibility of undetected or unproved violations compared with the risks inherent in continued testing in the absence of a test ban treaty.

There were also other political issues that tended to be submerged by the concentration on the technical questions. One was the fact that detection of a violation is only one part of demonstration of a violation. As Fred Iklé put it:

Yet, detecting violations is not enough. What counts are the political and military consequences of a violation once it has been detected, since these alone will determine whether or not the violator stands to gain in the end. In entering into an arms-control agreement, we must know not only that we are technically capable of detecting a violation but also that we, or the rest of the world, will be politically, legally, and militarily in a position to react effectively if a violation is discovered. If we focus all our attention on the technicalities of how to detect a violation, we are in danger of assuming that our reactions and sanctions will be adequate.[12]

Beyond that were questions such as: Would the Soviet Union accept any detection or inspection teams on her soil? How can U.S. demands for assurance of compliance with the treaty be squared with Soviet needs to maintain secrecy? Are there ways of devising means for operating a control commission that would be accepted as neutral by both sides? Would disputes arising under the treaty undermine the very increase in trust that was considered one of the purposes of the agreement? Of the greatest significance of all, is there enough of a genuine community of interest between Russia and the United States to make an agreement requiring international inspection and control viable?

These questions did receive attention, but the overemphasis on the technical solution resulted in consternation and confusion whenever clever new technical ideas were invented whereby a nation conceivably might be able to evade the control system. Some of these new technical ideas were important, but they rarely were given their proper weight in relation to the basic political issues of the negotiations. Instead, they caused the attention and effort of the government to be diverted to a consideration of the marginal technical gleam in someone's eye rather than to remain focused on the central issues.

It must be acknowledged that the fear of Congres-

[12] Fred Charles Iklé, "After Detection; What?," in *Arms and Arms Control*, Ernest W. Lefever, ed. (New York: Frederick A. Praeger, 1962), p. 221.

sional reaction to a treaty that could not have nearly foolproof control provisions strongly influenced the Administration in its handling of the subject. However, overconcern with the technical situation went well beyond an anticipation of Congressional objections. In fact, it was the scientists who were the most assiduous in pointing out that science could not solve the barriers to agreement. They were the ones who repeatedly emphasized that the real issues dividing the U.S. position from that of the Russians were political, not technical.

Given this essential inseparability of the technical and political elements of the test ban issue, it would seem logical at first glance to conclude that the device of a conference of technical experts as a preliminary to a political negotiation is unwise. This is not so. What would be unwise is a belief on the part of the policy maker that a conference of technical experts is apolitical.

In any negotiation, the likelihood of agreement is not good if the objectives of the two sides differ in important ways. The possibility of agreement is actually enhanced in technical negotiations, even if objectives differ, if the negotiations are on known or reasonably certain technical facts. When the subject is arms control, the technical negotiators must inevitably be speaking hypothetically of the capabilities of a given system in particular situations. In other words, there will always be uncertainty; it is not possible to foresee all contingencies.

The implications of those uncertainties are political as well as technical. Hence, technical negotiations on arms control issues are as likely to be affected by differences in political objectives as are political negotiations. All that can be expected of technical negotiations is to lay out the agreed facts and systematically to make explicit the uncertainties. To expect more is to ignore the fact that the differences between two nations' technical estimates of the future, and of the implications of those estimates, are quite likely to be the result of differing political assumptions and objectives. The forecasts of scientists and engineers can also be affected by political predelictions and desires.

With adequate understanding of this reality — that technical negotiations dealing with future developments cannot be divorced from political assumptions — technical conferences of experts can be a valuable negotiation technique that takes advantage of the relative precision and objectivity of science. Such conferences can serve to "clear away the underbrush" by establishing a base of technical facts and, even agreements on what the technical uncertainties are and how they might be removed.

The difficulty with both the test ban conference of experts, convened in Geneva July 1, 1958, and the experts' conference on surprise attack, convened November 10, 1958, was that the American delegations did not have this "adequate understanding." The Americans found themselves up against Russian delegations better prepared with regard to the political implications of their deliberations but rather less knowledgeable about the technical facts.[13]

---

[13] Even though better prepared, the United States suffered from insufficient technical data. George Kistiakowsky, who took part in the suprise attack conference, wrote:
   The negotiations on nuclear test cessation have shown the

The test ban conference did not turn out as badly from the U.S. point of view as might have been expected. In fact, the Russians made most of the concessions at the meetings. The conference's major shortcoming, and a most serious one, was that it did not present the kinds of technical alternatives for the subsequent political negotiations that might have speeded those negotiations. Instead, it presented a fully worked out control system that in the light of subsequent developments became a stumbling block for both the United States and the Soviet Union.

In other words, in the area of arms control and disarmament, there has been recognition of the relevance of scientific considerations, although there has not always been a clear understanding of the proper relationship of the scientific considerations to the basic issues. At times there has been an abdication to the scientific uncertainties rather than an assimilation of those uncertainties.

After 1961, the situation became much improved, as the new President and his advisers re-evaluated the test ban issue and quickly developed a better perspective at the top of the policy-making pyramid. The improved appreciation of the proper role of the technical elements of the test ban issue helped to make possible the 1963 treaty that banned all but underground tests.

---

importance of scientific and technological factors for the formulation of national policy in this area. These factors had to be evaluated by *ad hoc* groups that found a dearth of experimental data on which to base their conclusions.

"Science and Foreign Affairs," *Bulletin of the Atomic Scientists,* Vol. XVI, No. 4 (April 1960), p. 115.

INTELLIGENCE

On May 5, 1960, the world was startled to discover that the United States had developed for intelligence purposes a plane (the U-2) sufficiently advanced in technology to have been able to make overflights of the Soviet Union for four years without damage from Russian defenses.[14] Eventually, the U.S.S.R. developed defensive weapons that were able to match the capabilities of the U-2; it was presumed to be Russian action that finally brought down one of the planes and dramatically brought its existence to public attention.

This was not the first example of the use of advanced scientific capabilities for intelligence purposes (though it may be the most publicized), nor will it be the last. Atmospheric collection of nuclear test debris and analysis techniques developed specifically for the purpose made it possible for the United States to detect the first and subsequent Russian nuclear tests and to deduce detailed information about Russian nuclear bomb design. Massive new radars in Turkey made possible the monitoring of Soviet missile tests. The design and development of advanced computer systems have been undertaken for deciphering communications intelligence. Now, with the U-2's over the Soviet Union grounded, an earth satellite system dubbed SAMOS has been developed to attempt to obtain the same kind of photographic information the planes sought.[15]

These capabilities were brought into being by the allocation of scientific and technological resources to intelligence objectives. The development of special intelligence systems represents the most obvious and

[14] *The New York Times,* May 6, 1960, p. 1; May 11, 1960, p. 1.
[15] "Spying and Space," *New Republic,* Vol. 142 (May 30, 1960), p. 3.

direct way of employing science and technology to help achieve the vital security objective of knowing the strength and weakness of potential enemies (and friends).

Enlisting R & D resources for intelligence purposes appears to be an obvious tack, but, as with military weapons technology, it took many years before the full potentialities were appreciated and before good working relationships with the scientific community could be established. Indeed, to capitalize on science and technology for intelligence objectives is not simply a matter of establishing requirements and asking industry or government laboratories to meet them. Requirements are not independent of technical possibilities. Rather there must be scientific competence within the intelligence community that can match needs with technical feasibility and that can see new needs or new applications of scientific knowledge that might not otherwise emerge as formal requirements.

But the development of intelligence "hardware" is not the only way science relates to intelligence objectives. Intelligence is quite commonly thought of as the collection of secret information about a country through clandestine or unethical methods. In fact, intelligence methods are much more varied, and a good percentage of them are thoroughly innocuous as far as collection techniques are concerned. The end purpose is to know enough about a country to be able to make informed judgments about the country's likely response to specific situations, its ability and intentions with regard to development of certain kinds of weapons, the forces for change within the country, and so forth. These matters may depend in part on information not publicly available, but they will also depend on information and knowledge available to anyone who takes the trouble to look or to ask. This is particularly relevant to science, for as a nation's strength in science and technology has come to be a major determinant of its power and wealth, so too has knowledge about its science and technology assumed more importance as an intelligence target.

Information about science in another country, as opposed to technology, very rarely requires clandestine activity. A quite natural side product of contacts and travel of scientists, of international distribution of scientific journals, of cooperative programs of research and of international scientific conferences is the information gained about science and technology in other countries. This information will consist of, for example, impressions about individual and laboratory competence, the likely rate of progress and present state of knowledge in particular fields, comments on quality and quantity of research equipment and of research organization, and some feeling for special priority areas in science that may have been established. The information is diffused among many individuals but can be collected and evaluated if desired and if the individuals who have the information cooperate. It must be assumed that governments do collect this information that grows out of the natural intercourse of science.

The possibility exists for reversing the motivation of these scientific activities and carrying out some activities primarily for intelligence purposes. If there is a special intelligence target — a field of science, or an institution in another country — about which more information is sought, one way, in principle, of achieving that objective is to find a legitimate scientific reason for a scientist to visit the institution or to make contact with scientists in that field.

The Soviet Union is strongly suspected of doing precisely that in some areas of the scientific exchange program between the United States and the U.S.S.R. How important this motivation is in determining Russian policies on the exchange program is not known, although it seems to figure prominently in some fields of science and technology.

The United States learns a great deal in these exchanges with the Soviet Union as well and receives information that puts in better perspective the state of Russian science and technology relative to that of the United States. This is not the primary motive for U.S. participation in the exchanges, but it is a useful result, for a calm appraisal of Soviet science and technology has helped to eliminate the near-hysteria of the post-Sputnik era when it was believed that the U.S.S.R. had overtaken the United States in many fields of science. More extensive contacts have shown that even though Soviet science is strong, the United States is equal or maintains a continuing advantage in most fields and in the organization for R & D itself.[16]

[16] Two remarkable testimonials to the relative position of physical science in America and in the Soviet Union have been given by prominent and influential Russian scientists. In 1961, astronomer L. A. Artsimovich in an address to the Physics-Mathematical Sciences Department of the Russian Academy of Sciences characterized the situation in the following way:

> . . . but a careful analysis leads one to the conclusion that our lag may be analogized as follows: it is as if two ships are plowing along the same uncharted river at the same speed, but one of them keeps moving a ship's length ahead of the other; this allows the crew of the better ship to make almost all the important discoveries.

L. A. Artsimovich, "The Twenty-Second Congress of the CPSU

Although exchanges or other programs can be used to learn more about specific intelligence targets, such attempts require the cooperation of the caliber of scientist who would naturally be involved in the project even if it had no intelligence motivation. Scientists are reluctant to waste time on visitors who cannot contribute to their work, so it is likely to be of little value to send a second-rate man to collect scientific information. A visitor who cannot contribute as much as he receives is likely to find after a while that he is shown or told very little, not because of suspicion, but because it is a waste of time.

Some scientists, in the West at least, are hostile to efforts of their country's own intelligence agencies to collect open information from them and refuse to take part in projects for which they suspect an intelligence motive. This attitude grows out of the conviction that the freedom of science from political interference is essential to science and to maintaining free and open communication in the worldwide scientific community. Consequently, many scientists believe that any policies that seem to imply distorting science for a highly political motive, especially one as ethically questionable as

---

and the Tasks of Soviet Physics, Mathematics, and Astronomy," *Uspekhi Matematicheskikh Nauk,* 17:2 (104), 1962, translation for the Department of State.

Late in 1965, the physicist P. L. Kapitza, in a widely reported speech at a general meeting of the Academy of Sciences, U.S.S.R., summed up the situation by saying:

> We must not be afraid to say that in the past several years the science gap between our country and America has not only ceased to diminish but has increased.

P. L. Kapitza, *Theory, Experiment, Practice,* (Moscow: Znanie 1966) Series IX, Part 5, translated by P. C. L. Hodgson, Jr., for Professor D. J. de Solla Price, Yale University.

intelligence, are to be resisted at all costs.[17] These scientists see requests from intelligence agencies for open information as first steps in that subversion; they obviously see projects carried out largely for intelligence purposes in that light.

While some would argue that this attitude is naïve, it is only an extension of the basic tenets that most scientists believe to be necessary for the health of science. It is therefore an important constraint on scientific projects that may be launched primarily to garner intelligence information. Scientists conduct their international activities on the assumption that their colleagues are also interested in advancing science. Whatever other motives a scientist may have, they must have no influence on his primary scientific commitment. This is not idle sentimentality. It is a necessary condition growing out of the need for objectivity in observation of physical phenomena. If a scientist's objectivity is suspect, his science is suspect, in which case his collabo-

---

[17] A letter in *Science* is typical of a segment of the scientific community:

> . . . A . . . consequence of a relationship between scientists and the CIA would be to limit the freedom of discussion between American and foreign colleagues. No one speaks to an official . . . as freely as one speaks to a friend. We have all had the experience of talking to foreign scientists who were certainly part-time intelligence agents and part-time scientists, and these conversations are so stultified as to be a travesty of the usually free exchange and argument of a scientific discussion. Any general or indiscriminate questioning by the CIA of scientists . . . increases the danger that American scientists will be regarded by their foreign colleagues as government agents . . .
>
> As the scope of these [intelligence agencies] enlarges, anything can become grist for their mill; let us hope that academic freedom is not included.

Patrick D. Wall, *Science*, Vol. 136 (Apr. 1962), p. 173.

ration is of questionable scientific value. To be successful as an indirect intelligence source, any given exchange or project must be able to stand on its scientific justification alone.

In technological subjects, the situation is quite different. Information tends to be more immediately useful than in science, and the same traditions of openness and freedom to publish that are a major aspect of the scientists' credo do not apply to most engineers. The latter often expect to be under restraints imposed by their company or by the government and consider those restraints as a normal part of their work. For this reason, intelligence targets in technological fields may at times have more of the characteristics of the cloak-and-dagger operation. Even then, so much is published and freely available, especially in this country, that intelligence collection is in good part a library research job.

Special exchanges and programs can be of help in collecting information in technological subjects, too, though it is obviously difficult for the United States or the U.S.S.R. to agree to an exchange in a politically important technological area in which either believes it is ahead. The U.N. Space Conference that was discussed earlier would have been useful to the United States for the pressure it could have put on Russia to release information on space technology.[18] The Atoms for Peace Conferences in fact had as by-products the loosening up by both the Soviet Union and the United States of the secrecy that surrounded their atomic energy programs. These special opportunities are few and far between.

[18] See discussion in Chapter 2.

Even in technological areas, projects involving engineers of other countries need to be justified first on technical grounds if they are *also* to provide useful intelligence information. Information sources tend to dry up when the flow of information is patently in one direction only.

Thus, science and technology are part of, and can contribute to, intelligence objectives of the nation. Scientific considerations must figure prominently in policy making and in operations in the intelligence area. In particular, the policy maker must know and understand the scientific enterprise and the scientific community if he is to be able to tap them for new tools for his craft and for information about science in other countries.

Moreover, in intelligence analysis, a special competence is required to evaluate the significance and political implications of the information collected. It is not enough to say China could theoretically have the following list of weapons in x years on the basis of her present scientific competence. The analysis, to be useful, must go on to say how many on the list could be produced in parallel, which would prove the severest drain on technical and other resources, which would require outside data the Chinese could not develop on their own, and so on; in short, to present the choices as the Chinese planners might see them.

To achieve this capability requires a blending of scientific, economic and political talents in the intelligence function not unlike the blending of scientific and political elements required in the broader foreign policy process itself.

7

Bilateral Relations

At the end of 1964, General de Gaulle warned the French nation against becoming "colonized by foreign investments, inventions and capacities."[1] He was expressing the same sentiments as those published in greater detail the previous September by a French government body that argued that the battles of price in the conquest of markets are being replaced by battles of innovation, in which scientific and technical superiority is the only effective weapon. Consequently, the maintenance of political independence, which relies on industrial strength, necessitates a strong technology. Only this can resist subordination to a foreign domination exercising control of certain critical economic decisions.[2]

[1] Bernard D. Nossiter, "France Ponders U.S. Restraint" *The Washington Post and Times-Herald,* Jan. 12, 1965.
[2] "Recherche Scientifique et Indépendance," *Le Progrès Scientifique,* No. 76, Sept. 1, 1964, Délégation Générale à la Recherche

This issue of technological superiority, which the French like to call the problem of the "technological balance of payments," is but one example of the growing role of science and technology as new and often significant backdrops to country-to-country relations. This role has two main aspects. First, as a natural outgrowth of the general expansion of research and development, has come greatly increased international movement and activities of scientists and engineers. Scientific relations have become a larger portion of the totality of relations between countries.

Second, the disparities between nations in the breadth and competence of their scientific enterprises has become larger. First-rate scientific competence can be, and is, found in any nation. But the ability to capitalize on science, to keep abreast of many fields at once, to be in the forefront of the search for knowledge across the scientific spectrum, depends on the size and quality of a nation's scientific establishment and on the ability to commit adequate resources to it. The more a nation starts with, scientifically speaking, the faster will it advance.

This second aspect works very much in the favor of the United States, and it is this, of course, that worries the French and other nations. The present pre-eminence — in breadth and usually in depth — of science and technology in the United States has created a situation in which the rate of progress of science and technology in other countries is heavily affected by the extent of contact between their scientists and engineers and American work and progress. (The United States

Scientifique et Technique, and summarized in *International Scientific Notes*, Department of State, Dec. 1964.

benefits from these contacts as well, but the reliance does not tend to be focused on one nation as it does for others.)

It is difficult to measure information flow. Nevertheless, using patents and license agreements as an indicator of the movement of technological information, it is evident that there is a strong net flow from the United States to other countries. One estimate shows a roughly 5 to 1 ratio of payments to receipts (payments for technical know-how, licenses, and patents) for France, Germany, and England in dealings with the United States.[3] This probably understates the situation, for the flow of information not codified in licenses or patents would be expected to follow industrial investment trends, which are heavily weighted toward American industrial investment in Europe.

Another measure, which in part explains the European lag and points up the extent of the gap, is a comparison of the numbers of research workers in each country. In 1961, the number of research workers per 10,000 citizens in the United States and U.S.S.R. was 23 and 18.5, respectively, as against roughly 10 in Great Britain and 6.4 in France.[4]

The French argue, and the argument is echoed in Germany, and, to a lesser extent, in the United Kingdom, that the technological lead of the United States gives American industry important competitive advantages. The French even assert that, as this heavy R & D investment is largely from the government in space and

[3] C. Freeman and A. Young, *The Research and Development Effort in Western Europe, North America and the Soviet Union,* OECD, Paris: 1965, p. 53.

[4] *Le Progrès Scientifique,* No. 77 in *Reviews of National Science Policy—France,* OECD, Paris 1966, p. 26.

defense fields, it constitutes unfair competition and gives the French Government the right to take unilateral action to ward off impending American industrial domination.[5]

To date, the French have done nothing more than scrutinize American industrial plans in France more carefully. On the other hand, what is the validity of their basic argument? Is there a technological gap in fact? Is it growing? What are its economic and political implications? Some of the latter are evident as far as France is concerned: the American refusal to sell unclassified computers to France because they were intended for the *force de frappe* is not an incident to be taken lightly, given the current French frame of mind.[6] This is especially so when American industry now completely dominates the computer industry in France as a result of IBM's extensive activities and General Electric Company's large investment in 1964 in the last sizable French computer firm, Machines Bull.[7]

French arguments would appear to be overdrawn in economic terms even if they have political validity. Although there are undoubtedly many more civilian spin-offs of an attitudinal and educational nature than the critics of space and defense spending aver, it is hard to justify the assertion that such R & D expenditures are the primary basis for the greater economic power of

[5] M. P. Cognard, Chef du Service du Plan à la Délégation Générale à la Recherche Scientifique, "La Recherche Scientifique et les Échanges Internationaux," a paper delivered before l'Institut Européen d'Administration des Affaires, Fontainebleau, September 5–11, 1965.

[6] Howard Simons, "American Newsletter," *New Scientist*, No. 426, (Jan. 14, 1965), p. 97; *The New York Times*, May 22, 1966, p. 43.

[7] *The New York Times*, July 24, 1964, p. 31.

American industry. Moreover, foreign industrial investment and the purchase of patents and licenses may be
the fastest and most economical way to introduce new
technology into an economy.

The current French argument may be overdrawn, but
that is not the end of the matter. Several potentially profound trends are at work that may make a great difference in the future. Is it likely that the United States and
possibly the Soviet Union will pull so far ahead of other
countries technologically that there will develop a new,
subtle, and very powerful form of domination? Does
the U.S. national interest lie in seeing this situation
develop or in taking measures that will help to bridge
the gap? Right now, the countries less advanced in
technology must defer to the technology developed in
the advanced countries as they attempt to carve out a
national identity and maintain an independent culture.
Often the less-advanced nations say they would like
modern technology without the social values that have
grown with the technology, but the former seems to
bring the latter along with it. Will even the advanced
nations of Western Europe be in the same relative position in a few years?

President Johnson was responding to this concern on
the part of the Europeans when he proposed, during
Chancellor Erhard's visit in December 1965, solar and
planetary probes to be mounted jointly with European
nations.[8] Part of the offer, a joint solar probe, was suggested specifically for U.S./German cooperation, and
was intended both as an attempt to offer the Germans
a modern alternative to nuclear weapons, and as an

[8] *Ibid.,* Dec. 22, 1965, p. 10; Howard Simons, "American Newsletter," *New Scientist,* No. 477, Jan. 6, 1966, p. 18.

opportunity to meet the fears of the European nations that they would be left behind in the industrial development and exploitation of sophisticated technology.[9]

Some shorter-range issues related to this question of technological domination also arise. For example, complaints about the "brain drain" to the United States are common knowledge, but is there a parallel "knowledge drain" to the United States when a country's scientists and engineers are employed in their own country by an American subsidiary? In that situation, the results of the work of the scientists and engineers may be channeled to the benefit of U.S. industry rather than industry in their own country. The argument is also made that because the really important projects are always carried out only in a company's home laboratory, scientists and engineers working in an American subsidiary in France or England or any other country are unlikely to be engaged in projects in the forefront of their fields. In effect, then, a country's scarce technical talent is being employed on projects of secondary interest.

Thus, the very scale of scientific and technological activities in, or conducted by, the United States creates novel and important issues for American foreign relations. But in a sense that is the negative or passive side of the coin. The increasing relevance of science and technology to a nation's bilateral relationships also implies that these fields may offer fruitful possibilities for positive initiatives that can help to advance specific political objectives.

The President's suggestion to the Germans of a joint solar probe was an example of such an initiative. Op-

[9] Howard Simons, *ibid.*

portunities for and the problems of the use of science and technology in this way as instruments of foreign policy are sufficiently important to warrant more extended discussion. This can be done by a look at several of the past efforts to utilize science and technology to alter relations between the United States and another country.

INITIATIVES WITH THE SOVIET UNION

The traditional desire of scientists for free communication on scientific matters with scientists in other countries, regardless of the state of political relations between their governments, provides both problems and opportunities of a political nature. Some of the problems have been discussed in relation to the responsibility of those concerned with foreign policy to support science.[10] But the political opportunities are also significant, most vividly exemplified in the programs designed to support (and to spur) American scientists to establish close communications with their Russian counterparts.

The expected political gains from such close communication are straightforward; in the short term, better lines of communication to the Soviet Union and possibly (but not very hopefully) some reduction in tension between this country and the Soviet Union as a result of the growth of greater understanding on both sides; in the long term, some evolution of the Russian political system toward the substance, if not the forms, of Western democracies as the contacts with the West

[10] See Chapter 4.

introduce new ideas and new wants, and reduce old fears.[11]

Programs designed to develop these communications links have been established in many professional fields, not in science and technology alone.[12] The practitioners in each field claim for themselves a special ability to communicate with their colleagues in Russia and hence an important political influence in U.S./Soviet relations. This is as true of musicians, of editors, of artists, of labor leaders, of farmers, and, of course, of athletes, as it is of scientists. Each group has some justice to its claim, for in terms of establishing meaningful contacts, individuals with similar professional interests can more rapidly establish good personal relationships.

There are reasons for believing that relationships among scientists and engineers have some unique values in political terms, however, that do not accrue in other fields. These should not be overrated, because the evidence as to special political payoffs in scientific and technological fields is not overwhelming. The evidence is not entirely negligible, either, and there is little doubt that in the ranks of the present Soviet leadership, scientific and technological subjects excite considerable personal interest.

[11] "A Summary Report on the U.S. Exchanges Program with the Soviet Union," Soviet and Eastern European Exchanges Staff Department of State, Washington, D. C., April 18, 1964; Stephen S. Rosenfeld, "Soviet-American Exchanges,—Tit-for-tat Goodwill," *Science*, Vol. 143 (Mar. 27, 1964), p. 1413.

[12] The so-called Lacy-Zaroubin exchange agreement between the United States and U.S.S.R. of Jan. 1958 (renewed periodically since then) covered a variety of subjects such as science, the performing arts, motion pictures, and radio and television. Most of the science exchanges come under subsidiary agreements, such as those between the two Academies of Sciences and the two Atomic Energy Commissions.

The factors that give scientific relations special political value can be listed briefly. Some (the first four) apply primarily to relations with the Soviet Union; others have more general validity.

1. Russian scientists and engineers have been politically influential in their own right, providing at times direct entree to Russian political leadership, and exercising an independent role and broader influence on Russian society as a whole.[13]

2. The Soviet Union recognizes science and technology as major determinants of its future growth and international position; it also recognizes, privately, U.S. leadership and has been willing to accept at least some U.S. conditions for freedom of contacts in the interest of having contacts at all.

3. The present Russian leadership includes several with primary training in science and engineering; for example, First Secretary Brezhnev received his early training in metallurgy, Premier Kosygin is an engineer, and the latter's son-in-law, J. M. Gvishiani, was Deputy Chairman of the U.S.S.R. State Committee for Science and Technology.[14]

4. The Soviet Union, apparently for prestige purposes, feels it must participate in some inter-

[13] A startling example of the broader influence of scientists in the U.S.S.R. was the account in the *The New York Times* of Feb. 25, 1966, p. 10, of the avant-garde art exhibit displayed at the U.S.S.R. Academy of Sciences in Moscow at the same time that the government had mounted a campaign to suppress modern art and literature.

[14] *Ibid.*, Oct. 16, 1964, p. 15; *ibid.*, Nov. 18, 1964, p. 17.

national scientific activities it might otherwise ignore. This can provide a useful lever on Russian policy. (The 1955 Atoms for Peace Conference is a case in point.)

5. The subject matter of science is objective so that there is equivalent experience and interests in technical matters among scientists and engineers in different countries, and thereby direct communication is possible.

6. There is a strong tradition of internationalism in science, though a weaker one in technology.

7. There is a genuine international community of scientists with a culture and structure of its own, a communications network, a habit of reliance on the work of others without regard to nationality, extensive international meetings and projects, and common standards of achievement and recognition, all of which lend themselves to ease of understanding and establishment of common interests and goals.[15]

8. Almost all advanced countries are making major investments in science and technology to advance their power and wealth — making the subject matter central to a country's future international position and to its present national programs.

9. The great number of opportunities for cooperative work on subjects of genuine interest and genuine benefit in science and technology makes it easier to identify common interests among diverse nations.

[15] Michael Polanyi, "The Republic of Science: Its Political and Economic Theory," *Minerva*, Vol. 1, No. 1 (Autumn 1962), p. 54.

These points have been well recognized so that, in addition to the scientist exchange programs begun in 1958, there have been several other soundings of possible cooperation with the Soviet Union. The extensive initiatives and not-so-extensive agreements in space exploration discussed in Chapter 2 are prominent examples. In the late 1950's, U.S., Soviet, and European high-energy physicists discussed a possible joint high-energy accelerator of mammoth size that, it was thought at the time, would be too expensive for any one country or group of countries to build alone. Cooperation in the Antarctic has been going well on a modest scale for several years. Desalination technology is the popular field now, with exchanges of high-level delegations between Russia and the United States, and possibilities for more extended cooperation.[16]

Perhaps the most impressive aspect of these cooperative endeavors is the fact that very limited cooperation is actually in effect in each area. The scientist exchange program is almost the only one proceeding about as planned.

By and large, it has been the Soviet Union that has been reluctant or uncooperative, and has held back from American urging for greater cooperation, although the degree of American enthusiasm might also have cooled on some projects if actually put to the test. The exact reasons for the Russian attitude can only be surmised. Presumably, the Soviets calculate that the price of cooperation is too high for the gain they would expect to make. The gain the Soviet Union expects, the

[16] Dan Cooper, "Desalination is the new arena for science prestige—and cooperation," *International Science & Technology*, No. 33 (Sept. 1964), p. 95.

Department of State hypothesizes, is to obtain scientific and technical information, and to publicize a favorable picture of the Soviet Union and Soviet policies.[17]

The price, presumably, is the loss of information and perhaps the appearance of some further cracks in their closed society. For the relatively successful scientist exchange program, the calculation on the part of the Soviets must be that the subject matter is sufficiently removed (and the subject matter of the exchanges is tightly controlled) from short-term security interests that the loss of information and any long-term effects of allowing extensive access to the Soviet Union by American scientists are not as important as the gain in information. This is not a calculation that can be made with any degree of confidence. Certainly the United States feels that the greatly increased knowledge about Russian science, the scientific benefits of the exchange, and the considerable loosening up of Russian controls on their scientists have more than justified the program. Apparently, both sides consider the program a net gain in terms of their own objectives.

In other areas, particularly space, it is easy to understand Russian reluctance for cooperation in view of the close relationship between their civil and military programs. Indeed, for cooperation with the United States, many fields of science may simply be *too* important to Russia's central objectives to allow, without accompanying political adjustments, the degree of access that must accompany joint projects.

Still, what limited contacts and cooperation have been stimulated with the Soviet Union seem to be of value. A much healthier and open relationship exists at

[17] "A Summary Report," Department of State, *op. cit.*

present between American and Soviet scientists than was the case ten years ago, and this may have carried over to contribute in important ways to the détente of the early 1960's. The validity of the political meaning of these contacts cannot be proved. But the fact that there has been political fallout is illustrated by an incident during the test ban negotiations that also demonstrates the political risks.

The Soviet Union in 1962 finally agreed to accept three on-site inspections per year of suspicious underground seismic events in the expectation, apparently, that the United States would agree that three inspections were sufficient. This expectation on the part of the Soviet Union purportedly grew out of discussions between a few influential Russian and American scientists. The Russian scientists asserted later in private conversations that they had used their personal contacts and prestige in the Soviet government to convince the Soviet political leaders that the United States would be satisfied with three inspections per year. The Russian scientists pleaded, on the basis of their discussions with the American scientists, that the U.S. demand for some minimum inspection was motivated by substantive arguments and domestic U.S. political concerns, not by intelligence objectives. The American scientists involved say that they tried to impress their Soviet colleagues with the sincerity of the U.S. position but did not say the United States would accept three inspections per year. In the give and take of informal discussion, the Americans did apparently make the argument that on technical grounds alone a very small number of inspections, even three, would be sufficient but that politically the United States could not accept that small a number. However, the subtleties of the argument were missed by the Russians. When the Soviet Union announced publicly that it would accept three inspections and the United States countered with a proposal for twelve (later reduced to seven), the Russians reacted strongly. Premier Khrushchev claimed that he had been deceived and that this proved the United States was not seriously interested in a test ban agreement unless the treaty allowed broad access to the Soviet Union for espionage purposes.[18]

The risk of this kind of misunderstanding on the part of individual scientists not versed in diplomatic negotiation is not the only risk inherent in greater cooperation. For example, it is possible that attempts at intimate cooperation on a major technological or scientific project would ultimately cause more friction rather than produce a sense of cooperation and community of purpose. Disputes over who should construct necessary equipment, or how to provide quality control under widely different industrial-security systems, or how to insulate the project from fluctuations in the political climate might in the end exacerbate the political relationships the cooperation was intended to improve.

Also, international cooperation, especially with iron curtain countries, can be a serious impediment to the timely performance of a specific job. The reason is a pragmatic one: delays and possible frustrations are likely that, at the very least, will slow the progress of the joint effort. It is hard enough to work with one government; to work in detail with two or more that have conflicting political goals could create enormous

18 Norman Cousins, "Khrushchev Looked Worried," an account of an interview with Nikita Khrushchev on April 12, 1963, *The Boston Globe*, Nov. 22, 1964.

difficulties. It is interesting that the American physicists who were strong proponents of the large, joint, high-energy accelerator in cooperation with the Soviet Union and Western Europe, when the costs seemed much too large for a single nation to bear, lost a good bit of their ardor for the project when it appeared a few years later that the United States would be willing to finance accelerators of a similar size on a purely national basis.

Finally, the effects of cooperation with the Soviet Union on relations between scientists and the government in the United States may be undesirable. Even in the simple exchange program with the Soviet Union, the U.S. Government found it necessary to exercise a degree of control over visiting scientists and over the subjects of the exchanges that American scientists found distasteful. The controls were instituted to avoid a situation in which the Soviet Union would be gleaning all the benefits and the United States gaining little, either scientifically or politically, from the exchanges. The Department of State required a degree of reciprocity in the exchanges — approximately equal numbers of visits each way, in approximately the same fields, and to the same number of institutions — as a means of ensuring equitability. In addition, the Department excluded Russian scientists from specified areas in the United States in retaliation for similar Russian restrictions on Americans, in the hope that this would create pressure on the Soviet Union to ease its restrictive policies.

These controls were highly unpopular with American scientists, who argued that they were ineffective and time-consuming, that one could not measure reciprocal benefits in science, and that they gave an inaccurate picture of the benefits of the U.S. system to visiting Russians. Most important, the American scientists argued that the controls were antithetical to the concepts of a free and unfettered science and were imposing an overlay of government control of science that was alien to American traditions; in fact, were altering American science and society to conform to the Russian pattern, rather than influencing Russian science and society to move in the direction of the American pattern.

The situation is now improved because the Department of State has been administering the reciprocity principle more liberally and has attempted to modify the closed areas policy. At the same time, the National Academy of Sciences (NAS) has helped the Department to avoid the more damaging situations that arise and has helped to educate American scientists as to why some measure of control is necessary for bargaining power if the exchanges are to continue and if they are to evolve in directions desired by the United States.

The risk inherent in cooperative programs with the Soviet Union and the difficulty in mounting any large-scale programs to date do not mean that such programs are unwise. Quite the contrary, for the risks and difficulties only demonstrate that such cooperation does touch important nerves in the Soviet Union. The reasons that make cooperation in science and technology politically useful remain valid, but initiating such projects is neither easy nor automatically productive of favorable political results domestically or internationally.

It is obvious, therefore, that if the United States is to try to use science and technology in relations with the Soviet Union in more substantial programs than are in existence today, it must have deep understanding in the foreign policy process of the technical as well as the political ramifications of the subject. It is all too easy to call for scientific cooperation without adequate realization of the factors that must be considered if the offer is to be more than a gesture and if the cooperation itself is to be successful in scientific *and* political terms.

It is interesting to speculate as to whether scientific contacts can play anything like the same role with China. It is not likely that scientists have the same political influence in that country, if for no other reason than that so many Chinese scientists have been educated in the West and are likely to be politically suspect to the regime. However, science and technology are extremely important to China and will become more so as that nation attempts to achieve its aspirations to be a major world power. To the extent that the United States would like to begin to modify its China policy by establishing a few "nonpolitical" contacts with that nation, science probably offers one of the more fruitful fields. Recent liberalization of American policies so as to allow contacts between Chinese and American scholars are an acknowledgement of that fact.[19]

China is in need for its own purposes of scientific relations with the rest of the world, and American scientists have strong scientific motivations in fields such as meteorology, geology, and biology for including the Asian continent in their studies. If the Chinese were willing (an unsurmountable "if" at present), it would be relatively easy to use the international mechanisms of the scientific community to establish relations, leaving the U.S. Government with a minimal involvement in

[19] *The New York Times*, Apr. 15, 1966, p. 1.

the action. At the same time, the United States would begin to learn more about that great colossus of the Asian mainland that must inevitably be one of this country's major foreign concerns for many years to come.

The subject of communication between Russian and American scientists cannot be complete without mention of one of the most interesting forms for East/West contact that has developed in recent years: the Pugwash movement. In 1955, Bertrand Russell, with the support of Albert Einstein and a small number of other particularly eminent scientists, issued a manifesto to the "scientists of the world and the general public" appealing to them to join in urging governments to renounce war as a means of settlement of disputes.[20] The purpose of the manifesto was, in Lord Russell's words, to "bring together men of science of the most divergent political opinions — Communist, anti-Communist and neutral — in a friendly atmosphere in which it was hoped that a scientific spirit would enable them to find a greater measure of agreement than the politicians had found possible."[21]

This appeal found a sympathetic response in the politically active segments of the scientific community and resulted in the establishment of a continuing forum for meetings of scientists of East and West devoted to the arms race and disarmament. Originally dubbed the "Pugwash movement" because of the location of the first conference in July 1957 at the estate of financier

[20] Bertrand Russell, "The Early History of the Pugwash Movement," in Seymour Melman, ed., *Disarmament: Its Politics and Economics*, (Boston: The American Academy of Arts and Sciences, 1962), pp. 18–31.
[21] *Ibid.*

Cyrus Eaton in Pugwash, Nova Scotia, the movement now has an official title (Conference on Science and World Affairs, COSWA) but has never shaken the informal, more colorful name. Periodic meetings are held, most concentrating on disarmament subjects, but at times questions of international scientific cooperation or science in economic development are the main topics. A "continuing committee" under Professor Joseph Rotblat in London serves to provide the necessary organization and arrangements.

The Pugwash movement is a curious and interesting phenomenon, for it is the only major international scientific group avowedly devoted to political subjects. At first, its Western members included a large contingent of prominent "ban-the-bomb" scientists who were entirely unsympathetic to American and Western military and foreign policies and who had little or no connection with their governments. Gradually, the Western delegations, and particularly those from the United States, were taken over by more moderate scientists with greater experience in political/scientific affairs. Often the American scientists, including some social scientists, who took part were familiar with the military and arms control policy deliberations within the government and understood the issues as they were seen by responsible political leaders. In many instances, these scientists were in the forefront of academic and government studies that were breaking new ground in the complex field of arms control.

The Russian and other Communist delegations, whatever their original motivation for participation in the Pugwash meetings, also came to include scientists influential in government circles and familiar with the deliberations on arms control and disarmament matters in their own countries. Up to and including the meetings held in Moscow in the fall of 1960, even the Communist Chinese sent representatives to almost all of the sessions.

As a result, the Pugwash movement became a useful nongovernmental channel for East/West communication on disarmament matters; it was, in fact, the only channel that existed in which differing points of view and positions could be discussed and debated in depth and in privacy, without commitment of governments. The original purpose of the Pugwash organizers, to influence governments through mobilization of public opinion, has not been served particularly well by the Pugwash meetings (although at each session there is an argument about the wording of a final communiqué), but a much more important purpose of providing a unique forum for reasonably objective discussion of political/scientific matters has been achieved.

It is not possible to evaluate with any precision what political value this communication channel has had. Certainly, the suspicion shown by the Russians at early Pugwash meetings of all attempts to apply sophisticated analytical methods to the design of arms control proposals, especially those that did not lead directly to general and complete disarmament, was gradually modified as time went on. Persistent and competent studies by the American scientists of the details of arms reduction and control proposals slowly brought the Russians around to a willingness, at least in that forum, to discuss these studies on their merits.

In particular, test ban issues received major attention in Pugwash meetings during the course of the political negotiations at Geneva. At the least, Pugwash provided a means for each side to try to explain to the other the sometimes suspicious shifts in position taking place at the negotiating table. At times, the frank, substantive talks at Pugwash may have served to advance gradually the sophistication with which both the United States and the Soviet Union approached the negotiations. At times, as noted earlier in the incident over how many on-site inspections the United States demanded, misunderstandings arising at the Pugwash meeting may have slowed the negotiations. Still, the existence of the Pugwash communication channel undoubtedly helped to keep the test ban negotiations alive — a major contribution to the final agreement.

In disarmament matters, Pugwash no longer has such a unique role to play, largely as a result of the United States/U.S.S.R. détente that has served to open up other channels for objective contacts. Some of the scientists in the Pugwash movement are now turning increasingly to other areas of world affairs to which science can make a contribution. In particular, the interest in applying science to problems of economic development is growing. The meeting over the New Year's holiday of 1965–1966 in Addis Abbaba was devoted exclusively to that issue.[22]

Pugwash may have a relatively unique role to play there as well as in disarmament. The nature of the organization as a private group of scientists focused on political problems, but including individuals from both East and West, may make it possible to hold meetings and discuss issues that would not be possible or proper

[22] "The 15th Pugwash Conference," *Pugwash Newsletter*, Oct. 1965 and Jan. 1966, Vol. 3, Nos. 2 and 3, pp. 25–61.

under the auspices of individual countries or even of international organizations. The scientists can act without great concern for political propriety, for national borders, for overlapping jurisdictions of international agencies, for sensitive bureaucracies, and so forth. Any other truly international group of scientists could in principle do the same, but Pugwash is the only one that exists with this degree of independence.

Of course, Pugwash's greatest strength is also its greatest weakness: the independence and informality of scientists in Pugwash also means the scientists are unable, directly, to mount operations or programs. On the other hand, if they can raise the right issues and exert some influence as individuals in their own governments, their indirect accomplishments could be substantial.

INITIATIVES WITH TECHNOLOGICALLY ADVANCED WESTERN NATIONS

In distinction from relations with Communist nations, most bilateral scientific contacts and cooperation with the advanced nations of the West and Japan flow naturally as a result of private activities or as an outgrowth of an established international program. Only rarely are special initiatives needed or taken with Western nations that have as their primary motive some particular political purpose, as opposed to a technical program objective. When such initiatives are taken, the reason will usually be found in some political problem that has arisen and that will not be reached by the ordinary workings of the scientific community. However, as will be seen, the initiative must first be valid in scientific terms alone if it is to be successful and also to serve political objectives.

An excellent example of such a scientific/political initiative exists in the current U.S.-Japan Cooperative Science Program. The superb natural scientists of Japan, and particularly the physicists, have tended as a group to lean heavily to the left in their politics and to view with distrust American activities and policies. Their general attitude is that both the United States and Japan support science for military purposes only. This view is heavily conditioned by the military use made of science by the Japanese government during and before World War II, and by the firsthand Japanese experience with the military application of science by the United States. Politically, the Japanese scientists have become an important influence on the public and youth of Japan. Therefore, the political attitudes of many of the scientists is a source of concern to the United States with regard to the future development of Japanese foreign and domestic policies. In recent years, these scientists have had poor relations with their own government and few contacts with the American government or with American activities.

In 1961, the American Ambassador to Tokyo, Mr. Reischauer, suggested to President Kennedy, prior to a visit to Washington by Japanese Premier Ikeda, that the two leaders propose the creation of a joint U.S.-Japanese science committee. The mission of the committee would be to develop a series of cooperative research programs that would be carried out jointly by scientists of the two countries and would be financed jointly by the two governments. The objectives were to bring the scientific communities of the two coun-

tries into closer contact with each other and, in cooperation, to carry out research that was, in the words
of President Kennedy, "dedicated to the service of
humanity and to the arts of peace."[23] The assumption
was that these closer contacts would show, as words
and statements could not, the inherently peaceful objectives of American and Japanese policies and the desire of those governments to support science for the
general good of the people of both countries.

The idea was accepted and the proposal made in the
communiqué after the Kennedy-Ikeda meetings.[24] Implementation proved to be a delicate political task because of the suspicions of the Japanese scientists. The
value of a good science attaché at an American embassy was demonstrated repeatedly throughout the development of this cooperative effort, for without such
an individual who was sensitive both to the American
and Japanese political concerns, trusted by the Japanese scientists and close to the American Ambassador
and his political staff, the likelihood of success would
have been small.[25]

The committee has attracted the participation of
prominent American scientists and has sponsored excellent scientific programs. However, not many of the
projects are in the fields (largely physics and mathematics) of the scientists with whom the United States
was most anxious to make contact. This has happened

[23] "Joint Communiqué of the U.S.-Japan Committee on Scientific
Cooperation Dec. 15, 1961," The Department of State, Dec. 19, 1961.
[24] "Joint Communiqué Issued by the President and Prime Minister
Hayato Ikeda of Japan, Following Discussions held in Washington,
D. C. June 20–21, 1961," The White House, June 22, 1961.
[25] Dr. Otto Laporte, physicist from the University of Michigan
held the Tokyo post of Science Attaché during this period.

because valid scientific opportunities and political objectives were not coincident. The Science Committee, with the wise backing of the governments, realized that unless the projects suggested were basically sound from a scientific point of view the whole effort would collapse. Scientific proposals that were not justified on their own terms would only intensify the suspicions of the Japanese scientists of the American government's motives in supporting science. Therefore the scientific community had to be depended upon to develop the proposals according to the scientific opportunities as they saw them. Not many proposals emerged in the fields of physics or mathematics; most are in the earth and biological sciences.[26]

This situation does serve to point up one of the dangers that could arise in attempting to use science in as direct a way as this to serve political ends. In this case, science in Japan is first class. Legitimate opportunities, in scientific terms, exist for scientific cooperation in many, though not all, fields. The research carried out under the cooperative program will almost surely be competitive in quality with other research supported within the countries, highly competent scientists will be attracted of their own free will, and the subject matter of the research is likely to justify support by governments.

[26] In addition, there are programs expanding exchanges of scholars and scientific information and providing for joint work on scientific education. "A Brief Summary Report on the U.S.-Japan Cooperative Science Program," NSF, Washington, D. C., Feb. 1, 1965. Cooperation in medical research, air pollution, and pesticides will be further expanded as a result of another meeting between the American Head-of-State and the Japanese Premier, this time President Johnson and Premier Sato, early in 1965. *The New York Times*, Jan. 14, 1965, p. 5.

What if the managers of the effort, in their zeal for political payoffs, attempted to influence the proposals along lines of their own preconceptions? Or what if the resultant projects, interesting though they may be, had the effect of distorting natural scientific avenues of development because they were not in directions in which American or Japanese scientists would normally have moved? Or what if other countries demanded similar bilateral approaches to the development of cooperative projects and the United States felt constrained for political reasons to go along? This U.S./Japanese cooperation, as in the U.S./U.S.S.R. case, represents at the very least a departure from the norms of international scientific planning, norms that emphasize participation on the basis of scientific competence and scientific interest, not nationality.

In addition, this program affected scientific planning within the United States, for the National Science Foundation found it necessary to earmark funds to be sure the United States could follow through on the projects agreed upon. These were funds that were supposed to be awarded on the basis of scientific merit to American scientists. As it developed, the projects set forth by the U.S.-Japan Committee on Scientific Cooperation were competitive in quality so that supporting the American portion of the projects presented no major problem.

The principle is an important one, however. In effect, the U.S. Government was willing to use funds to support science for political as well as for scientific purposes when the projects developed under the program might not have measured up in quality to domestic proposals that would, as a result of the commitment to the joint program, have been denied funds. Is this wise? To be sure, the Japanese program is not a large one, and was almost sure to be of high quality. Still, this problem can be serious in other situations unless, as discussed in Chapter 3, the U.S. Government can make some different provisions for establishing criteria and providing support in this gray area where political and scientific motives intermingle, provisions that do not detract from domestic support.

These concerns cannot be taken lightly, for they exemplify the fears of the scientific community when suggestions are made to use science and technology for political purposes. They are legitimate concerns, involving as they do possible distortion and damage to science. Those responsible within the government for programs designed to capitalize on science and technology for political purposes must be highly sensitive to these issues at the same time that they are cognizant of the political advantages to be realized by following through wisely and carefully. Aside from competence, trust and respect are required on both sides in the relationship between the scientific community and the government on projects and programs such as the cooperative effort with the Japanese.

INITIATIVES WITH LESS-DEVELOPED NATIONS

In quantitative terms it is likely that the bulk of the opportunities for capitalizing on science and technology for foreign policy objectives arise in America's relations with nations that are less developed economically and scientifically. The same reasons that make science and technology attractive for political initiatives with advanced Western or Communist countries also apply to the less-developed countries. The difference is that with the generally lower level of scientific activity of the less-developed countries, fewer contacts take place naturally and there is greater need for outside technical help than in advanced countries.

One kind of initiative with less-developed nations immediately emerges as being of obvious importance: opportunities for using science and technology to assist in achieving economic growth objectives. Such initiatives can be seen best in the broader context of U.S. foreign economic assistance objectives and hence will be left to Chapter 9 for discussion.

However, there are opportunities for employing science and technology that are useful for achieving other political objectives in relations with less-developed nations, such as solving a problem that causes friction in relations between this country and another, or diverting attention from festering political disagreements, or establishing a community of interest and a habit of cooperation with another nation. A few examples can demonstrate this most effectively.

In 1959, the Department of Agriculture banned the importation of cured Argentine beef to the United States. This action was taken on the grounds that the Department had discovered in its Plum Island laboratory that the virus that causes foot-and-mouth disease could, theoretically at least, survive standardized curing methods.[27] This action caused some economic distress in Argentina, but even more political resentment

[27] "Report of the Scientific Mission to the Republic of Argentina on Foot and Mouth Disease," President's Science Advisory Committee, Washington, D. C., Jan. 31, 1962.

because the reason for the Department of Agriculture order was considered to be only an excuse to protect American beef interests. The situation persisted for several years, with the Argentines unhappy, but the Department of Agriculture was adamant that it had an overriding responsibility to prevent entry into the country of any beef possibly tainted with the virus, no matter how remote that possibility.

President Kennedy in 1961 asked his Special Assistant for Science and Technology to look into the situation and explore possible solutions. A special task force, chaired by Dr. George Harrar, President of the Rockefeller Foundation, was set up to carry out this examination and studied the matter first in the United States and then in concert with Argentine scientists. The net result was the recommendation of procedures that would allow cured beef to be imported safely, and the outlining of short-term and long-range research programs that would determine the extent of the immediate problem and facilitate progress toward longer-range solutions.[28]

There was nothing very startling in this solution. But by establishing the right political ground rules so that the technical aspects of the matter could be attacked without bias, a way out of a situation was found without having to deal overtly with related and difficult political questions. The Department of Agriculture, in principle, could have done the same thing long before. However, the variety of domestic pressures on that agency does not lead it to seek solutions to foreign policy questions that would complicate its domestic situation. In any case, the Argentines would probably

[28] *Ibid.*, p. 21.

have considered any recommendation by the Department of Agriculture to be biased. This way, the President was able to get the objective cooperation of the Argentines and to find an acceptable solution.

An unsuccessful example of a different kind was an attempt to find a way to defuse the Lauca River dispute between Bolivia and Chile. The Lauca River, a small stream in the Andes that describes an erratic course through Chile and then into Bolivia, became a source of controversy when Chile diverted some of the river water for agricultural and other purposes. Bolivia argued that Chile had no rights to the water and took the dispute to the Organization of American States (OAS) in April 1962.[29] The OAS attempted unsuccessfully to mediate, and when the Organization took no further action, Bolivia withdrew from the Council of the OAS. (She returned in 1965.)

At one point in the course of the controversy, which had its beginnings in 1939, an attempt was made to have the two countries agree to postpone the dispute by having a complete hydrological survey made of that region of the Andes. It was hoped that the Lauca River dispute could then have been put in the context of plans for water development of the entire area. But positions had become too fixed and the attempt failed.

President Kennedy is responsible for an illustration of how an initiative in science and technology can help divert attention from lack of agreement on other issues. In a July 1961 meeting with President Ayub Khan of Pakistan, President Kennedy offered to have American

---

[29] "Background Information on the Diversion of the Lauca River by Chile and the Bolivian Reservations," Document of the Delegation of Bolivia, Council of the OAS, C/INF-47, 20 Apr. 1962.

scientists study the waterlogging and salinity problems of West Pakistan.[30] The problem in Pakistan had been called to the attention of Dr. Wiesner, President Kennedy's Special Assistant for Science and Technology, in early 1961 by Dr. Abdul Salam, who served as science adviser to President Ayub. At that time it was thought to be a fairly straightforward technical problem, for which some recent technical developments in the United States might be applicable.

The importance of the problem to Pakistan, and the possibility that American scientists could help, was communicated to President Kennedy prior to President Ayub's visit to the United States. With a host of other sensitive and irreconcilable policy differences between Pakistan and the United States, the offer made by President Kennedy to ask his Science Advisory Committee to study the salinity problem for Pakistan was received as a welcome positive step that represented an issue on which the two Presidents could fully agree, and which was also important in its own right.

Closer to home is an excellent example that grew out of a dispute between the United States and Mexico over the effects of a new irrigation system on the Colorado River. The new system, located in Arizona, produced a substantial rise in the salt content of water reaching Mexican farmers south of the border and caused extensive damage to crops. The issue embittered U.S.-Mexican relations and became a factor in anti-American campaigns by Mexican nationalists.

President Kennedy, in 1961, characteristically turned to the scientists to ask if there was a technical solution

[30] Joint Communiqué of President Kennedy and President Mohammed Ayub Khan, *The New York Times,* July 14, 1961, p. 4.

to the problem. By the time of his visit to Mexico City in 1962, he and the President of Mexico were able to say: "In relation to the problem of salinity of the waters of the Colorado River, the two Presidents discussed the studies which have been conducted by the scientists of the two countries . . . They expressed their determination, with the scientific studies as a basis, to reach a permanent and effective solution at the earliest possible time. . . ."[31] A solution was achieved, involving American construction of a diversion canal, and the two nations signed a final agreement on March 22, 1965.[32]

President Johnson has been an avid employer of science and technology for international political purposes, consistent with his omniverous approach to most areas of government responsibility. For example, in February 1964, at his address at the Weizmann Institute dinner in New York, he called on science and technology as a means of emphasizing common interests between this country and Israel as well as of advancing the solution of an important problem. At that time, he suggested that the United States would help Israel meet its water needs through joint development of large-scale saline water conversion equipment. A cooperative program with Israel is now in progress, although economic desalination of sea water is still a promise for the future.

In October of 1965, the President expanded the desalination program with announcement of a "massive, cooperative, international effort to find solutions for

[31] Communiqué of the meeting of President Mateos and President Kennedy, June 30, 1962; *Ibid.*, July 1, 1962, p. 1.
[32] *Ibid.*, Mar. 23, 1965, p. 9.

Man's water problems." He called this the beginning
of a "Water for Peace Program."[33]

Similarly, in 1965, President Johnson took the occasion of Korean President Park's visit to the United
States to offer to send a team under his science adviser,
Dr. Donald Hornig, to help Korea apply science and
technology more effectively to its development problems.[34] Also early in 1965, the President used scientific
and technological initiatives to provide a concrete result from a visit by Premier Sato of Japan, calling for
"a greatly expanded program of cooperation" in medical research, air pollution and pesticides.[35] When President Ayub Khan of Pakistan visited at the end of 1965,
President Johnson announced (during the dinner toast
— a new dais for program announcements) the dis-
patch of his science adviser once again, this time with
the mission of improving medical training to serve rural
health and public health needs.[36] And, as noted earlier,
President Johnson in 1966 offered space cooperation to
Western European nations as a means of easing concern over the growing technological gap between the
United States and Western Europe.

Initiatives of these kinds with science and technology
are not likely to solve major political issues. But they
can ease big problems, or solve minor ones, in the short

[33] Text of the "Remarks for the President at Signing of U.S.–
Mexico–IAEA Agreement," White House Press Release, Oct. 7, 1965.

[34] "Joint Communiqué Between President Lyndon B. Johnson
and His Excellency Chung Hee Park, President of the Republic of
Korea, Following Talks in Washington, D. C., May 17 and 18, 1965,"
White House Press Release, May 18, 1965.

[35] The New York Times, Jan 14, 1965, p. 5.

[36] "Exchange of Toasts Between President Lyndon B. Johnson
and President Mohammed Ayub Khan of Pakistan," White House
Press Release, Dec. 14, 1965.

run and in some cases have long-term political effects of considerable importance. They offer excellent examples on a small scale of the benefits and some of the limitations of employing science and technology as instruments of foreign policy. The imaginative and proper use of science and technology for political purposes requires adequate recognition within the policy process of both the benefits and limitations.

8

International Organizations and Military Alliances

INTERNATIONAL ORGANIZATIONS

... international organizations exist simply because they are needed ... while nations may cling to national sovereignties ... science has created a functional international society, whether anyone likes it or not.[1]

Thus did Harlan Cleveland, former Assistant Secretary of State for International Organization Affairs, make the point that one of the aspects of the rapid advance of science and technology is the creation of new technologies or the multiplication of the scale of application of technology, so as to *require* some form of international regulation, cooperation, and control.

Some technologies simply cannot be effectively ex-

[1] Harlan Cleveland, "The Political Year of the Quiet Sun," *Department of State Bulletin* L, No. 1291 (Mar. 23, 1964) p. 455.

ploited by individual nations without prior international agreement. The use of electromagnetic frequency spectrum is a prime example, and the International Telecommunications Union was brought into being to facilitate achieving the essential international agreement. Other technologies, such as public health, have taken on new and urgent international importance as a result of the revolution in transportation that makes the spread of disease across national borders a more serious problem than ever before. One of the major functions of the World Health Organization (WHO) is to help control that spread, a task that no nation could do alone.

Moreover, the application of technologies to the needs of people who could not develop the technologies on their own has also become in part an international function. The WHO, the Food and Agriculture Organization (FAO), and other organizations are also concerned with this aid role as well as with their regulatory and control functions. The International Atomic Energy Agency (IAEA), too, has a split function: to further the peaceful uses of nuclear energy, and to help prevent the diversion of nuclear fuels to military purposes, though in this case the agency's regulatory function stems from the objective to control nuclear energy rather than from a technological imperative.

These agencies — the Specialized Agencies of the United Nations and others set up to meet specific technological needs or perform technological tasks — make up the functional international society to which Harlan Cleveland had reference. However, even those international organizations set up primarily for more broadly political or economic purposes, such as the United Nations itself, or the Organization for Economic Co-operation and Development (OECD), or the Organization of American States (OAS) often have important scientific or technological objectives and activities. Many have science programs of their own; all become at one time or another the forum for discussion of issues with important technical aspects such as radioactive fallout, peaceful uses of atomic energy, arms control, space exploration, or pollution.

It is not necessary to belabor the obvious that to make policy for participation in these international organizations of both the functional and political type requires intertwining of technical and political factors. Whether it be the meteorological program of the World Meteorological Organization (WMO), or the science program of the OECD, or the fallout debate in the United Nations, U.S. policy will serve short and long-term political objectives only if the technical aspects are viewed and understood in their political context.

This is not easy to accomplish in practice for the enormous volume of technical activities of international organizations makes it impractical (and unwise) for the foreign policy machinery of the government to attempt to be cognizant of and control the technical details of every program or issue. As a general rule, in the U.S. Government, the department or agency whose mission conforms most closely to the mission of a particular international body is delegated authority and responsibility, with guidance by the Department of State, to prepare the U.S. policy toward that body and to maintain substantive contact with it. For instance, the Weather Bureau is the primary agency to work with the WMO, the Department of Agriculture with the FAO, the Department of Health, Education and Welfare with WHO and so forth.[2] Complete responsibility for establishing the U.S. policy toward those bodies cannot be delegated to the technical agencies, although in practice, except for budgetary control and general policy guidelines, the technical agencies are in charge.

This is a reasonable procedure to follow for the great majority of issues. Nevertheless, for some — and it is always the important ones that are the exception — unless the foreign policy organs of the government have some independent competence to monitor technical activities and relate technical issues to broader political objectives, the technical agencies of the government will have effective control even of those issues with important political implications. It is not solely how well the policy process works for specific issues that is of concern. Rather, it must be recognized that international organizations are likely to be an increasingly central preoccupation of every nation's foreign policy in the future because the international political system as a whole has to cope with an increasing number of subjects that require some degree of decision making and action at the international rather than the national level.

U.S. objectives toward international organizations cannot be narrowly technical, even when an international organization may appear to be so; nor are the objectives only short range. U.S. objectives must in-

[2] UNESCO presents a special situation, and the State Department has kept the technical policy making for that body largely in its own hands. Even then, a separate part of the Department is responsible for substantive matters rather than the Bureau responsible for U.N. matters as a whole.

stead include the strengthening of international organizations so that they will be prepared to meet possible future tasks, such as inspection for arms control or competence to control and regulate new and possibly dangerous technologies. And U.S. objectives must include supporting the organizations in such a way that they have the stature to meet current political and technical needs, providing a safety valve to deflect conflict issues or offering a neutral forum for communication between states (or even providing a platform for making known American policies and achievements).

Science and technology can be conscious instruments of policy to contribute to these broader political objectives for international organizations in three general ways:

1. Programs in science and technology can serve to strengthen an international organization by giving it a needed (and appreciated) task that leads to increased international participation in the organization, greater respect for it, and the development of a pattern of international action. In addition, such programs can bring more funds, better personnel and greater influence for the organization.

2. Initiatives based on science and technology can force the development of needed new machinery within international organizations and provide operating experience that may be useful later for carrying out arms control or other peace-keeping roles. (The development of safeguards machinery for the control of fissionable material by the IAEA is a good example.

3. A particular political objective, such as enhanc-

ing American prestige through greater exposure of peaceful space accomplishments, can be advanced by specific technical programs undertaken in international organizations.

There are numerous examples of U.S. initiatives taken in international organizations that have had one or more of these political goals in mind. A discussion of two of these in some detail will serve to highlight the opportunities, and the problems.

UNCSAT Conference. The U.N. Conference for the Application of Science and Technology for the Benefit of the Less-Developed Areas, held in Geneva in February 1963, was a massive affair (over 2,000 papers and 1,600 participants) that is considered by some a highly successful exercise in U.S. diplomacy, and by others a caricature of what happens when science is overcommitted as an instrument of foreign policy. The objectives envisioned for the conference cut across many facets of U.S. international policy, and as a result the history of the conference idea within the U.S. Government is an excellent illustration of the issues surrounding an attempt to utilize science and technology for foreign policy objectives. It also is an interesting commentary on the role of scientists in the formulation and execution of foreign policy in the United States.

The idea for the conference was first broached in a meeting of the U.N. Science Advisory Committee in 1960.[3] The inspiration came from the August 1960 conference held in Rehovoth, Israel, addressed to the role

[3] The United Nations' SAC is a committee of eminent scientists from seven nations, chaired by the Secretary General of the United Nations. The Committee originated at the time of the Atoms for Peace Conferences and was quite active under Dag Hammarskjold.

of science in the advancement of new states, especially the African nations. Some of the participants, in particular the British atomic scientist Sir John Cockcroft, believed that the experience in Israel warranted a much more extensive conference that would bring in a wider representation of countries; hence the approach to the United Nations, where Sir John was a member of the Science Advisory Committee.

Dr. I. I. Rabi, American Nobel Prize winner in physics, who was (and is) the U.S. member of the U.N. Committee immediately responded favorably to the proposal, in the belief that it represented an important opportunity both for substantive assistance to the developing nations and for enhancing American prestige. He brought the idea for discussion in 1960 to the President's Science Advisory Committee, of which he was a member, and on October 24, 1960, to a panel of that committee that was charged with responsibility for international subjects.

Both the panel and the Committee were interested in the proposal but skeptical of the value of the "massive" conference form. Neither group took any formal position. However, Dr. Kistiakowsky, then the President's Special Assistant for Science and Technology and Chairman of PSAC, allowed one of his staff to accompany Dr. Rabi during further discussions at the State Department, thereby implying a certain measure of approval for the idea.

At the State Department in the late fall of 1960 there proved to be no enthusiasm whatever for the proposal. The Bureau of International Organization Affairs (IO) of State, which had responsibility for following the work of the U.N. Science Advisory Committee saw the

cost and problems associated with another large conference and was not impressed with the chances the
conference might offer for advancement of a variety
of U.S. objectives. The Bureau had a rather negative
view of the results of the first two Atoms for Peace
Conferences, and were not likely to see much in this
new proposal, which had obvious similarities. The
lame-duck nature of the Administration also deterred
a commitment to what would inevitably be a fairly
costly and difficult effort.

The critical point in the life of the conference occurred in January 1961 at the next meeting of the U.N.
Committee held in Bombay. Had either the United
States or the Soviet Union come in with a strong negative view, the proposal would likely have ended there.
But the Russians said little, and the State Department
did not make a clear decision, so that Dr. Rabi, who
was strongly in favor of the conference, was able to be
noncommittal on the U.S. position until the following
Committee meeting.[4] By then, the idea had received
enough international discussion and publicity so that
it would have been politically costly for the United
States to have tried to stop the conference had it
wanted to do so.

With the advent of the new Administration, the U.S.
attitude changed markedly. Harland Cleveland, the
new Assistant Secretary for IO immediately agreed
that there were attractive opportunities in the idea of
the conference and gave his strong support to a positive U.S. position.

The objectives the government had in mind (very

---

[4] Private communication from Dr. Rabi, Mar. 7, 1965.

few were ever stated explicitly) as the conference preparations proceeded were several:

1. The conference would be an opportunity to examine, in concert with representatives of the developing countries, the great variety of ways in which science and technology could be applied to their needs and the conditions that were necessary to do so successfully.

2. As a corollary of the first, the conference would provide a chance to examine, in a neutral forum, the *limitations* of science and technology in order to put them in proper and better perspective for the less-developed countries and for the United States.

3. The conference would make it possible to learn more about the attitudes of recipient countries toward bilateral foreign aid and the repercussions from such aid in a forum in which national representatives could speak more freely than they could in a bilateral context.

4. The preparations for the conference, which would require drawing together a great body of U.S. experience in foreign assistance efforts, could serve as a useful and possibly unique opportunity for evaluation of past U.S. programs.

5. The conference could serve to increase the contacts between the scientific and technical leadership in the United States and that of the less-developed countries so as to provide more channels of communication that did not necessarily go through governments.

6. Simultaneously, the conference could stimulate awareness of and interest in development problems within the American scientific community.

7. It could have the effect of enhancing the United Nation's role in science and in economic development and thus expand the areas in which the United Nations is important to its member nations.

8. Finally, the conference could emphasize U.S. leadership by demonstrating clearly the great strength of the United States compared to that of any other nation in fields of science and technology important to development and by showing the breadth within the United States of development accomplishments that are useful for other nations.

To achieve these objectives required several things to happen in the United States, in the United Nations, and in less-developed countries. For one, the preparations for the conference in this country had to be undertaken as a major project with ample funding, with the full and active support of the State Department and the foreign aid agency, and with full appreciation of the interlocking of the scientific and political issues. For another, the U.N. staff responsible for the conference had to be competent and relatively free from cold war politics. For a third, the countries the United Nations and the United States were trying to reach had to be fully informed of the conference and had to participate actively in the planning so as to insure their full participation with the proper representation at the conference itself. Unfortunately, these requirements were fulfilled only in part; hence the objectives were only partially achieved.

Within the United States, the foreign aid agency (the International Cooperation Administration and later its successor, AID), beset with reorganization problems and in any case with great unconcern for the conference, took only a marginal interest in the preparations. AID did pay the bill, but the U.S. government staff responsible for preparing the American input to the conference was set up as a separate entity and had almost no communication with the foreign aid agency itself. The State Department, notwithstanding Harlan Cleveland's interest, became involved only when specific political problems emerged. A high-level Public Advisory Board to the Department of State was established under the chairmanship of Dr. Walsh McDermott, Head of the Department of Public Health of the Cornell University Medical College. It worked hard and was successful in helping to assemble a superb U.S. contribution to the conference; but the Board operated largely independently of the Department.

The U.N. staff for the conference was not strong, as measured by several of its decisions that adversely affected the success of the conference. It allowed the over-all size to grow beyond sensible limits and greatly overorganized the actual meetings. In fact, the less-developed countries literally revolted at the conference itself and forced a relaxation of the procedures that were preventing any spontaneous discussion. In addition, the United Nations did not provide in advance the kind of information that was required to bring adequate participation from the countries to whom the conference was primarily directed.

The meeting was not a failure, but neither was it the success its originators had hoped. Certainly the amount of useful information exchanged at the conference was a disappointment, and domestically the sought-for feedback to AID was not achieved. Some of the other objectives were realized, however, notably that of arousing the critical interest of many of the less-developed countries in the subject. In addition, the conference succeeded in demonstrating the great scientific and technological strength of the United States, in large part as a result of the fast footwork of the U.S. delegation led by Dr. McDermott. When the less-developed countries rebelled at the rigid organization of the conference, the U.S. Delegation responded by organizing a conference on the side in which U.S. experts held discussions on problems of direct concern to selected groups of countries. The depth and breadth of the U.S. delegation and its ability to produce information on almost any subject made a deep impression on the others. Cold war issues were also avoided in the conference as a whole, which may assist future U.N. activities in this field.[5]

Whether there will be any lasting impact of the con-

[5] The avoidance of cold war issues was aided by deft handling of an incident at the beginning of the conference. Dr. Jerome Wiesner, President Kennedy's Special Assistant for Science and Technology, was the United States' principle speaker at the opening formal session. He followed Mr. Federov of the Soviet Union who had presented an address heavily weighted with ideological and political propaganda. Dr. Wiesner opened with the statement that he was "glad to be able to address this *scientific* conference . . . ," which brought a storm of applause and laughter. That turned out to be the last of the overt propaganda from the Soviet Union.

ference remains to be seen. Within the United States, the answer is apparently that there will not be. Internationally, it is not yet certain. The less-developed countries exerted pressure of their own after the conference for some kind of U.N. initiative in the field. They talked first of a new U.N. agency, but this idea was successfully diverted by the advanced countries. Instead, a special committee of experts was established under the U.N. Economic and Social Council that may be able to produce useful results.[6] Other possibilities are being considered, and UNESCO, which was shocked at the conference by the low esteem in which it was held, has substantially altered its program format in science to build on the work of the conference.

In sum, the conference achieved some movement internationally, and some prestige for the United States. It fell down with respect to usefulness to the less-developed countries and to feedback effects on the domestic scene. It was a valiant effort, and had there been more active participation by the foreign policy organs of the U.S. Government and more of a political commitment by the United States, the over-all record would almost surely have been better.

The initiative came in this case originally from scientists. The idea was not fully developed when they made the suggestion, but they did see the primary connection to political objectives. However, they clearly

[6] A provocative and potentially useful report was prepared by this ECOSOC committee at their May 1965 meeting: *Second Report, Advisory Committee on the Application of Science and Technology to Development*, Economic and Social Council, Official Records: Thirty-Ninth Session, Supplement No. 14, UN E/4026, May 1965. Since then, the Advisory Committee has continued to meet at regular intervals, but with some apparent falling off of national interest.

gave too little weight to the political problems and dangers and underrated the importance of a strong U.S. Government commitment that was most unlikely to be forthcoming, given the problems of the foreign aid agency in 1961 and 1962 (the "turnaround" period in the evolution from ICA to AID). It is also fair to say that the scientists underrated the complexity of the problems of development and the lack of any clear conception of the actual role science and technology play in the development process. If the conference resulted in any more attention to analyzing and understanding that role, it may prove to have been a success in the long run.

U.N. Program in Meteorology and Atmospheric Sciences. The UNCSAT conference was an initiative conceived by scientists with political payoffs in mind. For comparison it is worth while to examine the history of a scientific initiative conceived by nonscientists with political payoffs in mind. Such an example is the proposal made to the United Nations in September 1961 by President Kennedy for a major new international effort in meteorology and atmospheric sciences to take advantage of the new tools for research and application offered by space technology.[7]

From the early days of the Kennedy administration, with the International Organization's Affairs Bureau in the State Department playing a leading role, the U.S. Government was anxious to explore all possibilities for strengthening the United Nations. In the spring and summer of 1961, the "new team" in the Department searched for ideas that could form the basis for initiatives at the U.N. General Assembly meeting that

[7] *The New York Times,* Sept. 26, 1961, p. 14.

fall. Among the ideas proposed, largely by politically oriented Department officers, was a program for greatly expanded weather forecasting and atmospheric sciences research.

The program was envisaged as a substantial effort in which would be included a worldwide "weather watch" (global weather forecasting services) and a large-scale research program in the atmospheric sciences. The objectives in mind were approximately the following:

1. To strengthen the United Nations and its Specialized Agencies by involving those organizations in a new science, a new technology and a new public service.
2. To prepare the U.N. family for possible regulatory and control functions as the possibilities for weather modification came closer.
3. To advance, under a U.N. umbrella, a field of science and technology of value to all people and of interest to the United States, one which requires international cooperation.
4. To remove one more potentially contentious issue from cold war debate: the claim by the Soviet Union that U.S. weather satellites were "spy" satellites.[8]
5. To gain prestige and propaganda returns by further exploitation of the successful TIROS weather satellites.

When the proposal was formulated, there was insufficient time to evaluate it fully on scientific grounds

[8] *Ibid.*, July 24, 1961, p. 1.

although a hastily convened panel of scientists did give their approval to the general concepts. As far as weather forecasting was concerned, there was little doubt that the time was ripe for a major step forward and little doubt that the WMO was the organization that should take charge of the effort. The situation on the atmospheric sciences research side was much less clear either on substantive or organizational grounds.

First and most important, the research portion of the proposal was premature. Scientists had not yet absorbed the sudden great increases of data from the first TIROS weather satellites and had not yet evaluated the implications for atmospheric research of the availability of earth satellites as a new research tool. In effect, they did not yet know what direction research should take in the years to come and were not quite ready to decide.

On organizational grounds, tying atmospheric sciences and weather forecasting together in the same proposal to the United Nations made it very likely that the whole package would go to the WMO. This might seem logical on the surface, but actually the WMO had little research experience, representing as it did the Weather Bureaus of the member countries, and it had a poor reputation among atmospheric scientists. It is essential for sound scientific programs that the detailed research plans be worked out by scientists. In this case, no time was available for such detailed scientific planning before the proposal was made. Therefore the possibility that the responsibility for the program would go to an organization that had little experience in science or science planning was of great concern to the scientists involved.

As feared, the WMO acted quickly and successfully after the proposal was submitted to the United Nations; the final resolution as it was passed gave primary responsibility for the whole package to the WMO.[9]

The appropriate procedure in principle would have been *first* to ask the international scientific community, through the International Council of Scientific Unions (ICSU), to work with national and international groups of scientists to lay out proposals for research. These proposals could then be weighed by governments and by international organizations representing governments, such as WMO and UNESCO, to arrive at agreed plans for cooperative research. But in the press of the need to formulate ideas for proposals to be made when the President addressed the United Nations in September of 1961, there was no time to follow "normal" procedures — not an unusual occurrence in government.

The U.S. Government, concerned about the turn the organizational developments were taking, in January 1962 enlisted the aid of the National Academy of Sciences to develop what American scientists would consider to be a scientifically desirable international research program.[10] The Academy, in an effort led by Dr. Sverre Petterssen of the University of Chicago, produced a plan that formed the basis of subsequent government deliberations to determine what the United States would be willing to support in an international program.[11] The Academy also attempted to alert the

[9] U.N. Resolution 1721 (XVI), Dec. 1961.
[10] Letter from Dr. J. B. Wiesner, The President's Special Assistant for Science and Technology, to Dr. D. W. Bronk, President of the National Academy of Sciences, Jan. 25, 1962.
[11] "An Outline of International Programs in the Atmospheric Sciences," National Academy of Sciences/National Research Council, No. 1085, Washington, D. C., 1963.

international scientific community through ICSU to the need for scientific planning of the program but met with some indifference, partly on the grounds that, as WMO already had charge of the program, there was little the scientists could do that would be worth while. This indifference later turned into a jurisdictional dispute between two scientific groups — the ICSU Committee on Space Research (COSPAR) and the International Union of Geodosy and Geophysics — as to which one should have the leading scientific role.

The creation of this difficult and, from a scientific point of view, unnecessary situation might have been avoided at the beginning if the State Department had thought to mobilize American scientists at an early stage to help formulate the proposals and prepare the groundwork in other countries. The fact that the scientific proposal was politically motivated was perfectly legitimate *as long as* it allowed reasonable time for detailed planning by scientists. The deficiency arose because there was inadequate appreciation, before presentation of the proposal, of the conditions necessary for this scientific planning and of the need for governments and governmental organizations to remain interested but aloof until the detailed scientific plans were made and the needs more clearly seen.

In this example, it can also be seen what happens when the Department of State is in the position of relying for all its technical information on an interested government agency. The U.S. Weather Bureau in this situation was an interested party and had its own motives for wanting to build up the WMO in the atmospheric sciences as opposed to giving that part of the over-all proposal to UNESCO or any other international body that might have been created. The

Weather Bureau knew the scientific problems well but believed, in contrast to others, that WMO could handle them; in fact, it had a vested interest in relying on the WMO because of the Bureau's extremely close ties to that organization. It therefore gave little thought to any alternatives to WMO and opposed them when questions about alternatives were finally raised. Because the State Department was so dependent on the Weather Bureau, it was not alerted to the possibility that there might be a problem until it was too late to take effective action.

MILITARY ALLIANCES

In December 1957, with much fanfare, the Heads of Government of the members of the North Atlantic Treaty Organization (NATO) announced the formation of a Science Committee to "increase the effectiveness of national efforts through the pooling of scientific facilities and information and the sharing of tasks."[12] This step, with the United States in the vanguard, was one of NATO's most visible responses to Sputnik. It was taken in recognition both of the military importance of strong science in Atlantic nations and of the belief that science and technology could and should be better integrated among alliance nations. It was also taken as a dramatic gesture that appeared to respond to the post-Sputnik political situation. The history of science in NATO and of the creation of the Sci-

---

[12] "Declaration and Communiqué Issued at the Ministerial Meeting of the North Atlantic Council." Paris, 16–19 Dec., 1957 in *NATO: Facts About the North Atlantic Treaty Organizations,* NATO Information Service, Paris, Jan. 1962.

ence Committee can illustrate well the variety of ways that science and technology can impinge on a major military alliance.

In the early years of NATO, fairly ambitious ideas for cooperation in military research and development were explored under NATO auspices. The first was at a conference of NATO research directors convened by Dr. Theodore von Karman in Washington in 1951.[13] The report of that conference included the following statement:

> In many countries during and since World War II, the important part played by research and development in defence planning has been recognized, and close working arrangements between science and defense have been established. Within the defence organization set up by the North Atlantic Treaty nations, the contribution which science can make to military planning must not be overlooked.

As a result, the Advisory Group for Aeronautical Research and Development was established in 1952 to further cooperative R & D among NATO countries, and to advise the military on technical matters.

In 1954, the post of science adviser to SACEUR, the Supreme Allied Commander, Europe, was established, and the same year the SHAPE Air Defense Technical Center was formed in The Hague as the first cooperative defense laboratory under a military alliance.[14] (Its function has now been expanded to include other defense subjects, and its name correspondingly shortened to SHAPE Technical Center.) In addition to these new posts and organizations, much time and

13 *Ibid.*, p. 133.
14 *Ibid.*, p. 131.

effort has gone into joint planning of technical force requirements and the setting of common technical standards for military weapons.

This and subsequent work, although productive of useful results, never fulfilled the original concepts of bringing about substantial integration in military R & D. The reasons for the lack of full success are complex, but the underlying factor was the basic reluctance, or lack of commitment on the part of member governments to move in a really serious way to integrate defense planning, R & D, and production. Each nation wanted to preserve freedom of action in its defense planning, wanted to be as self-sufficient as possible in science and technology, and wanted to capture an important share of the production contracts for itself.

By 1956, the lack of progress in tying the science and technology of member countries effectively to the needs of the alliance stimulated a call by the NATO "Three Wise Men" for a conference on scientific and technological cooperation and a study of possible new measures that could be undertaken.[15] A task force was set up in June 1957 under Dr. Joseph Koepfli of the California Institute of Technology to make specific recommendations; a report was issued in November 1957.[16]

Before the study was completed, there was considerable doubt in the study group that the recommenda-

[15] The "Three Wise Men" were Martino of Italy, Lange of Norway, and Pearson of Canada, who were installed by the NATO Council in May of 1956 as a "Committee of Three on Non-Military Cooperation in NATO."

[16] "Report to the Council by the Task Force on Action by NATO in the Field of Scientific and Technical Cooperation," Nov. 1957, *NATO: Facts,* pp. 289–293.

tions would have any chance of adoption. The Russian Sputnik of October 1957 changed the atmosphere. The shock of that event, with its intimation of rapid Russian scientific and technological progress as compared to the West, caused sudden new attention to the health of science and technology in the Atlantic nations. President Eisenhower, with the strong concurrence of his new Special Assistant for Science and Technology, Dr. James R. Killian, urged the adoption of the task force recommendations at the NATO Heads of Governments meeting in December 1957. The other Governments agreed, and the chief operational recommendations that a Science Adviser to the Secretary General should be appointed and a Science Committee established were adopted.

But for all the fanfare with which the new steps were announced, a basic decision by member countries to develop real collaboration in science and technology was not taken. The Science Committee of NATO since its inception has developed useful programs of joint research, fellowships, and scientific conferences; it has focused attention on domestic measures in member countries necessary to strengthen scientific and technological competence; the Science Adviser has stimulated closer ties between science and the military, notably by bringing together on a regular basis those responsible for military R & D in member countries (now established as a separate Committee); and the Science Committee and the Science Adviser have served to develop a respectable nonmilitary role for NATO in science to implement Article 2 of the North Atlantic Treaty.[17]

[17] The text of Article 2 is:

These measures alone, though useful, do not amount to extensive scientific collaboration. Without accompanying political decisions of a fairly basic nature that make possible a genuine sharing of scientific personnel, weapons information, and development and production facilities by all the countries involved, such collaboration was bound to be restricted in its scope. And those political decisions were not forthcoming.

Curiously, it may have been the French who were the only ones to see the kinds of political decisions that had to be involved if there was to be genuine scientific integration and who said they were willing to act. At the 1957 Heads of Government meeting and repeatedly in the Science Committee, the French proposed the creation of a Western Foundation for Scientific Research which was intended to be a major central source of financing of research in NATO countries.[18] Funds alone were not enough, but the French argued that through such a common enterprise with the leverage of large amounts of money it would be possible to develop much greater collaboration and integration among NATO nations, to bring about changes in the conditions and environment for scientists where necessary to influence the development of important scien-

---

The Parties will contribute toward the further development of peaceful and friendly international relations by strengthening their free institutions, by bringing about a better understanding of the principles upon which these institutions are founded, and by promoting conditions of stability and well-being. They will seek to eliminate conflict in their international economic policies and will encourage economic collaboration between any or all of them.
NATO: Facts, p. 198.

[18] Communiqué, NATO: Facts, op. cit., p. 283; see also Proposal for an International Institute of Science and Technology, Report of the Working Group appointed by the Secretary General of NATO, May 1962, p. 48.

tific fields, and to provide an impetus for strengthening science and technology throughout the Atlantic Community.

The political fallout from such a Western Foundation could have been immense. But the other NATO countries, and particularly the United States and United Kingdom, dismissed the French proposals as visionary and impractical. Undoubtedly they were so at the time but primarily because the United States and United Kingdom were not willing to create such an international mechanism, which would have been of great help to France in particular but which also would have had resources large enough to influence materially their own scientific development.

This history points up an important conclusion with regard to the use of science for international political purposes. It is that science is too closely bound to a central objective of government — that of providing for the defense of the nation — for a country ever to let control over its scientific development be shared with other nations *unless* a prior decision has been made to integrate defense responsibilities substantially with those other nations. Truly intimate scientific cooperation and integration cannot ever be very far in front of intimate defense cooperation and integration. The degree of defense integration in NATO, though unprecedented for an alliance, is still not great enough to allow or require thoroughgoing scientific cooperation.

In 1957, the NATO countries were talking as though they wanted this level of integration. But the cavalier way in which the French proposal for real scientific cooperation and planning was treated belies their words.

9

Foreign Economic Assistance

Perhaps the most challenging and controversial development in American foreign policy after World War II was the recognition that America's new position in international politics carried with it a vital concern for the political stability and economic growth of the entire non-Communist world. This concern was first given substance in the Marshall Plan to assist the recovery of the battered states of Europe. Later, it led to President Truman's Point Four Program, inaugurated in 1949, that in effect symbolized the acceptance by the United States of a measure of responsibility for the evolution to viable, stable nationhood of the underdeveloped countries of Latin America, Africa, and South Asia. The Marshall Plan rapidly achieved its objectives in Europe, but the Point Four Program, which started wholly as a technical assistance effort, gradually developed into the broadly based economic, technical, and military programs of today.

Whether this foreign assistance program be thought of in short-range terms as one of the many tactical instruments of foreign policy or in longer-range terms as a fundamental objective of American foreign policy, it is in essence a program aimed at nation building. Behind it lies the conviction that economically viable nations are more likely to be politically stable; in turn, political stability is more likely to guarantee the kind of peaceful, productive, and free world society the United States believes necessary to be able to pursue its own social goals.[1]

[1] The character of the U.S. interest is subject to wide interpretation and much dispute that is only indirectly relevant to this discussion. Hollis Chenery, former Assistant Administrator for Program, Agency for International Development (AID) presented a semi-official view as follows:

In the most general sense, the main objective of foreign assistance, as of many other tools of foreign policy, is to produce a political and economic environment in which the United States can best pursue its own social goals. The long-term economic and social progress of other countries can be regarded either as a prerequisite for the kind of international community that we need for our own selfish interest or as an end in itself. In either case, we should be concerned to promote rising levels of income, modernization of economies, independent political systems, and other features of societies that satisfy their own citizens as well as the international community.

The second objective, which concerns the immediate future, is internal stability, which is sought by giving financial support in times of economic crisis, by preventing internal disorders, and by other measures that help existing governments to stay in power. The measures taken to preserve economic and political stability may or may not also promote long-term economic and social development. The conflict is acute when the existing government is not development-oriented and a change might be more conducive to growth.

The third major objective of foreign assistance is security of the United States and its allies from external aggression. This objective is sought directly by the provision of armaments, the security of military bases, and where critically important, the preclusion of Soviet bloc penetration. External security is both a short-term and a long-term objective. It is supported

To many, the foreign aid program is the nation's number one foreign policy problem: a program of great importance but one characterized by uncertain methods, contradictory results, and little public support within the United States. In fact, given the lack of theoretical understanding of how economic development takes place, the always uneasy relation between a donor and a recipient of aid, and the difficulties inherent in influencing societies by manipulation of external resources, the U.S. foreign aid effort has been remarkably effective. It has helped some countries to the point of self-sustained growth (e.g., Taiwan, Greece, Israel) and others have a good chance of reaching that goal (e.g., India, Pakistan). It is no criticism of the program to observe that the problems of bringing about self-sustaining growth and political evolution are much greater than was generally realized in the early postwar period. General progress has therefore been slower than originally expected but almost surely better than would have been achieved without American aid.[2]

The role of science and technology in foreign aid ef-

in the long run by the economic development of the United States and its allies and in the short run by the maintenance of political stability.

Hollis B. Chenery, "Objectives and Criteria for Foreign Assistance," in *Why Foreign Aid?*, Robert A. Goldwin, ed. (Chicago: Rand McNally & Co., 1963), p. 33.

[2] There are, of course, widely disparate views of the effectiveness of U.S. aid efforts, held even by those who are wedded to the view that the United States has a responsibility to assist the emerging nations. This debate has no definitive conclusion at present and is not germane to the discussion here. The viewpoint of the author starts from the position that the U.S. foreign aid program has been useful, is essential for American interests, and needs to be increased in emphasis and resources.

forts has been as uncertain or perhaps more uncertain than any other element of the program. At the time the Point Four Program was launched, the general concept was that technical aid, sometimes called transference of American know-how, was all that was required to remove the barriers to economic growth. This belief was gradually supplanted by almost the opposite view that science and technology were almost unimportant by comparison with infusion of capital resources, economic planning, and general budgetary support.

Neither extreme is useful, and the AID program and foreign assistance policy in general now steer a middle course, attempting to relate science and technology more appropriately to foreign assistance efforts. But the barriers and the problems are formidable because a clear body of theoretical knowledge relating science to economic growth is yet to be developed, and even seemingly straightforward problems of the transfer of simple technologies often turn out to be complex and intractable.

The economic assistance portion of the foreign aid program now regularly accounts for about two-thirds of the total AID budget, or approximately $2 billion per year at the appropriation levels since 1955.[3] Of that amount, some 10 per cent, or between $200 and $300 million, is allocated for technical assistance projects, the remainder being made up of budget support, development loans, capital assistance, and other items.[4]

[3] "Proposed Mutual Defense and Development Program, FY1965, Summary Presentation to the Congress," Apr. 1964, inside cover; and "Facts About the Foreign Aid Program for FY1967, New Initiatives in Agriculture, Education, Health," Agency for International Development, Mar. 1966.

[4] *Ibid.*

Not only in the technical assistance programs, however, but throughout the economic assistance category, scientific and technical elements figure to some degree.

To understand this relationship better, it is useful to break down the relevance of science and technology to foreign economic assistance into three major categories: (1) the transfer of technology process, central to many aid projects and programs; (2) the question of allocation of resources for science by the less-developed countries; and (3) the need for research to support the economic assistance program as a whole. These categories will be discussed in turn, though a brief discussion of this complex and little-understood subject can do no more than highlight relationships and pinpoint areas of uncertainty requiring expanded study.

TRANSFER OF TECHNOLOGY

One of the central tasks of economic assistance or of foreign aid in general can be viewed as the successful transfer of technology from the economically advanced to the less-developed nations. Perhaps it would be more appropriate to use the term "transfer of the principles of technology," for, as will be seen, it is the exception when a technology can be transferred without some modification required in the technology itself. Sometimes even complete "reinvention" is necessary of all but the basic principles. Quite clearly, the transfer of technology is the motive for that part of the foreign aid program labeled technical assistance, but it is a major purpose in other parts of the program as well.

Technical assistance, which includes projects such as introduction of new farming methods, establishment of light industry in villages, aid for the development of a technical university, or help in the application of new public health measures, obviously is concerned with the transference of known technologies to the environment of other countries. Capital assistance programs, such as support for the construction of a steel mill, hydroelectric plant, or fertilizer factory, are also in an important sense concerned with the transfer of known technologies from the United States to other economies. In both cases — for technical and for capital assistance — the underlying scientific and technological knowledge is almost always well known and familiar, at least to American scientists and engineers.

But the fact that the underlying science and technology is known is in practice only a part of the problem of transferring the technology. Several other factors complicate the task:

1. The technology must be adapted to the local environment, and the local environment to the technology. For example, seeds must be adapted to the local soil and climate conditions, possibly requiring changes in plowing or sowing methods; steel mills must be adapted to the types of steel needed, the availability of raw materials, the limited foreign exchange situation, and the kinds of trained manpower available, while local infrastructure may have to be built to provide access to markets and power.

2. Sometimes the underlying science may be known, but a specific, needed technology may not exist in advanced countries. Considerable R & D may be necessary before a suitable tech-

nology is available for application: low-cost small power generators are not a major need in advanced countries but could be of importance in countries with large, poor, rural populations that have an inadequate electric power distribution system.

3. All technical needs of a country cannot be met at once nor can all problems be worked on simultaneously. A very difficult selection process must take place. There must be a priority ordering based on (a) the importance of the need or the problem to development objectives, (b) the existence of knowledge and people that can be applied to the project, and (c) a judgment of the relative costs and benefits of the project when compared to alternate uses of the same resources. Such a selection process implies a high degree of technical and economic sophistication, if it is to be done well, on the part of both donor and recipient of the aid, with the primary task falling on the latter.

4. The nontechnical environment must be understood. The local social, cultural, economic and political situation in the last analysis may be the dominant factor in attempts to transfer technology. These factors clearly must be taken into account in the design of any innovations or the design of the means by which technologies will be introduced. For example, the subsistence farmer in Pakistan is not likely to mortgage his land to introduce fertilizers unless he has a guarantee that a bad year for water would not mean foreclosure; the Turkish peasant is

not going to take kindly to substituting horses, much less tractors, for oxen if he depends on the body heat of an ox to supplement scarce winter fuel in his home.

The problem of transfer of technology or, more appropriately, technological innovation in less-developed economies is much more than a technological problem. Contrary to the early assumption of the Point Four Program, doing nothing more than to make technology available has little value. There must be adaptation, selection, genuine R & D, and great sensitivity to the special characteristics of the environment into which the technology is to be introduced.

Moreover, the introduction of new technologies, because of their intimate relation to the nontechnical environment, are bound to have important effects on that environment. Technological innovations will sometimes bring about new political patterns and institutions, just as they have done in advanced nations. It is these institutions and patterns that will in the future determine the course of a society's internal development, so that meddling with a nation's technology is indeed meddling with a nation's future form and character. As yet, however, the societal effects of technological innovation are so little understood that technological intervention could not be part of a grand design.

Knowledge of how to innovate technologically, and of the effects of such innovation, is advancing slowly, with a host of opportunities for social science research. Most of the time, action cannot wait for study, and questions that arise must be decided on an ad hoc basis relying on a mix of technical, social, economic and political judgments. Even when relevant studies of the implications of technological innovation are available, they can serve only to reduce the areas of uncertainty, not to eliminate them.

The most important observation may be that whenever possible (that is, whenever resources and the political situation permit), attempts to transfer technology should be approached on a trial-and-error or experimental basis. Given the complexity of the problems and the usual lack of relevant information, there is little reason to expect that the first solution selected for a problem of technological innovation in a society is the right one.

In fact, no one would expect in ordinary physical problems that solutions could be found without a process of repeated experimentation, trial and error, and research. That is the essence of what "development" means. Yet in complex social systems in which the problems are extraordinary, it is somehow assumed that good common sense can be applied and come up with the right answer to any problem the first time. On the contrary, whenever possible, the "scientific" method — experimentation to test hypotheses — is a much wiser approach.[5]

An interesting illustration of the breadth of the problem of transfer of technology and thus of the interrelation of technological factors and the broader ele-

[5] The M.I.T. Conference on Productivity and Innovation in Agriculture in the Underdeveloped Countries came very strongly to this conclusion:

> . . . the fundamental problem confronting agriculture . . . is to build into the whole agricultural process—from the farmer to the university research institute, from the field extension agent to the minister of agriculture—an attitude of experiment, trial and error, continued innovation and adaptation of new ideas.

Policies for Promoting Agricultural Development, Center for International Studies, M.I.T., Jan. 1965, p. 28.

ments of economic development is offered by the study undertaken at the initiative of President Kennedy to study the waterlogging and salinity problems of West Pakistan.

In July 1961, President Ayub Khan of Pakistan came on a state visit to Washington. One of the subjects he discussed with President Kennedy was the hydrological situation in the Punjab region of West Pakistan that was turning 50,000 to 100,000 acres of arable land per year into salt deserts.[6] It has already been noted in Chapter 7 that President Kennedy responded to President Ayub by offering to have the Science Advisory Committee study the problem for Pakistan, thinking of this as a useful initiative that was important to Pakistan and would also serve U.S./Pakistan political relations. The study was set up under Dr. Roger Revelle, then Science Adviser to the Secretary of the Interior.

Before and during the meeting between the two Presidents, the problem was thought of as primarily a technical one having to do with such questions as the means of lowering the water table, providing better irrigation, preventing water seepage from the British-built canal system, and so forth.

It quickly became evident to Dr. Revelle and his team that the problem was much broader: "Waterlogging and salt accumulation are only one of the problems besetting agriculture in the [Indus] Plain. The scanty yields that hold the countryside in poverty are not the consequences of any *single* deficiency."[7] Instead, the

---

[6] *Report on Land and Water Development in the Indus Plain,* White House/Department of Interior Panel on Waterlogging and Salinity in West Pakistan, The White House, Washington, D. C., Jan. 1964, p. 63. Hereafter called the "Revelle Report."

[7] *Ibid.,* p. 2.

issue was one of agricultural productivity as a whole and involved questions of water use by the farmers, agricultural techniques, fertilizer availability and use, crop selection and seed development, land ownership patterns, agricultural credit, and village political structure. The waterlogging and salinity could have been ameliorated somewhat by technical means, but in isolation such improvement would have been of limited value in terms of the development goals of the region.

The study, which started as a search for a known technology that could be used to solve a vexing but narrow technical problem, ended up putting the technical problem in proper perspective with the broader goals and problems of economic development. Only in the context of those broader goals could decisions be taken on the technical problem: What resources should be devoted to it; what alternative technical solutions should be examined that might have a bearing on the solution of related nontechnical problems; what social or economic or other measures must be taken concurrently to make the technical measures meaningful, and so forth.

The final recommendations presented a dramatic plan for carving out million-acre project areas in the Punjab within which a series of related measures for solving agriculture, water, and social problems would be taken concurrently.[8] The first of these project areas has been incorporated in Pakistan/U.S. plans. President Ayub Khan in a 1965 visit to the United States referred in glowing terms to the study and to progress in implementing it.[9]

[8] *Ibid.*, summary.
[9] White House, "Exchange of Toasts Between President Lyndon

A related need emerged from the experience of the Revelle Panel. The group found, as is a common experience in underdeveloped countries, that the available data tended to be sketchy or unreliable. The Panel found it necessary to spend a great deal of time with individuals of many disciplines in developing basic information before they could make reasonable analyses of the actual situation and develop any plans for action. Even then, the validity of the underlying data was of concern because it had to be assembled so quickly and sometimes from uncertain sources.

The study took well over two years, and then the team was disbanded. How much more valuable it would be if a continuing capability were to exist so that the analysts in the Revelle Panel and others like them could, in an organized way, maintain contact with a region, to follow the changes and developments, continue to identify bottleneck problems of research or of data, and be able to bring to bear recent research developments to the projects as they developed.

Creation of this kind of broad, semipermanent analytical capability is not a simple task, but it represents one of the important ways in which science and technology could be part of and contribute to the aid process. Very little of this nature is done in the foreign aid program at present.

INVESTMENT IN SCIENCE

Closely related to the problems of transfer of technology, and in many ways more fundamental in terms

B. Johnson and President Ayub Khan of Pakistan," White House Press Release, Dec. 14, 1965.

of long-term growth, is the question of what type and level of investment in science is appropriate in a developing country? This is a controversial subject that has yet to yield to hard, quantitative analysis. It is important to donor nations in formulating policy for economic assistance, and of much greater moment to the developing countries themselves as they attempt to allocate their scarce resources in the face of ignorance about the relative economic returns of such investments.[10]

What are some aspects of the issues involved in determining the level and kind of resources that should be devoted to science and technology?

1. Underdeveloped countries cannot rely on advanced nations to solve all their technical problems for them; the problems are too numerous and too dependent on local conditions. This, then, requires an indigenous capability, at least

[10] Much of the available literature is hortatory in nature, for example, the Report of Working Group IV of the 12th Pugwash Conference on Science and World Affairs entitled "Science and Technology in Development," Feb. 1, 1964; and the American papers prepared for the UNCSAT conference, contained in Vol. IV and Vol. XI of *Science, Technology and Development,* U.S. Papers Prepared for the U.N. Conference on the Application of Science and Technology for the Benefit of the Less Developed Areas, GPO 1963. Theodore W. Schultz of the University of Chicago and Stevan Dedijer of the University of Lund, Sweden, have done some of the most interesting, more quantitative work to date, but even they would surely agree that the field has been barely touched.

Stevan Dedijer, "Research and the Developing Countries," Paper read at the Royal Swedish Academy of Engineering Sciences, Nov. 13, 1961, and Theodore W. Schultz, *The Economic Value of Education* (New York: Columbia University Press, 1963), and R. S. Eckaus, "Notes on Invention and Innovation in Less Developed Countries," paper prepared for a meeting of the American Economic Association, Dec. 30, 1965.

in adaptive technology and in applied research.

But what kind of a capability and with what mix of fields? What scale of investment is warranted as measured against alternative uses of scarce human material and financial resources? Is the time required to develop economic returns on such investment commensurate with alternative investment possibilities? Answers in anything like quantitative terms are not now available.

2. The need for an indigenous capability in adaptive technology and applied research may imply, in addition, some basic research capability. If so, how much?

Some scientists will argue that basic research is absolutely essential if the technologist and applied scientist are to be able to do their job reasonably well.[11] This view is based on the requirement that an education system be up to date if it is to produce competent and knowledgeable applied scientists and engineers and if those scientists and engineers are to have intellectual resources at home to enable them to remain abreast of pertinent developments in other countries.

But is this argument really valid? Did not the United States itself find it possible to advance rapidly in technology without an extensive commitment to basic science? Even if the situation today is different to that in nineteenth-century

[11] For a typical argument, see: Michael J. Moravcsik, "Technical Assistance and Fundamental Research in Underdeveloped Countries," *Minerva*, Vol. II, No. 2 (Winter 1964), pp. 197–209.

America, so that some basic research *is* essential for applied research and technological development, what kinds of quantitative guidelines should be followed in investment decisions in basic science? Certainly large-scale investment in fundamental research (and there are economies of scale in many modern scientific fields) means diversion of human talent — normally the scarcest of all resources — from alternative uses that are of immediate relevance to growth. For many small countries, the scale of human and other resources required, even for a minor basic research program, is simply beyond their means. In other words, guidelines that can be accepted with confidence are not available here, either.

3. Economic arguments are not the only ones pertinent; another is the issue of technological independence. As Caryl Haskins, President of the Carnegie Institution of Washington, D.C., put it:

> . . . since no country can understand so well the subtle requirements and the new opportunities for technology within its own lands as the people who actually employ it and must live with its consequences, the effective adaptation of technology to local use requires, in the most pragmatic sense, both a living and a practical native science. It is no overstatement that, in the long run, a nation can be reckoned truly strong and independent only if it possesses both a vital technology and a vital science in appropriate balance.[12]

[12] Caryl P. Haskins, *The Scientific Revolution and World Politics*, Council on Foreign Relations (New York: Harper & Row, 1964), p. 35.

For technological innovation, as previously noted, affects and is affected by the social and cultural patterns of a nation. Choices made now will determine the development of those patterns in the future. The identification, selection, and adaptation of technology is not a process that one nation can leave indefinitely in the hands of another if it is to be truly independent.

4. Foreign trade aspirations are also relevant. If a nation intends eventually to trade in world markets in industrial goods, and if its exports are to be competitive, it must develop product sophistication. This sophistication will depend on the scientific and technological competence developed in the nation, a competence that takes many man-years to build.

5. The educational systems of the traditional societies are obviously crucial to their modernization. They are not only crucial in producing the technicians necessary to operate a modern society but also crucial to the introduction of new ideas and attitudes.

The basic tenets implied by science — that man is master of his own fate, that his environment is controllable — are perhaps the most powerful forces for change in a traditional culture. Science therefore has a central place in an education system at all levels, not just to produce scientists but to produce modern man.

Good science education that does not itself take on the cast of "revealed" knowledge is difficult to achieve. The quality of each level of education depends to a considerable extent either on resources outside the country or on the quality of the next higher level, the level of teaching the teachers and providing the curricula. Science education at all levels in a country that maintains a self-contained education system depends ultimately on the quality of the apex to the pyramid — the graduate school level where research and teaching are one.[13]

6. Inevitably, a certain number of a nation's most competent people will want to pursue scientific careers. Unless the country has research opportunities available, most of these will leave or will be disaffected. If congenial policies are followed, some of these first-rate individuals will be encouraged to remain and can make important contributions not only in their scientific fields but also to education, to government planning, and to the intellectual climate of the country.

7. In some of the newer countries, notably in Africa, the new elites see the gap growing between their nation and the United States, and

[13] Dr. Jerome B. Wiesner stated it forcefully at the UNCSAT conference:

    . . . but the higest level of the educational system is especially important because it sets the goals for the future of the whole educational system and hence for the future of the nation. You cannot have a truncated educational system and still meet future needs for growth, change, and intellectual challenge. Science plays an important part in this, for fundamental research is one of man's noblest intellectual endeavors; to neglect it on any grounds, but particularly on the ground of irrelevance to a nation's growth, is in my estimation sheer folly.

"Planning Policies for Investing in Scientific and Technical Education," in *Science, Technology & Development, op. cit.,* Vol. XI, p. 127.

they believe the disparity to be based on differential capabilities to employ science and technology. They want to have their science or technology, whether it has economic justification or not. This is in contrast to many countries with a background of hispanic culture in which the elites are inclined to place a low value on technology and believe it degrading.[14]

8. Last is the elusive question of national pride. There is clearly some importance to a nation to be able to point with pride to the activities and accomplishments of its own people, to take part as an equal in international activities, to demonstrate its emergence as a modern nation, and to hold up to its own people the example of acknowledged excellence. Science, as the symbol of the age, is the most appropriate field in which to meet this need for recognition.

This does not mean, as unfortunately it so often tends to do in practice, that scientific projects should be undertaken with pride or prestige as the only motive. In those cases, there is a risk that the resources will be largely wasted. But useful scientific projects can be devised that will also serve the legitimate need for recognition. In fact, as Dr. F. J. Weyl, former head of the AID research program, has remarked, an important task of American scientists is to "realize and make clear to their colleagues in the developing countries that the

[14] W. S. Stokes, "The Drag of the Pensadores," in J. W. Wiggins and H. Schoeck, eds., *Foreign Aid Reexamined, A Critical Appraisal* (Washington D. C.: Public Affairs Press, 1958) pp. 56–89.

scientific problems encountered in their world can be just as challenging intellectually as the research problems currently popular in the United States and other advanced countries."[15]

These are some of the qualitative arguments associated with investment in science that have to be considered in a country's policy process. Aside from the lack of objective criteria for making such judgments, another serious impediment exists in many of the underdeveloped countries: the lack of individuals who understand science and its potential benefits, and the lack of well-designed and politically powerful science policy machinery to represent science adequately in government councils.

These deficiencies may sometimes result in overinvestment or unwise investment in science, which can stem from a feeling that science is a magic wand that can cure all ills. That is a dangerous misconception, just as dangerous as the more common situation: believing that an indigenous capability in science and technology is not necessary. The right middle ground is not easy to find, nor is it well defined. For it is as much a question of *what* policies are followed for science as it is of *how much* is allocated to it.

The question of investment in science is most certainly a tangled and uncertain one (not exactly unique in the area of foreign aid) and one of prime importance to the underdeveloped countries and to American programs for those countries. It is also relatively neglected because it appears to many, quite wrongly, to be far

[15] As quoted in "Meeting Notes, American Political Science Association," *Science,* Vol. 147 (Feb. 19, 1965), pp. 924–925.

removed from economic growth objectives. Its proper role, however, has yet to be accurately assessed.

RESEARCH

The lack of solid knowledge about the appropriate level of investment in science in less-developed countries, or about the necessary conditions for effective transfer of technology, is symptomatic of most of the foreign aid program. Information about the countries the program is trying to help is incomplete; only the rudiments of understanding are available on how, with certainty, to spur economic development; and few guidelines exist for the best allocation of American or indigenous resources. This situation need not occasion surprise, for foreign economic assistance is a relatively new endeavor for the United States or any government, and one of the most complex ever undertaken. Nor does this lack of full understanding mean that useful programs are not possible. The design of programs must and can proceed on the basis of the best information currently available coupled with individual judgments based on experience, imagination, and common sense.

The relatively poor intelectual underpinning of foreign aid leads to another role for science in foreign aid: the application of science itself to finding solutions to important problems, to advance theoretical understanding of critical economic and social relationships, to develop background information and knowledge necessary for effective programs, and to experiment with programs designed for advancing development objectives. Science in this context obviously includes not only natural science and technology but the social sciences as well.

Euphemistically, these functions are referred to in AID as research. More precisely, they involve systematic study, analysis, review of experience, hardware development, and experimentation. It is not exactly a novel concept that a major government program would benefit from these kinds of activities; the natural sciences and engineering have been employed in this way in support of government objectives in defense, agriculture, health, space, atomic energy, and other fields for many years. But in the past, research has been supported only in a minor way by the Federal Government in furtherance of foreign policy objectives in foreign aid (or more broadly, in other foreign policy fields).

The reasons for this relative lack of research support are several, but undoubtedly one of the major factors is that much of the research would have to be in the social sciences. It is true that the state of development of the "soft" sciences is not comparable to that in the physical sciences. The subject matter of the social sciences is highly complex and difficult to reduce to a manageable number of variables. Controlled experiments are difficult or impossible to conduct, and the validity of the results of systematic study in social science subjects is not necessarily seen by many operators in the field or in Washington to be superior to judgments based on experience or common sense. Moreover, the problems of relating the often imprecise results and highly qualified projections of most social science research to operational needs are frequently great.

These are not insuperable barriers, however, and the

strides made in many of the social sciences in recent years justify their selective use as aids in the formulation of foreign policy. In particular, the U.S. foreign aid program, directed at major tasks of nation building, has many problem areas in which additional study or analysis could in fact provide a better framework for action. At times the problems call for research in the physical or life sciences or in technology. At times they call for research in social science fields. Most often, they are multidisciplinary, involving, as in the case of the Revelle study in Pakistan, simultaneous and related work in several disciplines.

Considerations such as these led to the initiation of a study in 1960 by a panel of the President's Science Advisory Committee to examine the need for a research arm in the U.S. foreign aid agency. The panel's report in the spring of 1961 after the Kennedy Administration took office was favorably received by the new Administration and by some elements within the aid agency who had been working toward the same goal.[16] It resulted in the creation within the new AID of a research program with a charter for sponsoring research in support of the Agency's mission. The authorization in the Act for International Development of 1961 read:

The President is authorized to use funds made available for this part to carry out programs of research in less-developed countries and areas, into the factors affecting the relative success and costs of development activities, and

[16] "Research and Development in the New Development Assistance Program," Report of the Development Assistance Panel, President's Science Advisory Committee, *Mutual Security Act of 1961, Hearings before the Committee on Foreign Affairs*, House of Representatives, 87th Congress, 1st Session, Parts I–III, June 7–July 6, 1961, pp. 971–982.

into the means, techniques, and such other aspects of developments assistance as he may determine, in order to render such assistance of increasing value and benefit.[17]

The program got off to a slow start. By Fiscal Year 1966, it was sponsoring studies totaling only about $9 million per year. The PSAC report recommended a program that would after a few years be close to $100 million.[18] It is unlikely that this level will ever be reached.

The problems that have limited the program, and are likely to continue to, have stemmed in part from unfortunate administrative decisions and practices in the early years and from Congressional and agency skepticism. In addition, the difficulties of identifying and mounting research programs in support of AID's operational needs have proved to be formidable. Reliance wholly on unsolicited proposals from the research community, the initial practice, has not been adequate to meet the agency's needs. The alternative of generating projects within the agency for study by outside contractors in turn requires a degree of internal competence and effort that has been difficult to mobilize. Some of the projects supported by the AID research group have been superb, notably in the fields of agriculture and education, and have been closely tied to agency objectives. A large number of others have been less successful, either in their intrinsic worth or in their relation to agency needs. Slowly, with increased internal competence within AID and with the help of a strong external Research Advisory Committee, the qual-

[17] S. 1983, 87th Congress, 1st Session.
[18] "Research and Development in the New Development Assistance Program," Report of the Development Assistance Panel, PSAC, op. cit.

ity of the research program as a whole has been moving steadily upward so that there is promise for the years to come.

The PSAC envisioned that one of the by-products of launching a substantial research program, and one that has yet to be realized in any significant way, would be the increased involvement of the nation's academic and scientific resources in the intellectual problems of foreign aid. By and large, the aid effort as a whole has not been able to mobilize the competent technical resources of the nation in the way other major U.S. programs — notably in defense and health — have done. An extensive and well-run research program could provide that needed entree to the problems of aid that would interest a much larger segment of the intellectual community. It would also serve to introduce into the graduate training in American universities some of the fascinating and challenging issues with which AID is constantly being faced. In time the result could be not only to engage the interest of the intellectual community more fully but also to draw in an increased number of the advanced students in many different disciplines who are interested in following careers in fields related to foreign economic assistance.

As of 1966, the AID research program remains small. But it has the strong support of the AID administration and the imaginative leadership of Dr. Albert Moseman, who was brought from the Rockefeller Foundation in 1965 as Assistant Administrator for Technical Cooperation and Research. There are thus renewed hopes that this vital program, designed to provide a better base of knowledge and understanding for American foreign aid efforts, will prove its worth.

10

National Influence
and Prestige

The United States is concerned with its general prestige in
the world and its image as a dynamic and progressive
society not out of national vanity but because the effectiveness of our leadership on crucial issues is involved. Today
it is recognized that unless governments effectively communicate their policies and actions to all politically influential elements of foreign populations, their programs can
be impeded and their security placed in jeopardy.[1]

This general statement of the importance of a nation's
prestige made by President Eisenhower's Committee on
Information Activities Abroad would probably be en-
dorsed by most political commentators. Paul Nitze goes
further and states "Today it would appear that the

[1] "Conclusions and Recommendations of President's Committee
on Information Activities Abroad" (Sprague Committee), White
House press release, Jan. 9, 1961.

most important tool of foreign policy is prestige."[2] Hans Morgenthau lists the policy of prestige as the third of his basic manifestations of the struggle for power, defining its purpose as "to impress other nations with the power one's own nation actually possesses, or with the power it believes, or wants the other nations to believe, it possesses."[3]

Whether prestige is *the* most important tool of foreign policy, as Paul Nitze avers, or one among a few important tools, it clearly has a central role to play in a nation's foreign affairs. It is a difficult role, especially in a democracy, which can exercise little influence over the dissemination of negative information about itself. It is also a much misunderstood role, conveying at times an aura of sham or deceit. And it is a role in which science and technology now figure prominently.

The elements that make up a policy of prestige have been changing, in parallel with the changes in the elements of power itself, as a result of the advances of science and the increasing application of science to national purposes. A nation's military and economic strength is now so dependent upon the quality of its scientific resources that demonstrations of scientific capabilities have become the vivid symbols of a nation's existing and potential power.

The Soviet Union demonstrated this relationship well in 1957 when it quite directly linked in public pronouncements its capability to orbit an earth satellite to

[2] Paul H. Nitze, "The Secretary and the execution of foreign policy," in *The Secretary of State*, Don K. Price, ed., The American Assembly, Columbia University (Englewood Cliffs, N. J.: Prentice-Hall, Inc., 1960), p. 15.

[3] Hans J. Morgenthau, *Politics Among Nations*, 3rd ed. (New York: Alfred A. Knopf, 1961), p. 73.

its military capabilities.[4] The American reaction to Sputnik, especially the sudden sharp increase in military spending, served to support the validity of that linkage.[5] Demonstrations of scientific competence have implications beyond military power. They have also become the commonly accepted measure of a nation's vitality, of its ability to fulfill its economic and political, as well as military commitments, and of its future status and strength.[6] The logic for this is straightforward if incomplete: science has come to represent the key to future progress; the nation strongest in science is the one that holds that key, the one most likely to dominate in the future; therefore, it is the one most to be emulated, feared, and respected. Raymond Aron put it well:

. . . [science] has now become a *sine qua non* of power and prosperity. Nations which deliberately reject scientific development are choosing to leave the path of history and to stagnate in a backwater. Those which reject it unwittingly would appear doomed to final annihilation.[7]

The Russians have also played this theme intensively. In their propaganda they emphasize their very real technological accomplishments as proof of how far they have come in science in but forty years or so under Marxism.[8] By implication, communism is supposed to

[4] *The New York Times*, Oct. 8, 1957, p. 1.

[5] "Fiscal Year 1959 Budget Message," *Ibid.*, Jan. 14, 1958, pp. 17–20.

[6] Vernon Van Dyke, *Pride and Power, The Rationale of the Space Program* (Urbana: University of Illinois Press, 1964) pp. 130–133.

[7] Raymond Aron, "Rationality of Modern Society," *Bulletin of the Atomic Scientists* Vol. XX, No. 1 (Jan. 1964), p. 23.

[8] In the original announcement of Sputnik I, the Tass statement concluded with . . . it seems that the present generation will witness how the freed and conscious labor of the people of the new Socialist society turns even the most daring of men's dreams into reality," *The New York Times*, Oct. 6, 1957, p. 43.

represent the wave of the future; if Russia under communism has overtaken the West in such a brief span in as fundamental and necessary a field as science, imagine what the future has in store.

The United States has not been idle in displaying its own scientific achievements as symbols of its strength and vitality. The monumental investment in space in effect signals acceptance of the concept that a nation's political power is in some sense determined by its ability to compete in a major scientific and technological endeavor. President Kennedy saw competition in space as a battle between the United States and the Soviet Union conducted with the world looking on and making comparisons *whether or not* the United States decided to compete. He felt the nation had no choice but to accede to the challenge. The United States could not accept politically the onus of always being second in space accomplishments. The choice of the lunar program as the major vehicle for competition was based on its inherent drama, as well as on the long time span that gave the United States a chance to be the first on the moon.

Both space and atomic energy are fields that are peculiarly relevant to a nation's foreign policy interests. They require massive investment of resources, they require advanced scientific and technological competence, they are dramatic and symbolic of the age, and they are related to military capability in fact and even more so in the public's view. In short, they provide an arena for highly visible accomplishments in science and have come to represent a nation's competence and capability far beyond the actual programs themselves. They are obvious instruments of a policy of prestige in an age when surrogate demonstrations of power must serve instead of the real thing.

Other fields of science and technology, especially those that relate directly to the needs and desires of less-advantaged people all over the globe, can also be relevant to a nation's prestige and influence. Accomplishments in medicine, in agriculture, in education, and even in transportation (every country wants its own airline, and most use American aircraft) can have important psychological effects, in addition to their utilitarian value, on attitudes toward present U.S. power and future influence.

Clearly, the policy maker concerned with enhancing a nation's prestige now must reckon with science as an important element in that task. But what considerations must be taken into account in the policy process? How can America's great scientific and technological strength be used appropriately and effectively for prestige purposes?

One consideration is the apparent interest of the public only in what is dramatic and understandable. This means that it is the applications of science rather than science itself that gain maximum attention. Hence, it is the technological feat or accomplishment that is the actual gauge used to measure science.[9] It is not an accurate gauge, for it is possible to concentrate resources in narrow areas of science and technology and on specific technological accomplishments that do not reflect broad scientific capability. Accurate or not, the policy maker must look to visible technological feats most of the time except when he can devise ways to

---

[9] Testimony of George V. Allen, Director USIA, before House Science and Astronautics Committee, *Ibid.*, Jan. 23, 1960, p. 1.

dramatize the basic accomplishments of science as well. This situation emphasizes the need for exhibits, fairs, or other programs that present a cross section of technology and provide a more accurate picture of the breadth of the nation's scientific and technological capability. A second consideration is that any program utilizing science and technology as a means of projecting an image must have solid technical achievement that relates to the interests or problems (or fears) of the intended audience. For pragmatic reasons, if no other, frauds or fakes or gross exaggerations are unwise. They are likely, in an open society, to be easily debunked. Even if the truth does not catch up to the original claim, subsequent real achievements will be debased.

The scientific and technological strength of the United States would seem to provide a great number of possibilities for legitimate "exploitation" beyond space and atomic energy. In fact, the selection of suitable subjects is far from simple. It seems to require an uncommon blend of scientific knowledge and of political/psychological common and scientific sense. It is easy to look for the obviously spectacular, such as a cure for cancer (frequently cited by nonscientists as a technical objective suitable for image-building purposes), but much harder to keep abreast of current scientific and technological developments and select those that can have some impact. The problem of how to exploit appropriate developments with taste, effectiveness, and reasonable accuracy equally requires a rare blend of competences.

Not all, or even most, image-building programs utilizing science need to be focused on the exploitation of specific advances or achievements in science or technology. Some can attempt to project an image through a substantive effort to provide useful materials or information such as textbooks, agricultural information, or other material directly related to the needs or interests of the peoples in other countries. In such programs the scientific and technological information must be accurate; it must be relevant to the situation of the audience (as a general rule it is not possible without adaptation to supply information or texts commonly available in the United States); it must be presented in appropriate and useful ways (providing textbooks at American prices in less-developed countries is not particularly useful); and it should preferably be part of a longer program of aid and contact rather than an isolated effort.

Furthermore, it cannot be forgotten that the image of a nation held by others is determined by all of the activities of that nation, not just those activities carried out primarily for prestige reasons. In particular, the international technical activities of U.S. government agencies and of the private sector will influence the impression the nation gives of its scientific competence and strength. Thus, in scientific operations overseas, in the conduct of technical aid programs, in participation in U.N. programs, in carrying out the American share of cooperative scientific endeavors, there must be recognition of the relationship between U.S. actions and the image created of American scientific achievement.

Providing appropriate recognition of this relationship in the policy process is difficult. It is easily overdone, and an all too common argument in Washington for U.S. participation in this or that international scientific program is the cry that not to do so would be an irretrievable blow to American scientific prestige. There may be good arguments for participating in most international scientific programs, but it cannot be true that the United States *must* participate in any and all of those that are proposed. The evaluation of each must be made on the basis of scientific, budgetary, and political considerations taken together.

But what are, in fact, these political considerations? What elements in another country is the United States trying to reach? The international scientific community is, by and large, well aware of the scientific pre-eminence of the United States. Which, then, are the groups most important to U.S. objectives who will be affected by a knowledge of relative scientific competence? And what impression does the United States want to produce: fear, respect, appreciation, envy?

The social sciences can be useful here, for modern survey research can provide data and analyses that relate directly to the choices the policy maker faces. Aside from broad questions of what constitutes image building, social science research can also provide background data that can aid decision making at the more detailed level: What subjects or programs are most effective for making a lasting impact in other countries? Are relevance to need or frequency of observation important, or do they fade into insignificance next to space spectaculars. (For example, what is the relative value for prestige purposes of a water pump that replaced oxen-powered wells in a village as compared to communication and weather satellites?) Has Sputnik pre-empted the field? That is, has it in effect reduced in significance, and hence in impact, all subsequent space achievements? How does the significance of hybrid corn, American jet planes on world airlines, or American agricultural productivity compare in impact with space spectaculars?

To answer these questions requires more data and analysis of the significance of elite and mass opinion in other countries and of how relevant groups can be reached by a variety of American programs. Research into these subjects can provide much more useful background information for use in the policy process than is now available.[10] A little is being done, much of it supported by private funds; much more, with support from public as well as private sources, is amply justified.

The appropriate use of science as an element of a policy of prestige raises a critical question of another kind: Should the nation ever commit scientific and technological resources primarily on the basis of expected returns in foreign prestige, and if so, how much? The issues raised in practice range from whether a program that is already in train should be altered or accelerated largely for political prestige purposes, to consideration of mounting an entirely new program that might otherwise have been deferred, ignored, or initiated at an entirely different support level. The water desalting research program of the Department of the Interior was increased in size and emphasis in 1961 largely as a result of prestige motivations. The space program, also, would assuredly have been considerably smaller were it not for prestige considerations.

---

[10] For a discussion of the research needs and of some research in progress in this area, see *Communication and Values in Relation to War and Peace*, Ithiel de Sola Pool, Institute for International Order, New York (undated).

Seeking to enhance this nation's international prestige is as valid a political objective as any other; the extent to which that objective is achieved bears a close relationship to the achievement of other political objectives. It is therefore entirely proper to commit scientific and technological resources to the goal of enhancing national prestige and influence.

What disturbs scientists and others in the prospect of carrying out research and development primarily for prestige objectives is the inherent danger of distortion of scientific or technological programs by diversion of scarce technical resources from the nation's "true" needs to a possible satisfaction of the uncertain and probably ephemeral goal of prestige. But this argument in effect denies the validity or importance of prestige objectives, for those objectives, too, represent a nation's "true" need.

In other words, this question is essentially an allocation of resources problem in which the goal of prestige must be accepted as legitimate but must somehow be weighed against other national objectives. Individuals may rightly be suspicious of prestige as a major objective because of its vagueness, its uncertain results, and its occasional quality of sham. But these need not be qualities of well-formulated programs, and "well-formulated" when science and technology are involved means that as a prerequisite science and technology are represented fully and competently in the policy process. To allocate scientific resources to projects that are unsound in technical terms is both wrong and foolish, whatever the motive. It may be justifiable to allocate resources to projects that are technically sound but primarily serve prestige goals if the benefits and the costs have been realistically compared to alternative uses of the resources. Such comparison is difficult to achieve with any precision (especially if the prestige projects are spectacular in nature). It is, in the end, a matter of informed judgment.

Scientists are concerned because they believe that the scientific considerations involved in such a judgment are often not adequately understood or taken into account. The space program has aroused the most reaction in the scientific community because it has such a large impact on many elements of the American scientific enterprise: on the availability of technical resources for other national tasks, on American higher education, and on the balance among scientific fields in the United States. Dr. James Killian, in 1960, expressed the sentiments of many in the scientific community when he said:

We should insist on a space program that is in balance with our other vital endeavors in science and technology and that does not rob them because they currently are less spectacular. In the long run we can weaken our science and technology and lower our international prestige by frantically indulging in unnecessary competition and prestige-motivated projects.[11]

The scientists are right to be concerned about the effectiveness of the representation of scientific factors. They particularly fear decisions that seem politically rewarding in the short term but in the long term would distort or undermine the very scientific and technological progress that the nation's real strength will re-

[11] "Making Science a Vital Force in Foreign Policy," Text of an address given at the M.I.T. Club of New York, Dec. 13, 1960.

quire. Their concern is a valid one, but the question should be: how to represent the proper range of issues effectively in the foreign policy process, rather than whether prestige is a valid criterion for setting R & D objectives.

PART IV

Science in the
Foreign Policy Process

The process by which American foreign policy is formulated is complex and constantly changing, with many individuals and groups sharing influence and authority. The final responsibility, of course, rests with the President, although his influence over the policy process is not always commensurate with that responsibility. For those issues in which the scientific aspects have a major influence on the policy choices, the discussion of the preceding chapters has shown something of the character of the perplexing and novel problems now facing the foreign policy maker. The nature of the scientific aspects of issues and the character of their interaction with other elements of central issues of foreign policy dictate a degree of integration of science and technology in policy making that has been difficult to achieve in practice.

221

In particular, the ability of the Department of State to meet the technical agencies of government on equal terms when necessary appears to be declining steadily as the issues with which the Department must deal involve increasingly sophisticated scientific and technological elements. At the Presidential level, the requirements for staff competence to balance and challenge agency positions have grown steadily with the corresponding growth in complexity and technical sophistication of important issues.

In both the State Department and the White House, significant innovations in organization have been made in recent years in an attempt to cope with the interaction between science and foreign affairs. Changes have taken place in other parts of the government as well, but those changes most central to foreign policy matters and most important for the issues under discussion here are found associated with those two foci of responsibility and authority.

With the substantive discussion of Parts II and III in the background, it is useful now to analyze and evaluate in some detail, first for the Office of the President and then for the Department of State, the mechanisms by which scientific elements are introduced in the foreign policy process. Some ideas for improvement or change in the system will also quite naturally emerge.

11

The President and
His Official Staff

The President, in fulfilling his constitutional responsibility for the nation's foreign affairs, relies on multiple sources within the government to bring issues to his attention, to provide the information necessary to reach decisions, and to carry out his policies. This has always been true to a degree, but until recently only a few government departments have had extensive interest or activities in international affairs, with the Department of State normally playing the dominant role in foreign affairs. Today, the scale and complexity of America's overseas commitments and involvements have forced the President to consult with and depend upon a much wider range of advisers inside and outside government. In turn, to organize and evaluate this advice, to provide better assurance that the right issues are coming to his attention with the relevant information, and to follow through on decisions, the President has also found it necessary to build a personal staff in the White House.

Conflicts in authority and influence inevitably arise between this staff and the operating departments, but a permanent pattern has not been, and surely never will be, established that determines who has the major voice in advising a President on foreign policy matters. Quite clearly, Harry Hopkins had more influence on President Roosevelt than did Cordell Hull. On the other hand, Secretary of State Dean Acheson earned the role of chief policy adviser to President Truman, as did John Foster Dulles with President Eisenhower. Under President Kennedy, McGeorge Bundy and other White House staff members had more significant roles to play in foreign policy than did their predecessors under Eisenhower, and the influence of the Secretary of State was correspondingly reduced. Under President Johnson, the influence of Secretary Rusk appears to have risen sharply, although for both Presidents Kennedy and Johnson, Secretary of Defense McNamara has been a major figure in foreign policy debates.

The influence of the President's personal staff on the formulation of foreign policy is variable, but the need for a personal staff is no longer in serious contention. The President simply must have the help of individuals directly responsible to him who can survey the government from his vantage point and who can help in his endeavor to make American foreign policy truly governmental or Presidential policy rather than State, Defense, Commerce, or other Departmental policy.

The formal structure and informal relationships among the staffs of the White House and Executive Office of the President are quite fluid, matching at any given time the personality and operating patterns of the Chief Executive, and his personal relationships with his assistants and his Cabinet officers. Under President Kennedy, the three formal organizations in the President's Office that were most concerned with foreign affairs were the National Security Council (NSC) staff, the Bureau of the Budget (BOB), and the Office of Science and Technology (OST), with the NSC staff the most continuously involved over the entire range of foreign policy issues. In addition, various other Special Assistants to the President, e.g., Theodore Sorenson, Arthur Schlesinger and Richard Goodwin, and the President's military aides and advisers, were devoting a large percentage of their time to foreign policy problems. Under President Johnson, the NSC staff has retained its central role, but OST seems to be somewhat less closely involved. The President, in contrast to his predecessor, appears to be relying more heavily on the Department of State and the operating departments than on his personal assistants to protect and represent his interests in policy formulation. For example, at the time of the resignation of McGeorge Bundy as Special Assistant for National Security Affairs, President Johnson issued a new directive designed to bolster the Department of State's coordinating responsibility for foreign operations throughout the government.[1] This move had the appearance of transferring real policy influence from the NSC to the State Department, but how effectively the Department will be able to execute this responsibility is not at all clear.

In view of the pervasiveness of the science/foreign policy interaction, all of those at the Presidential level

[1] *The New York Times*, March 5, 1966, p. 1.

who are concerned with foreign affairs are perforce dealing with many issues that have high technical content. For most issues, the scientific and technological elements will have been considered (well or poorly) at lower levels in the policy process. For those most significant issues where scientific variables are crucial, the President's Special Assistant for Science and Technology, who is also Director of the Office of Science and Technology and has his own staff there, is expected to be concerned with the relevant scientific inputs.

The Office of the Special Assistant for Science and Technology, formally established in 1962 as OST, is the single most important structural innovation in the Federal Government in recent years designed to cope with the new relevance of science to national policy in all fields, both domestic and foreign. It has not as yet received a great deal of analytical attention, especially with respect to its foreign policy role; yet it is of central importance to an understanding of how scientific advice is obtained at the Presidential level. A discussion of the history and functions of the office and of present trends will serve to bring out the important elements.

THE SPECIAL ASSISTANT FOR SCIENCE AND TECHNOLOGY

As in so many policy areas touching on science and technology, the history of the Office of the Special Assistant to the President for Science and Technology effectively started on October 4, 1957, when the Soviet Union launched the first man-made earth satellite. That event, and the reaction in the United States, meant that, for the first time since before World War II,

American scientific leadership was in question. Moreover, the surprise of the event and its implied criticism of previous decisions in military technology led President Eisenhower to realize more forcefully than ever before that he was unable to rely wholly on the departments and agencies of government to bring appropriate issues before him. Especially was this so in military areas where many of the issues had important technical aspects, yet service and department bias and logrolling within the Department of Defense often prevented the President from knowing the real choices open to him or the implications of those choices.

The President responded to the situation by moving his Science Advisory Committee (PSAC), which had been performing a useful but limited role while housed in the Office of Defense Mobilization, into the White House and creating the post of Special Assistant to the President for Science and Technology with Dr. James R. Killian, President of M.I.T., as the first incumbent.[2] PSAC elected the Special Assistant as its chairman, a practice that has continued to the present day, although it retained the right to report independently to the President if circumstances ever required. In addition, a

[2] Address to the nation by President Eisenhower, Nov. 7, 1957, *The New York Times*, Nov. 8, 1957, p. 1; R. N. Kreidler, "The President's Science Advisers and National Science Policy," in *Scientists and National Policy-Making*, Robert Gilpin and Christopher Wright, eds. (New York: Columbia University Press, 1965), p. 114; The Science Advisory Committee while in ODM was the sponsor of, or helped to set up, several major studies for the President, such as the Technological Capabilities Panel in 1955 and the Gaither study in 1957. These studies themselves demonstrated the President's realization that he had to reach out beyond departments and agencies to analyze some major issues in military policy. He did not, however, draw the conclusion (until 1957) that he needed full-time help of this kind on the White House staff.

small staff was created to serve both the Special Assistant and the Committee.

The early charter, contained only in a letter from the President to Dr. Killian, gave the new office wide latitude in its activities and guaranteed access to information throughout the government.[3] The early activities of the office focused primarily on national security matters, providing for the President a technical appraisal of weapons programs and a continuing review of military strategy from the point of view of the impact of present and future developments in science and technology.

These subjects represented the President's immediate needs, but he quickly began to look to his science office for a much wider range of analyses and activities.

1. President Eisenhower's concern for the effectiveness and vitality of science in America, especially in relation to the meaning of Sputnik, encouraged the office to study questions related to the support of science by the Federal government and to become heavily involved in the growth of the National Science Foundation.

2. The reaction to Soviet space accomplishments led to the need for a new government agency to mount a space program. The President asked Dr. Killian to take the lead in laying out the structure and goals of what later became the National Aeronautics and Space Administration.[4]

---

[3] Interview with Dr. James R. Killian.
[4] Enid Bok, "Making American Space Policy, (1) The Establish-

3. The increasing pressure for a nuclear test ban led the President to turn to Dr. Killian for an analysis of the strategic significance of a test ban agreement and an evaluation of the feasibility of inspection and control measures. This study, as discussed in Chapter 6, led to the opening of the test ban negotiations in the summer of 1958, with the Special Assistant's office heavily engaged in establishing policy and providing backup for the technical negotiators. (Two of the three members of the U.S. delegation at the technical talks, Dr. James Fisk and Dr. Robert Bacher, were members of PSAC). During this period, and until 1963 when the limited test ban treaty was signed, the White House science office acted in effect as science advisers for the Department of State, as well as for the President, on this issue.

4. At the same time, PSAC established a standing Panel on Science and Foreign Policy under Dr. Detlev W. Bronk, whose first recommendation was that Secretary of State Dulles should re-establish, at a higher level, the science adviser's office in the Department that he had allowed to lapse some four years before. The Secretary accepted the recommendation and appointed a new Science Adviser early in 1958.[5]

In these activities, and the many others that the office gradually moved into, the Special Assistant and his

---

ment of NASA," unpublished Working Paper of the School of Industrial Management, M.I.T., Jan. 1963.

[5] *Department of State Bulletin*, XXXVIII (Feb. 3, 1958), p. 190.

staff functioned as a direct arm of the President. That is, they attempted to see the issues from his point of view, to anticipate problems, to bring to his attention important controversies that individual agencies might have preferred to sidestep, to bring to bear the best scientific talent in the nation on crucial problems, to provide the kind of analyses independent of department positions that clarified policy alternatives and their implications, and to follow through within the government on Presidential decisions. The staff, as staffs are wont to do, gradually established a network of contacts and information sources throughout the government that soon made possible early warning of potential problems and provided effective means for following important issues.

One of the unique features of this White House Office was the ability it had to bring in outside consultants on short notice for detailed and extended analysis of subjects of concern to the President. The Science Advisory Committee operated largely through a system of panels set up usually on an ad hoc basis to study questions set by the President or the Special Assistant. The panels were normally composed of a small number of PSAC members, with outside experts brought in on a part-time basis. Reports were evaluated and challenged by PSAC as a whole and then used for the guidance of the Special Assistant or the President, depending on the circumstances.

It was possible by this means to enlist the most competent individuals in the nation for thorough analyses of issues in subjects such as antiballistic missiles, strategic weapons systems, space science, civil defense, or U.S./Soviet science cooperation. The President, then, had a unique tool at his command, designed to supplement the work of the departments and agencies themselves and to enlist the help of the nation's leading scientists and engineers. One of the most important results of this mechanism was to force the departments and agencies, particularly the Department of Defense, to review and improve its own procedures, in the knowledge that a powerful group was in a position to challenge their recommendations at the White House level.

Of course, in all the subjects with which they became concerned, the primary task of the office, the Special Assistant, and PSAC was to represent the scientific or technical aspects of issues. But as is clear from the discussion and examples of Parts II and III, it is impossible to provide technical inputs on important issues in a political vacuum. In every case in which they had any influence, the Special Assistant or his staff, or PSAC, had to be aware (with considerable sophistication) of the nonscientific aspects of the subjects under study: of how specific technical characteristics of weapons systems would affect strategic or political matters; of the strategic implications and questions surrounding a test ban agreement; of the economic, political and social problems associated with the transfer of technology to less-developed countries; of the organizational and domestic political ramifications of a space program; and so on. Most often, they were dealing not with hard technical facts, but with expectations, judgments, and uncertainties about science and technology, all of which could alter significantly the nature of a political situation. To provide technical advice independently of the implications of that advice on the political variables would have been

tensive studies already performed by other organizations, whether by including their analysts as panel members or by asking them to present their studies and findings to the panel. In fact, through this mechanism, the President had available to him more readily and more usefully the results of the competent strategic analysis groups existing inside and outside government.

Technical/strategic analyses, though they remained for a long time the largest single consumer of the Special Assistant's and PSAC's time, steadily gave way to other public issues in which science and technology figured prominently. In fact, when John F. Kennedy assumed the Presidency, the entire science office went through what can only be described as an explosion in the scale and scope of its activities. Dr. Jerome B. Wiesner became Special Assistant for Science and Technology with a long-standing personal relationship to the new President. Both he and the President, although they had arrived at their views from quite different backgrounds, were imbued with a belief that the government had a responsibility to explore ways in which science and technology could serve public interests in all fields.

As a result, under the leadership of Dr. Wiesner and with the constant prodding of the President, the science office expanded its horizons to examine a host of areas that had not been tackled under President Eisenhower or had been touched only lightly. The possibility of developing a role for the Federal Government in stimulating science and technology in lagging civilian industries in the United States is an example of one of the new areas; reviewing and stimulating research in the Department of Agriculture is another; a broad and detailed involvement in developing Administration policy toward education is a third.

In foreign policy areas, the office took an active role in laying out science programs to be included in the Alliance for Progress, moved more positively into foreign aid policy and organization, worked with the State Department on a wider variety of current issues, and took the lead in formulating specific proposals based on science and technology that could contribute to foreign policy objectives. Among the latter, some of which were discussed in Parts II and III, were proposals for cooperation with the Soviet Union, the Pakistan salinity project, scientific cooperation with Japan, a proposed computer center in West Berlin, and many others.

The work in national security areas was continued, especially on arms control and test ban issues, although the time devoted to these issues decreased relatively as a result both of the wider range of activities of the office and the greater competence manifested within the Defense Department and the new Disarmament Agency. Dr. Wiesner's personal allocation of time remained approximately the same as his predecessors: the largest share was concerned with national security issues. This matched the President's direct daily needs and Wiesner's own concerns and interests. But his office and the PSAC found their attention much more diffused and their time increasingly spent on nonsecurity-related issues.

In general, it is a fair assessment that Dr. Wiesner and his staff responded to the attitude and approach of President Kennedy and became more aggressive than had been the case under President Eisenhower. There was a more conscious effort to reach out for issues and opportunities to which science and technology could contribute and a corresponding reduction in concern for bureaucratic boundaries and definitions of responsibilities. The new leadership of the individual departments and agencies of government also tended to embrace this attitude toward new departures and new approaches through science and technology. Very rapidly, with the urging of Dr. Wiesner, departments and agencies moved to strengthen their scientific organization at top policy levels. The Department of Commerce established an Assistant Secretary for Science and Technology; the Department of the Interior set up the post of Science Adviser to the Secretary; the Department of Agriculture conducted a special advisory study for the Secretary on science in the Department; the Department of Health, Education and Welfare gave new responsibilities for science to an existing Assistant Secretary, and so forth. In addition, Dr. Wiesner helped in the creation of the Arms Control and Disarmament Agency, which included a science and technology bureau, and provided the impetus for the State Department to reorganize and upgrade the Science Adviser's Office.

This increased activity and involvement of the White House science office carried with it the seeds of major change in the character of the office and a change in the influence of the Science Advisory Committee. The changes were symbolized by the creation of the Office of Science and Technology in 1962, but the full impact of the evolving situation was not fully appreciated at that time. These changes hold the key for likely developments in the future.

THE OFFICE OF SCIENCE AND TECHNOLOGY

One of the results of the activist role of the White House science office was its more widespread (and more evident) influence on the establishment of domestic policy toward science and technology. From the very beginning in 1957, Dr. Killian and PSAC had been charged with the task of working with the National Science Foundation, and overseeing government science policy more generally to ensure the health and vitality of science in the United States. Several of the early PSAC public reports were devoted to this question, and PSAC was responsible for the creation of the Federal Council for Science and Technology (FCST) by President Eisenhower in 1959.[7] This body, discussed briefly later, was designed to aid in rationalizing and coordinating government policies and programs concerned with science and technology. In addition, at an early point the Special Assistant began working with the Bureau of the Budget on questions of allocation of resources for science and technology.

All of these earlier efforts grew in intensity and scope during the first year of the Kennedy Administration, but through the entire period from 1957 through 1961 the Congress was essentially excluded from access to the key science decision makers and to their deliberations. As confidential advisers to the President, the Spe-

[7] "Strengthening American Science," PSAC, U.S. GPO, Washington, D. C., 1958.

cial Assistant and his staff refused invitations to testify before Congress on the grounds of Presidential privilege. This privileged stance was appropriate when the science office functioned only as advisers to the President, but as the Special Assistant and staff assumed an independent science policy role, Constitutional doctrine required a better means for the Legislative branch to question, challenge, investigate, and influence the making of policy. In fact, it became necessary, as science policy-making functions moved to this level, to provide for Congressional contacts and information if the necessary legislation and appropriations were to be forthcoming.

Moreover, the Congress, which had accorded science a veritable honeymoon period during which almost all requests for appropriations were honored or even increased with little question, was becoming restive. Funds for research and development were reaching levels that inevitably had economic and political implications throughout the country and reached far beyond the progress of science itself. The Congress often found itself voting on programs about which it had little understanding, and it had no way of being assured that the broader questions of science policy—effects on universities, geographical distribution of science funds, allocation of resources among scientific fields, etc.—were being adequately considered.

In addition to the question of the Special Assistant's relations with Congress, was the issue of how the general public, including scientists not involved with the Government, could gain knowledge of and access to the science policy-making process. Operating formally as a confidential adviser to the President, the public as well as the Congress was unable to participate in discussions of current and increasingly far-reaching issues of science policy in which the Special Assistant or his office may have played a decisive role and which might affect the nation or the body politic in important ways.

Accordingly, President Kennedy submitted his Reorganization Plan No. 2 of 1962, which was allowed to stand by the Congress, that created a statutory Office of Science and Technology (OST) in the Executive Office of the President. With a status roughly parallel to that of the Bureau of the Budget, OST now provided that essential tie to the Congress and the press. The Special Assistant became Director of OST, but at the same time retained his title as Special Assistant to the President and thus his relationship as a confidential adviser to the President. The Science Advisory Committee remained in the White House, but the staff and the many consultants now came under OST. Among other implications of the move, at least the formal continuation of the White House science advisory mechanism over changes in administration was now assured; a degree of permanence had been imparted to the structure. There was no sharp alteration of activities of the office at the time OST was created except for the occasional requirement for the Director or others to testify before Congress. But formal creation of the office was symbolic of its role in domestic science policy formation, a role that has continued to expand since that time.

The qualitative result of this heightened science policy responsibility has been to skew the office and staff increasingly toward domestic matters. The relationship with the Bureau of the Budget is close, with the Bureau looking to OST for judgments about science budgets throughout the Government. PSAC and its panels spend a large proportion of their time studying and advising on science policy questions and considering broader technical matters in relation to other domestic policy issues such as pollution, water management, use of pesticides, and so forth.

If anything, this trend has been accelerated by the accession to the Presidency of Lyndon Johnson because of his relatively greater interest in domestic issues. Dr. Donald Hornig, who succeeded Jerome Wiesner as Special Assistant and Director of OST, came to the office with relatively little previous involvement in security and foreign policy matters and with almost no previous acquaintance with the President. The result has been that Hornig was initially somewhat less directly involved with the President and was inevitably drawn most heavily into science policy and domestic issues that came to his attention as a matter of course. Although Dr. Hornig's relations with the President have become steadily closer, his initial emphasis on issues outside the national security area has continued.

This is not to say that President Johnson has not looked to science and his science adviser on foreign policy matters. Dr. Hornig and his office and PSAC continue to provide important analyses in security-related issues, and the President often turns to his Special Assistant in his practice of "gathering in" all available fields to help advance national objectives. In this way, with Hornig's assistance, the President has launched a "water-for-peace" program, has put new emphasis on spreading education, health, and technology to the less-developed countries, has sent Hornig on a mission to help Korean science, has expanded the Japanese cooperation program, and has given new direction to the Pakistan salinity program.

Notwithstanding the variety of these involvements, the office as a whole is now more heavily oriented to domestic and science policy issues than ever before. This trend is likely to continue, and one characteristic of this orientation is that an increasing percentage of time is spent on issues and policies that do not have to engage the President directly. It seems to be a reasonable prediction that OST and the Special Assistant will be less involved and therefore less influential in foreign policy matters in years to come. This estimate must be strongly qualified to recognize that White House relationships, which depend so heavily on personalities, are not predictable with confidence. It is entirely possible that a different President and/or a different Special Assistant would sharply alter the situation. Or the possibility must be considered that another Secretary of Defense will be less effective in rationalizing military strategy and weapons systems developments, and once again a greater premium will be put on an analytical, technically oriented, objective arm of the Presidency primarily engaged in national security issues.

At this time, however, the basic trend for OST and the Special Assistant appears to be away from foreign policy issues and toward domestic and science policy concerns.

One result of this conclusion is to put greater stress on building the capability of the departments and agencies of the Federal Government concerned with foreign policy, and particularly the Department of State, to inject scientific elements into the policy process within their own agencies. Even if the White House Office remained heavily involved in these issues, a strong science element within agencies would continue to be necessary. The need is now reinforced by the trends at the White House.

THE ROLE OF SCIENTISTS AND ENGINEERS IN PSAC

A brief note is in order about the characteristics brought into the foreign policy process at the White House level by the scientists and engineers who have been active in PSAC and OST. As with any sizable group, their approach to policy problems and to the politics of government is not uniform but encompasses considerable variation. Still, there are a few common threads that at times enhance, and at times detract from, the scientists' effectiveness.[8]

A scientist often enters government service with a strong sense of optimism that any problem once adequately defined can be solved. At the same time, he may underrate the complexity of the problems and

[8] There have been several interesting and provocative essays on the role of scientists in policy making in foreign affairs, though much of the existing literature is subjective in nature and could be usefully supplemented by more intensive research. One of the best and most detailed is Robert Gilpin's *American Scientists and Nuclear Weapons Policy* (Princeton: Princeton University Press, 1962), especially his first chapter that discussed in general terms the policy role of scientists. Several of the essays in *Scientists and National Policy Making*, edited by Christopher Wright and Robert Gilpin (New York: Columbia University Press, 1964), are also pertinent and good. See also the address of McGeorge Bundy before the American Association for the Advancement of Science, Dec. 27, 1962, reprinted in *Science*, Vol. 139 (Mar. 1, 1963), p. 805.

choices facing the government and the difficulty of obtaining solid information on which to base decisions. In turn, this often makes the scientists, especially those with little experience with the political process, appear naïve and unrealistic about the political barriers to "rational" action. For some scientists, the somewhat fuzzy and imprecise political constraints surrounding issues become intensely frustrating. They are used to examining a problem on its merits, and are annoyed when political considerations seemingly irrelevant to the substance of an issue prove to be a decisive barrier to a clear resolution of the issue. This same desire for objectivity and simple rationality carried over from science also tends to lead to impatience with the delays of political in-fighting and a certain reluctance to compromise when the technically "proper" decision on a particular issue appears perfectly evident.

Although these characteristics often detract from the inexperienced scientists' effectiveness in government and are the root of Albert Wohlstetter's criticisms, they quickly wear off for most as experience is gained. On the other hand, these traits are refreshing when injected in a staid and rule-bound bureaucracy and can lead to imaginative initiatives and innovations. The creative impact of the scientists in the White House was very useful to President Kennedy when he first came to office.

The scientists usually bring other attributes with them that are less equivocal in their effect. One is a tendency to what Warner Schilling has called the "whole-problem approach."[9] That is, a desire, on the

---

[9] Warner R. Schilling, "Scientists, Foreign Policy, and Politics," in R. Gilpin and C. Wright, eds., *Scientists and National Policy Making* (New York: Columbia University Press, 1964), p. 155.

part of the scientists to understand an entire problem so that they can decide for themselves what the important technical questions are. They are rarely satisfied to be asked to solve a narrow technical issue unless they are first allowed to determine whether that issue has real relevance. This attitude has been of great importance, particularly in some defense areas where compartmentalization of defense tasks among and within the military services tended for many years to obscure major problems in American defenses.

Another attribute found among the scientists is an emphasis on quantification and use of analytical techniques. This emphasis can, of course, be overdone, but in many policy areas, especially in weapons system matters, much more quantitative analysis was possible in 1957, for example, than the military services or the Defense Department was interested in applying. The result of the involvement of the scientists was an important gain in understanding of the costs and benefits of competing weapons systems. Similarly, the dedication of scientists to a logical, rational approach to the problems they face (although, in fact, in their own disciplines, scientists tend to be logical *after* discoveries are made, rather than before), can sometimes appear novel and useful when it appears in the frenetic, subjective atmosphere of Washington: the scientists in PSAC were the first in the late 1950's to make it possible for the President to examine the defense program in a logical, functional breakdown as opposed to a breakdown along military service lines.

Scientists bring another characteristic of value, although it is also one that is often hard to square with political reality. That is an experimental approach to problems, a willingness to try one solution and to quit and start over on another tack if the first attempt was unsuccessful. That is such a useful approach to public policy issues always surrounded by uncertainty that it can only be a source of regret that political constraints and expectations make it an unpopular tactic. Political leaders and decision makers are expected to have answers, not experiments, even when it is impossible to obtain answers without experiments. Scientists have been able to make some headway in legitimizing an experimental attitude toward action programs as a by-product of the large investment of public funds in the experimental fields of science and technology. But the attitude has not spread far into other areas of government policy.

Last, in terms of general approach to international affairs, scientists as a group do tend to have a fairly common point of view. Although there are a few exceptions, most of the scientists who have become involved in PSAC and its panel activities take an internationally oriented view to world politics. No doubt this is a carry-over from their own disciplines in which scientific facts remain constant regardless of national borders, in which close communication among scientists across political and ideological barriers is possible and in which Thomas Jefferson's "republics of science" continue to exist. No doubt it is also a reflection of the fact that many of the PSAC scientists had their fill of armaments and war and may have had some sense of guilt about their own involvement in the creation of new weapons. Whatever the cause, the scientists on PSAC have in general been oriented toward disarmament, toward fostering greater international communication, and toward control of the arms race.

To what extent, these political attitudes may have influenced their judgments on scientific and technical matters cannot be determined. Certainly the role of these scientists in strengthening the nation's military posture and world power, at the same time they were actively seeking ways of bringing the arms race under control, cannot be denied. All that is certain is that the possibility of contradiction between these activities was a source of torment to many.

THE FEDERAL COUNCIL FOR SCIENCE AND TECHNOLOGY

The Federal Council for Science and Technology, which came into existence on the recommendation of PSAC, has become one of the policy arms of the Director of OST, who serves also as Chairman of the Council. The Federal Council's mission is to develop uniform science policies throughout the government, to coordinate and integrate programs where appropriate, to be concerned about special problems in government science support, and in general to serve as the chief government body for bringing together the departments and agencies with substantial science programs.

President Eisenhower established the Federal Council by Executive Order in 1959.[10] Its membership includes the heads of the independent agencies: NASA, AEC, and NSF, and Assistant Secretaries for Science and Technology or their equivalent from DOD; Agriculture; Interior; Health, Education and Welfare; and Commerce. The Department of State, the Bureau of

[10] Executive Order No. 10807, Mar. 13, 1959.

the Budget, and the Federal Aviation Agency are observers.[11]

The FCST has been of mixed success, suffering the
vicissitudes of all interagency committees. The Chairman does not have formal authority over the Council
members; his weapons are persuasion, broad knowledge of what is needed, and, only rarely, the threat of
invoking Presidential support through his relationship
to the President. The trouble with interagency committees as a whole is, as Don Price put it, "the relative
independence of the federal departments and services
and bureaus, with their roots in the independent Congressional committees and the special interest groups
concerned."[12]

Nevertheless, the Council has been able to come to
grips with some issues, such as administrative practices in the government in the support of research or
the conditions necessary for recruitment and retention
of talented scientists for government service, that are
common to many agencies and that do not run afoul
of important agency interests. In a few cases, it has
been able to deal successfully with issues that touch
more sensitive chords within departments. The ten-
year plan for oceanography for the U.S. Government,
a program that involves some fifteen different agencies
of government is a good example.[13] The Council is, in
any case, a necessary mechanism, among several, for

[11] Presumably the new Department of Transportation will be a
full member.

[12] Don K. Price, "The Secretary and Our Unwritten Constitution,"
in *The Secretary of State*, Don K. Price, ed., The American Assembly,
Columbia University (Englewood Cliffs, N. J.: Prentice-Hall, Inc.,
1960), p. 181.

[13] "Oceanography, The Ten Years Ahead," Inter-Agency Committee
on Oceanography of the FCST, ICO Pamphlet, No. 10, June 1963.

the Director of OST as he moves more fully into the task of formulating science policy for the government as a whole.

The charter of the Council includes reference to the foreign programs of government agencies; one of the stated objectives is "to further international cooperation in science and technology."[14] Therefore, shortly after the Council was established, a standing committee called the International Science Committee was created under the chairmanship of the Department of State. The formal justification of the Committee was to provide a mechanism for coordinating the international scientific programs of government departments, and for airing common policy problems in overseas activities.

The Special Assistant's office saw still another justification for creating that Council committee: to strengthen the hand of the State Department in its efforts to monitor and influence the international scientific activities of other government agencies and to ensure that those activities were consonant with foreign policy objectives. It was hoped that by providing the State Department with an extradepartmental lever associated with the White House, the Department's own formal but, in practice, limited, authority could be buttressed. This has not worked out. The International Committee has been useful as a device for exchanging information on agency programs (an appreciable achievement in an area in which two agencies operating in the same foreign country in similar scientific fields often knew nothing of each others programs) and for developing uniform policies in a very few problem areas.

[14] Executive Order No. 10807.

Beyond that, however, the International Committee has not been notably productive. The problems it faces in bringing about substantial coordination of agency programs, or of surfacing ideas for new programs that can serve foreign policy objectives, or of halting or modifying existing international programs, are the same as those faced by the parent Federal Council, with the additional impediment of lower-level agency representation. Moreover, until the Department of State itself is stronger in its ability to monitor and oversee the international scientific activities of other government agencies, no interagency committee that it chairs can perform those functions for the Department. An interagency committee as a whole cannot be stronger than the one member of the committee that has the real stake in seeing the committee achieve its purpose.

12

The Department of State

At the Cabinet level, one department in particular
must be concerned across the breadth of its activities
with the interaction of science and foreign affairs: that
is, quite obviously, the Department of State. For that
department, at least as much as for any other and more
than for most, the scientific revolution has altered the
environment within which it must operate and has
drastically changed its former ways of doing business.
It is necessary only to reflect on the sudden emergence
of the United States as a major world power with unprecedented military strength or on the effects on the
conduct of diplomacy of the speed of communication
and transport to demonstrate the changed situation.

President Kennedy expressed his view of the impact
of this new situation on the Foreign Service in a talk
in 1962:

In my opinion, today, as never before, is the golden period
of the Foreign Service. In the days before the War, we dealt

with a few countries and a few leaders. . . . We were an isolationist country, by tradition and by policy and by statute. And therefore those of you who lived in the Foreign Service led a rather isolated life, dealing with comparatively few people, uninvolved in the affairs of this country. . . .

That is all changed now. The power and influence of the United States are involved in the national life of dozens of countries that did not exist before 1945, many of which are so hard pressed.

This is the great period of the Foreign Service, much greater than any period that has gone before. And it will be so through this decade, and perhaps even more in the years to come, if we are able to maintain ourselves with success.[1]

How well the Department and the Foreign Service have responded to the challenge is a matter of continuing debate, with the critics emphasizing the tradition-bound nature of the Foreign Service and the difficulty the service has encountered in attempting to adapt to the new conditions of the postwar world. Arthur Schlesinger is particularly caustic in his account of the early days of the Kennedy Administration, although the same Department with few changes of leading figures appears to be satisfactory to President Johnson.[2] This contrast emphasizes the need to recognize, in any evaluation of State Department performance, that the Secretary is first and foremost the President's

[1] President John F. Kennedy, "The Great Period of the Foreign Service," *Foreign Service Journal*, Vol. 39, No. 7 (July 1962), included in *U.S. Congress, Senate Subcommittee on National Security Staffing and Operations Selected Papers: Administration of National Security*, p. 20.

[2] Arthur Schlesinger, Jr., *A Thousand Days* (Boston: Houghton Mifflin Company, 1965), Chapter XVI, pp. 406–447.

adviser—sometimes the chief foreign policy adviser, sometimes one among many—and the Department's primary function is to serve the Secretary in that role.

Certainly, in the subjects touched on in this work, the Department has not shown the degree of flexibility, of adaptation, of appreciation of new situations and new relationships that the scientific age demands. The quality of the Department's advice to recent Presidents on issues with important technical components has not been what it should have been. Moreover, the Department has too often on such issues been the virtual prisoner of the views and desires of the technical agencies of government rather than an independent source of policy.

The latter situation is inevitable for the great majority of issues that arise. The sheer volume of activities and the edge in information and expertise available to operating departments mean that State cannot hope to be on top of every item. In addition, every agency now has its own small foreign service; sometimes they are not so small. The AEC, for example, had in 1965 approximately 125 people directly engaged in international activities.[3] It is obvious that under these conditions many international contacts, negotiations, and other activities are carried out directly by the operating agencies with only the most general guidance and knowledge of the Department of State.

For the great bulk of issues, it is entirely appropriate and efficient that the details be handled by a technical agency directly under the general policy guidelines of

[3] Personal communication from John A. Hall, Assistant General Manager for International Activities, AEC, April 1, 1965.

the Department of State. It is for the relatively small number of important issues, however, that the question of the ability of the Department to meet the technical agencies on approximately equal terms of knowledge and competence is important.

It is here, as well as in the more general problem of recognizing the implications of science for foreign policy, that the performance of the State Department has been occasionally satisfactory but all too often inadequate. The Department is not alone at fault; the scientific community shares an important part of the blame.

The attempts of the Department since World War II to cope with the scientific elements of foreign policies are instructive, for they show the difficult problems encountered as well as the shortcomings on the part of the Department and on the part of the scientific community. Hopefully, they can also point to necessary changes in the future.

WORLD WAR II TO SPUTNIK

The Department of State in the years immediately following World War II found itself faced with a series of major issues in which scientific factors figured in critical ways. The development of a plan for international control of the atom was the most prominent such issue, although others were also important: establishing policy for dealing with allies on atomic matters, rehabilitation of war-torn Europe, evaluating the desirability of H-bomb development, mitigating the aftereffects of the nuclear attacks on Japan, and others.

By and large, the scientific elements of these issues

were handled on a case-by-case basis until, in 1946, the Department established the post of Special Assistant for Atomic Energy, attached to the Under Secretary of State.[4] Edmund Gullion was the first incumbent, taking over the responsibilities largely exercised by an undesignated Special Assistant prior to that time.

This office, beyond its formal responsibility in atomic energy, served in effect as the ad hoc focus for the integration of technical elements into policy for the Department as a whole until 1951 when the Office of Science Adviser was established. Even then, the office of the Special Assistant to the Secretary continued to bear primary responsibility in atomic energy and space matters and, for a time, disarmament, until the bulk of the office was merged into the reconstituted Office of International Scientific Affairs in 1962.[5]

The creation of the office of the Special Assistant for Atomic Energy was an important landmark. Its usefulness to the Department demonstrated that a degree of specialization was required to couple the new developments in science and technology effectively to American foreign policy. And it demonstrated that special measures were required to reduce the dependence of the Department on other agencies of government for information that was essential to understanding policy alternatives.

The individuals who staffed the office were the first to recognize that their operation, good as it was, only began to meet the problem. Among other shortcomings,

[4] Information from Mr. Edmund Gullion, Dean, Fletcher School of Law and Diplomacy, Tufts University.
[5] "Director of International Scientific Affairs," Foreign Affairs Manual Circular, No. 84, Sept. 14, 1962.

they had no scientists on the staff; hence their contact with the scientific community and their ability to question the technical judgments of other government agencies were severely limited. Accordingly, in 1949 they welcomed the report of the State Department's Reorganization Task Force No. 2, operating under recommendations of the Hoover Commission which concluded:

The Department is dealing on the one hand with foreign policy matters which have a great effect upon U.S. scientific policy and on the other hand with international scientific activities which have an impact on foreign policy. These matters are being handled at various points without adequate scientific evaluation. . . . We believe that the extent of the Department's responsibility for international scientific matters requires top policy consideration and the aid of professional scientific judgment, and cannot properly be determined in the course of a necessarily hurried review of the Department's organization.[6]

The Task Force went on to recommend that a scientist of national repute be asked to analyze the situation and submit recommendations.

Acting on this suggestion, James Webb, then Under Secretary of State, asked Lloyd V. Berkner, a prominent American scientist active in international scientific affairs to head a study group with the mission to make recommendations on (1) the role of the Department in national science policy and (2) appropriate

[6] *Science and Foreign Relations;* International Science Policy Survey Group, Department of State publication 3860, Washington, D. C., May 1950, p. 1, to be referred to subsequently as the "Berkner Report."

organization and staffing required for the Department to carry out its responsibilities.[7, 8]

The report of the study group, submitted in 1950 and tabbed the "Berkner Report," made three major recommendations respecting organization: (1) that the Department establish a Science Office "at the policy level," (2) that Science Staffs be established at selected missions overseas, and (3) that the National Academy of Sciences be urged to appoint a committee of pre-eminent scientists to serve as an advisory board to the Department.

The Science Office, according to the Report, should serve a staff function to the entire Department, reporting directly to the Under Secretary of State. The head of the Office, with the title of Science Adviser to the Under Secretary of State, ought to be a prominent scientist with a "keen awareness of world problems and a deep interest in their solution." The staff, it was recommended, should have one representative apiece from the physical and life sciences and from engineering, with the expectation that the posts would be filled by working scientists serving on a temporary basis.

The Berkner Report was a major step forward in developing formal recognition by the Department of State, and by scientists, that there is a continuing relationship between science and American foreign relations that the government must be organized to meet. In retrospect, however, it did not go far enough in delineating this relationship. The emphasis was largely on the problems of international scientific communica-

[7] Departmental Announcement 201, Nov. 1, 1949.
[8] *Berkner Report*, p. 15.

tion rather than on the needs of the Department for scientific advice and participation in the formulation of foreign policy.

The recommendations of the Berkner Report were accepted by the Department, and during 1950 two consultants, Caryl Haskins and Herman Spoehr, consecutively acted as temporary science advisers as the program got under way.[9] In January 1951, Dr. Joseph Koepfli, Professor of Chemistry from the California Institute of Technology, was sworn in as the first Science Adviser; the Office of the Science Adviser was established on February 6, 1951.[10] Dr. Koepfli quickly moved to organize the office along the lines recommended in the Berkner Report and established a science attaché system at some four embassies abroad.[11]

However, when Secretary Acheson gave way to Secretary Dulles in 1953, interest in the office waned, and later in 1953 Dr. Koepfli resigned, with no one named as successor. The Office was continued with a Foreign Service Officer as caretaker, but for most purposes it ceased to exist. The formal reason for the virtual demise of the program was its low priority on a severely tightened State Department budget. McCarthyism has also been cited as a contributory cause.[12] In fact, though

[9] Private communications from Dr. Caryl Haskins, President, Carnegie Institution of Washington, and Dr. Joseph Koepfli, California Institute of Technology.

[10] *Department of State Bulletin,* XXIV, Mar. 26, 1951, p. 519.

[11] "What's Happened to Science in State?" *Chemical and Engineering News,* Vol. 34, Jan. 9, 1956, p. 112. The four were located in Bern, Stockholm, Bonn, Paris. A fifth, in London, predated the Office of the Science Adviser. A sixth in Tokyo was filled after Dr. Koepfli left office.

[12] D. S. Greenberg, "Science and Foreign Affairs, New Effort Under Way to Enlarge Role of Scientists in Policy Planning," *Science,* Vol. 138 (Oct. 12, 1962), p. 122.

these were contributory causes, more significant was the fact that under presure to cut back the leaders of the Department did not feel they were sacrificing a needed or important function.

Neither the policy officers nor the scientists at that time saw the breadth of the requirement. Rather, both groups thought of the job as being concerned primarily with international scientific activities and how these could be helped by the Department. In the early 1950's, before the IGY and the enormous growth of international conferences and projects, even that aspect of the job was not as significant to the Department as it is today. These factors, coupled with Secretary Dulles' independent manner of making foreign policy and with the lack of influential friends to turn to for support (PSAC was still housed in the Office of Defense Mobilization and not highly active or secure itself), left the Office of the Science Adviser highly vulnerable. It is not really surprising that it failed to put down roots or survive.

SPUTNIK TO THE PRESENT

Sputnik again was the turning point. With the reaction to the Russian achievement came the realization that, had there been adequate coupling of science and technology with foreign policy formulation, the United States might have been able to avoid a humiliating and dangerous incident in its history.

It is no doubt too much to argue that a scientist in the State Department in the general budget tightening and security-conscious atmosphere of 1957 could have influenced U.S. earth satellite programs appreciably, even if

he were convinced of the political significance of a successful Russian first shot. However, once the Russians
demonstrated the significance, a science adviser in State
should have had a major role to play in the policy
decisions with regard to the U.S. space program.

One of the first moves after PSAC was established in
the White House and the new post of Special Assistant
to the President for Science and Technology created,
was the recommendation to the Department of State
that the Office of the Science Adviser be re-established.
This time, the post was called Science Adviser to the
Department of State, which was considered a boost in
status in prestige-conscious Washington.[13]

Secretary Dulles asked Dr. Killian for suggestions for
the Science Adviser post and selected Wallace Brode, a
chemist well known in scientific circles and at that time
Associate Director of the National Bureau of Standards,
from the list prepared by the Science and Foreign Policy
panel of PSAC. Dr. Brode proceeded energetically to
reactivate the office and to restaff the science attaché
program abroad. But once again the realization of the
breadth of the job to be done was lacking.

The emphasis of the office during Dr. Brode's tenure
and, indeed, during the tenure of his successors, was
again on international scientific activities. Disarmament, space, and atomic energy were handled by another office: the Secretary's Special Assistant, at that
time Mr. Philip Farley. Other policy areas such as
military policy, foreign aid, international organization,
or information activities were all but ignored, or the
technical inputs were provided by the White House
science office. Had the Office of the Science Adviser

[13] *Department of State Bulletin*, XXIV (Feb. 3, 1958), p. 190.

shown the interest or inclination, it could have played a major role, working independently, or with Farley's office or with the White House science office, in providing scientific and technological inputs in those foreign policy areas, because neither Farley, nor his staff, nor anyone else in the Department claimed to have sufficient scientific support.

Dr. Walter Whitman, chairman of the Chemical Engineering Department of M.I.T. succeeded Dr. Brode in 1960 and also devoted his major efforts to international scientific activities and to problems of the scientific community.[14] Dr. Whitman at first had no choice but to concentrate on problems of and with the scientific community, for relations between the Department and American scientists had become seriously strained. A series of policy disputes and misunderstandings had arisen and had been allowed to reach crisis proportions over issues such as participation by American scientists in international organizations that had representatives from countries not recognized by the U.S. Government.

Dr. Whitman performed that fence-mending task brilliantly, quickly exploring and developing workable compromises. But he did not take the job of the office much farther. Though these problems of the international relations of the scientific community were and are clearly important, there was much more to be done, and the Science Adviser's Office was not doing it.

As the time approached for Dr. Whitman's retirement in 1962, Secretary of State Rusk asked Dr. Wiesner for his views of the future of the Office of the Science Adviser. Rusk appeared to understand well the inade-

14 *Ibid.*, XLIII (Sept. 12, 1960), p. 429.

quacies of the existing organization, particularly with respect to the creative use of science and technology for policy initiatives and to the timely prediction of scientific and technical advances that would have foreign policy implications.

The same panel of PSAC that had urged Secretary Dulles to re-establish the Office of the Science Adviser now prepared a proposed new charter based on experience since 1958 and on the situation in 1962. Dr. Whitman actively assisted in the discussions. Approved by the full PSAC, the new recommendations were transmitted in March 1962 and were accepted in principle by the Department.

On the organization side, PSAC recommended combining the Office of Special Assistant for Space and Atomic Energy with the Office of the Science Adviser, raising the rank of the Science Adviser, and designating him to be a principal officer of the Department.[15]

The PSAC wanted in this reorganization to emphasize the Science Adviser's status as an action officer in some fields, notably atomic energy and space, even though his primary role was to be as a staff officer for the Department as a whole. Even the staff function, however, PSAC hoped would be action-oriented as a necessary path to influence. As Richard Neustadt observed, in commenting on PSAC itself in testimony before the Jackson committee:

Mr. Wiesner and PSAC and OST (the Office of Science and Technology), taken together, have made quite an impact even though they aren't organized around an action-forcing

[15] "Director of International Scientific Affairs," Foreign Affairs Manual Circular, No. 84, Sept. 14, 1962.

process they can call their own. But I think this is partly because their full-time staff is still rather small. . . . More importantly, he and his associates have been able, up to now, to reach out and hook onto action issues in other people's bailiwicks for a rather special reason: his office has been able to do this with others because it can claim special expertise, because it can lay hands on technical resources, judgments, better or more readily or more confidently than they can.[16]

The Department rephrased the specific functions recommended by PSAC, making them on the whole less specific. The approved missions of the office, now to be known as the Office of International Scientific Affairs (later International Scientific and Technological Affairs, but with identifying initials SCI) appeared as follows:

The primary functions of the Director of International Scientific Affairs will be to bring to bear the impact of science and technology in foreign policy development and decision-making, and to provide advice and guidance to the Department, other Government organizations, and the science community on matters concerning science and technology in foreign affairs:

More specifically, his functions will be to:

a. Participate actively in general foreign policy development, ensuring that appropriate consideration is given to scientific and technological factors.
b. Advise and assist the Secretary of State and other Department officers in reaching decisions on matters having scientific and technological implications.
c. Participate in policy planning for and provide guidance to U.S. international science activities.

[16] Testimony of Richard E. Neustadt, *Hearings, U.S. Congress, Senate Subcommittee on National Security Staffing and Operations, Administration of National Security,* March 11, 22, and 25, 1963, Washington, D. C., 1963, p. 92.

d. Work with the Bureau of Educational and Cultural Affairs, regional bureaus, and other appropriate elements in formulating policy and planning programs for scientific exchange.

e. Recommend activities to further U.S. foreign policy objectives in the field of science and technology.

f. Provide guidance to the science attachés developed in collaboration with other Department elements, particularly the regional bureaus.

g. Serve as the point of coordination within the Department and between the Department and other organizations, governmental and non-governmental, on matters concerned with science and technology, including the non-military uses of atomic energy and outer space.

h. Represent the Department on appropriate interdepartmental committees.

ISA [later changed to SCI] will be staffed to enable the Director to carry out the above functions, and to provide professional staff support to other bureaus and offices of the Department on all scientific and technological matters.[17]

The only PSAC recommendation not fully implemented was that recommending complete integration of Mr. Farley's office. Instead, the military and some regional aspects of atomic energy and space were broken off and made the responsibility of the new office of political/military affairs or of relevant bureaus. This deletion of certain functions would not necessarily prevent SCI from becoming involved in military and regional matters but did not give them a specific, as opposed to a general, charter to do so.

In fact, the office could get involved in whatever matters it wanted, for the charter is obviously open-ended. Peculiarly, but in many ways comparable to the

[17] Foreign Affairs Manual Circular, No. 84, Sept. 14, 1962.

post of Special Assistant for Science and Technology in the White House, the success of the office in doing more than narrow scientific functions depends on the man at its head.

For, except for space and atomic energy, most of the issues discussed in Parts II and III of the present volume are the primary responsibility of another part of the Department or even another agency. The Director of International Scientific and Technological Affairs must force his way in; he must, in Neustadt's phrase, "hook onto action issues in other people's bailiwick," must show in practice the kind of contribution he can make, and must be prepared to develop new initiatives in detail with full cognizance of the technical and the *political* facts. He cannot wait for the opportunities to come; he must create them.

The new office and new charter were ready well before the summer of 1962, but the task of finding the man to fill the Director's post proved time-consuming. It requires, to say the least, an unusual combination of talents and experience unlikely to be completely satisfied in any one individual.

A three-month search finally settled on Dr. Ragnar Rollefson, Professor of Physics at the University of Wisconsin, who had had Washington experience with the Army and had shown considerable personal interest in foreign affairs. The new office and appointee were announced simultaneously in September of 1962.[18]

Unfortunately, the new incumbent and office did not expand the influence of the office to bear out the high hopes that were entertained for it in the, by now, quite

[18] *Department of State Bulletin*, XLVII (Oct. 1, 1962), p. 505.

sympathetic environment of the State Department. Most of the initiatives based on science and technology came from other parts of the Department or from outside the Department. The functions of providing advice and representing scientific and technological factors in policy making were performed by the office for a limited number of obvious policy areas, such as U.S./U.S.S.R. scientific exchanges, but they were not extended significantly beyond those the office had performed before. Its involvement in foreign aid, disarmament, and military matters was minimal. In space and atomic energy it was necessarily active, but even there NASA and the AEC continued to be politely but firmly in command in foreign operations except when major issues arose that required attention by other parts of the Department and by the White House.

Instead, the office emphasized, as before and with high competence, the monitoring and assisting of international scientific activities. It must be repeated that this is an important function but only a small part of the job. Moreover, this is the part of the job that seeks the office, for direct problems of science come to roost in SCI without effort required to seek them out.

Dr. Rollefson's two years were up in mid-1964 and he returned to Wisconsin. Since he left, the post has been filled in an "acting" capacity by Foreign Service Officers: first by Mr. Edward Kretzman, who had been Dr. Rollefson's Deputy, and, since Mr. Kretzman's retirement in December 1964, by Mr. Herman Pollack, who is scheduled eventually to be the Deputy Director to Dr. Rollefson's successor. The search for the right man has been on since September 1964, with no success up to the fall of 1966. It is worth noting that more serious efforts have been made to enlarge SCI's role under the leadership of a highly competent Foreign Service Officer such as Herman Pollack than in the several preceding years. But progress has been slow, and there is a natural limit (discussed in the next paragraphs) without the leadership and accepted scientific competence of a Director of scientific stature.

What should be the conclusion? After three incumbents since 1958 and with no important result, is the answer simply that too much is expected of a single office of this kind within the State Department? Is there still hope that a science office can meet the need?

THE FUTURE OF SCI

On the basis of the poor performance to date of SCI, relative to expectations, several conclusions are possible: (1) the need is overstated; State has no problem in coping with foreign policy issues heavily dependent on science; (2) the expectations were too high — no office could do in the environment of the Department of State what was expected of it, and SCI had done as much as was possible; (3) the job must be done in other ways than by a central science office; or (4) some reorganization of SCI or new leadership will enable it to do better.

The first alternative, that there is no problem of providing scientific inputs in the policy process, is belied by the sweep of the discussion of the earlier chapters, and will be considered no farther. The second conclusion, that expectations are too high, has more plausibility but can be rejected on two grounds: (1) SCI, notwithstanding its three Directors, has not yet had the leadership that would constitute a real test; and (2) there are specific examples of success for the science advisory function within the State Department to indicate that the over-all job can in principle be done well.

The third conclusion, that a central science office in State is not the way to do the job, bears closer scrutiny. The alternatives to a central office are either the provision of scientific capability throughout the Department or the creation of an outside group of consultants available as needed. The latter of these two can be rejected immediately as an alternative to a central office simply because such an outside consulting group would not have the close tie to operating needs necessary to be useful. Further, a panel of consultants available "on call" without effective points of contact would rarely, if ever, be used. Even if the outside panel were the President's Science Advisory Committee, the lack of a central focus in the Department would limit their involvement to a very few issues, and then as outsiders. In conjunction with a central office, such a group of consultants could be very valuable, however.

Diffusion of scientific competence throughout the Department is theoretically possible; for example, scientists could be stationed in every bureau in which issues arise that have important technical elements. But the chances of attracting competent persons with sufficient stature to such posts is small. Even if it were possible, the absence of a central focal point with sufficient status within the Department would make relations with the outside scientific community (necessary for special studies or detailed advice) much more difficult.

Combined with a central science office, to provide better access to the scientific community and to give added stature within the Department, some diffusion of scientific competence throughout the Department is not only possible but desirable.

Diffusion of scientific competence can be obtained in another way: through special training or preparation of regular Foreign Service Officers to be better able to handle the scientific elements of the issues they face. The need for this kind of preparation, referred to here as "science affairs competence," is later discussed more fully. But such training does not do away with the need for a science office for there must still be available within the Department a place where scientific information and help can be obtained. The development of Foreign Service Officers expert in science affairs is an important requirement, but only in conjunction with a strong science office.

Therefore, the discussion leads back to the conclusion that a central science office is needed. What should be its functions? What is needed to make the present office more effective?

The charter of SCI is essentially adequate. In effect, it gives the Director of SCI the authority to inject himself in almost any issue that he or the Secretary may deem to be important. How successfully he can participate in policy deliberations depends in part on his knowledge of what is happening, on his relationship to the Secretary and senior Department officers, and on his competence to contribute to the issue under discussion. But what are his primary functions? Which of the eight tasks listed earlier are most important?

In effect, SCI has three levels of functions to perform:

1. Participation in formulation of policy.
2. Execution of operational responsibilities, in-

cluding the science attaché program, interagency coordination, and service functions to
other government agencies.
3. Communication with the scientific community.

The first is by far the broadest, hardest, and most important. The second and third will happen almost automatically; the problem rather is to keep them from
swamping the first.

Participation in policy formulation is easy to demand
but hard to fulfill in practice. What it means is providing for the Secretary, other senior officers of the
Department, and the various bureaus the kinds of
scientific/political inputs that have been described repeatedly in this study. These inputs must be relevant to
the political choices facing the policy makers and timely
if they are to be meaningful. This is the key job of SCI,
and it must be performed not only for issues that happen to arise but also on the initiative of SCI when
opportunities are seen for using science and technology
to advance political objectives.

Of course, no small office can hope to do this for all
issues with scientific elements, nor even for the majority
of them. The Director of SCI must be highly selective
with regard to which issues he tackles, just as the President's Special Assistant for Science and Technology
must be selective. For, as has been noted often before,
relevant scientific information on politically significant
issues cannot be provided without full understanding of
the political variables of an issue. A small staff cannot
successfully follow a great variety of issues in depth at
the same time.

Staff size, however, need not be as much of a limitation as it would appear, for the Director has a powerful means to augment staff capability that has never been adequately tried by SCI: tapping outside scientific competence on a regular consultant basis. In this, the pattern adopted by PSAC is a pertinent model. PSAC meets regularly as a standing committee but establishes highly knowledgeable panels on specific issues as they arise, co-opting other experts according to need.

A similar pattern could be followed in State with a small advisory committee to the Director of SCI, or to the Secretary of State with the Director of SCI serving as chairman.[19] On specific issues of interest, ad hoc panels could be created or individual consultants brought in, to provide the Director with independent background and analysis and to work with other elements of the Department as required.

This pattern has many advantages: (1) it supplements necessarily limited staff time and competence; (2) it draws more effectively on the scientific competence of the nation; (3) it allows the Director of SCI to form scientific and technical judgments independently of the views of other government organizations; (4) it expands the net for developing ideas for creative innovations in policy; (5) it improves the sounding board for problem areas developing in the scientific community; (6) it gives the Director and his staff a personal forum for discussing problems they encounter and for obtaining, privately, critical reactions to their ideas; (7) it provides a spur to action to the Director

[19] The committee's formal attachment to the Secretary could be a device, as with PSAC, to allow for communication of any disagreement between the committee and the Director of SCI to the Secretary should the occasion arise.

and his staff; and (8) it provides a prestige symbol for the office and the Department that can be of value in meeting staff recruiting problems, in attempting to influence other government agencies, and in providing continuity when the position of the Director of the office changes.

Such a consultant relationship has been proposed to State by PSAC and others but has never been implemented. One of the objections has been that it would duplicate the panel structure of PSAC and that State should look to PSAC for such support. In operation, PSAC and its panels have occasionally served the State Department as outside consultants and will no doubt continue to do so on issues of wide national concern. But PSAC panels cannot perform for State all of the functions just listed, nor can they be expected to see issues from the State Department's viewpoint.

Consultants do not replace the need for adequate and competent staff, but they can greatly enhance the contributions of competent staff. In addition, over the years, an ancillary benefit would be the development of a pool of experienced people, possibly available for full-time stints in the Department or in international organizations.

This emphasis on the use of outside consultants should not be allowed to obscure the great difficulty any Director of SCI will have in practice, especially if he is inexperienced in the ways of the State Department, in carving out for himself a role in policy making. The Foreign Service is a competent, tradition-minded organization, with an ingrained suspicion of the newcomer and outsider, especially if he has somewhat different perspectives on world affairs. Whoever the Director of

SCI may be, he will require political help within the Department from his own staff and the active support and interest of the Secretary.

Another problem facing the office is the danger that daily operational responsibilities, and the need to be a communication link with the scientific community may pose severe time problems. The present (1966) staffing pattern calls for some twenty professional positions (not necessarily scientists) with the possibility of adding several more shortly.[20] This is not a large staff, and even if it were considerably enlarged it could easily be swamped in the details of the science attaché program, by the need to attend interagency meetings, in preparing the ground for detailed overseas operations by technological agencies, and the like.

The operational functions, however, cannot be separated from broader policy functions. Some interagency work is tedious and unrewarding. Some, however, will be essential to give the background necessary to exercise influence over agency activities overseas. Organizing and guiding the science attaché program may be time-consuming, but if that program is itself to be effective, it must have the staunch and informed backup of SCI in Washington.

One attractive solution that has been proposed to this danger of overburdening the Director of SCI with operational responsibilities is to give SCI the status of a bureau, with an experienced Foreign Service Officer at the head. He would then report to the Director of SCI or, as has been proposed, to a man in a new post of

[20] Personal communication from E. G. Kovach, Department of State, Office of International Scientific and Technological Affairs, Mar. 31, 1966.

Assistant Secretary for International Scientific Affairs. This arrangement would serve to raise the level of the science adviser's job once again and would remove the senior man from day-to-day management responsibilities. It would, however, still give him access to the staff resources necessary to carry out his tasks.

Raising the post to Assistant Secretary rank has other advantages as well. One of the difficulties in attracting a first-class scientist to the post now is the concern that the existing rank below the level of Assistant Secretary will not give the individual sufficient stature and influence within the Department to be able to carry out the primary tasks of the office. Undoubtedly, the personal relationship of a science adviser with the Secretary is the most telling determinant of his influence, but a rank commensurate with the scope of the job to be done is not an insignificant element in recruitment, if nothing else.

Whatever the title or organizational pattern, it is perfectly evident that the key to the operation is, not surprisingly, the competence and quality of the man selected for the science post. Judging on the basis of the performance since 1958, and the present extended vacancy in the Directorship, there are, apparently, very few who are qualified.

Need the Director be a scientist? In principle, no, but in practice, yes. A scientist has certain obvious advantages of being at home in quantitative subjects, of being able to understand the scientific considerations firsthand rather than through an "interpreter," of being able to exercise his own scientific judgment, of being able to anticipate developments himself, and of being familiar with the working of the scientific community and known to that community. But these arguments are not determining; there are a few nonscientists who can or have overcome the obstacles these requirements pose and who are also well equipped to represent science in foreign affairs with foreign affairs specialists.

The key point, at least until more confidence is gained, is that the man in the science post in State must have the scientific stature and reputation to command the unquestioning confidence of the Secretary and his senior officers. If the State Department is going to be in a position to question the technical judgment of another agency on an important issue, the Secretary must have no qualms about the competence of the scientific advice he has been given. Whether it is substantively necessary or not, the symbolism of established scientific reputation is important. It is primarily for this reason that the present leadership by a Foreign Service Officer, notwithstanding his competence, could not satisfy the role foreseen for the office.

CHANGES IN THE CHARTER

Accepting the conclusion that the existing organizational pattern is workable if directed properly, there are three areas in which the charter of the Office of International Scientific and Technological Affairs should be broader. The office is not prevented from moving in these areas now, but a more specific charge would be useful.

The first is in the area of policy planning, specifically, the need for planning for the impact of likely developments in science and technology. There are no certain ways of predicting the future, but SCI should have the responsibility to attempt to anticipate the likely political and social effects of technical advance and to keep abreast of other studies in the government and in the private sector that are attempting to systematize "technological forecasting."[21] Some developments with foreign policy implications are not hard to anticipate. It was not hard to forecast, for example, the advent of communications satellites as soon as NASA undertook their development, and to predict some of the policy issues they would raise. Similarly, it was not hard to anticipate well in advance the international political problems that would be raised by the deployment of an intelligence-gathering satellite system.

Much more difficult for precise prediction for planning purposes are the technical developments apparently on the horizon but fuzzy and unclear in application, such as the ability to alter the genetic makeup of man and animals; or man's growing knowledge about the atmosphere that will one day mean an ability to control the weather; or the exploding developments in drugs, with full applications yet uncertain.

Subjects of these kinds should be under surveillance in State (and in other places in government as well) by an office charged with the responsibility of following the progress of science and technology, relating anticipated developments to foreign policy interests, and ensuring that the proper planning and policy-making responsibility is assigned when the time is appropriate. The State Department as a whole cannot be expected to devote much effort to specific planning for a general-

[21] Two groups heavily engaged in improving the art of forecasting are the Hudson Institute, Harmon-on-Hudson, New York, and the Commission on the Year 2000 of the American Academy of Arts and Sciences in Brookline, Massachusetts.

ized scientific development ten years in the future, the practical applications of which are presently unclear. It *can* be expected to have a responsible office able to speculate about the implications of future developments and competent to assist in the detailed planning for developments that are reasonably clear in focus.

SCI is a natural location for this surveillance, study, and warning responsibility (serving also as a channel for ideas from its consultants and the scientific community generally), possibly working in conjunction with the Policy Planning Council, which would be the logical first recipient for the information. A focus of responsibility does not mean that ideas cannot enter from other sources, but it is insurance that important developments will not be missed, or possibly ignored, because the original warning did not adequately point out the foreign policy implications.

The conviction that foreign policy objectives should be a factor in the determination of "domestic" technological objectives leads to the conclusion that another new mission of the Office of International Scientific and Technological Affairs should be to represent State Department views in a broad range of government technological decisions. State Department participation in technological decision making is not a new idea; it did play a role in a few technological and even scientific programs in the past: as a result of the inadequate seismological information needed for the test ban negotiations, the Department helped in the establishment of Defense Department projects designed to improve ability to monitor underground nuclear explosions and participated in the setting of general goals for expanded research in seismology. Earlier, the State Department had a prominent role in the decision to proceed with H-bomb development. By and large, the Department does not participate in technological planning in this way but rather accepts the technological programs of the government as determined by others. The Department therefore concerns itself only with the implications of the results of the programs.

This is not adequate, for in Lincoln Bloomfield's words: ". . . without a better thought-out linkage between . . . respective values and purposes [of technology and government], statesmen and people the world over will continue to be confronted and increasingly threatened with the products of politically mindless choices made in the laboratory or on the drawing board ten years back."[22] There is ample justification for the State Department to work, for example, to see that new weapons systems are designed with arms control measures in mind, that space systems are designed to make multination operation easy, and that more emphasis is placed on developing low-cost sources of power useful in less-developed countries.

There are, of course, practical reasons why the Department only rarely takes an active role in policy planning in technological areas, the most important being its inadequate technical resources. Participation in technical program decisions without adequate competence would be worse than no participation at all, for it would then only result in unnecessary delays or in unwise program alterations (and violent objections on the part of the agencies involved). Such a technological

    [22] Lincoln Bloomfield, "Vital Interests and Objectives of the U.S.," Address to the National War College, Washington, D. C., Aug. 26, 1963.

role for the Department could not be carried out on a large scale in any case without a major commitment to staffing the Department with a sizable number of scientists and engineers. The likelihood of being able to attract a large number of sufficiently competent people to State for a technical task of this kind, even if the positions were available, is slim indeed.

This role could be exercised selectively, however, on important issues and at the right policy levels. To do so effectively would require on the part of the State Department restraint, sensitivity to the problems, statutory missions and views of other agencies, and, above all, some highly competent technical skills so that the Department's interventions are based on a thorough understanding of the underlying science and technology as well as of the foreign policy considerations. The intervention cannot be continuous — time would not allow — but it can be applied, if wisely done, at the strategic points in technical planning in major agencies. Once again, the logical place for this responsibility in the Department is in SCI. This task would put a premium on attracting to SCI a small number of first-class scientists and engineers in pertinent fields. Consultants can be used occasionally, but in most instances only full-time individuals, conscious of the wide variety of pertinent factors that govern technological planning could perform this technological planning function.

In the functions listed earlier for SCI, this task is not mentioned at all, except to say that the office will "serve as the point of coordination . . . between the Department and other organizations . . . on matters concerned with science and technology, including the non-military uses of atomic energy and outer space." Significantly more than coordination is intended here, though it must be noted that even the coordination function requires a high level of technical competence if it is to be performed well.

A third area of responsibility that SCI should have, but which is not specifically mentioned in its charter, is that of concern for the general ability of Foreign Service Officers to deal with the day-to-day interactions between science, technology, and foreign policy.

Quite clearly, if an adequate job is to be done in integrating science throughout the range of foreign policy issues, it is not enough to expect a small staff in SCI to be familiar in detail with policy throughout the Department and to be able to make thoughtful contributions to all policy issues. Special capabilities in science and foreign policy are needed in the individual bureaus and on the part of Foreign Service Officers more generally. This capability can be thought of as competence in "science affairs," a term intended to be roughly parallel to the more familiar categories of economic affairs and political affairs.

The elements of this science affairs competence would include the ability (1) to explore familiar issues and to identify new ones from the point of view of the impact of scientific and technological developments, (2) to determine the relevance of technical questions, (3) to ask whether science and technology can make special contributions to specific issues on the basis of some familiarity with science and scientists, (4) to ask scientists for advice and to build connections between that advice and political deliberations, and (5) to deal with technical organizations in and outside government on a basis of greater understanding (without the sense of inferiority a nonscientist often has when dealing with scientists on technically related subjects).

The competence would also include an understanding for the ways in which advances in science and technology are generated and how they can alter the power and influence of the United States. And it would include a reasonable appreciation of the nature and dynamics of science and of the broader social implications of the discoveries of science and their fruits in technology.

In short, it is suggested that a good part of the job of dealing with the intimate involvement of science and foreign policy and of realizing the opportunities and averting the dangers of that involvement can and should be done by some Foreign Service Officers (FSO's) themselves.

Each bureau or other element of the Department, depending on its size and the nature of its responsibilities but including many of the overseas missions, should be expected to have one or more relatively senior FSO's on the roster who, in addition to other duties and on the basis of special training received, would be competent in science affairs. These officers would be expected to be alert to opportunities offered by science and technology, to see the relevance of technical factors, and to know when to turn to SCI, or to the Science Attaché, or on their own outside the Department for scientific advice and suggestions. They would be the first to whom a head of a bureau might turn when technical inputs are needed, and they would then act as the bridge with SCI or as the agent for bringing SCI fully into the policy process. They would be qualified through training to work with SCI and technical agencies of government when developing technical proposals such as the U.S. program, discussed in Chapter 8, for outer space cooperation offered by President Kennedy to the United Nations in 1961. They would be sufficiently current on scientific and technical developments through understanding and familiarity with "popular" scientific literature (e.g., *Scientific American, Science*) to be conscious in broad terms at least of new technical advances and of the pace of scientific progress.

This capability in the Department on the part of regular Foreign Service Officers would not supplant the need for scientific competence but would rather enhance the usefulness of such competence by bringing it into policy making at the right time on the right issues, by handling the great multitude of more minor interactions on the basis of personal knowledge or contacts, and by providing some technical inputs, even if only in the form of questions, on issues in which no other technical exposure is possible because of staff or time limitations.

Science affairs can be studied and mastered as well as most subjects having to do with governmental affairs. However, as in any field, a little knowledge can sometimes be more dangerous than none at all. Hence the training provided to produce competence in science affairs must be carefully developed, with its limitations as well as its strengths understood.

Only a few individuals have today become expert practitioners in science affairs. Several who have in the Department of State have become so by necessity when their responsibilities and activities required it. But on-the-job training is expensive in policy terms, time-consuming, and inadequate in terms of numbers. Some who have become experts, both inside and outside government, were trained originally in the natural sciences or engineering, and some in other professions. Few have had the time or inclination to reflect about their work. This knowledge and experience, acquired the hard way and usually as a result of independent initiative or chance circumstance, ought to be able to be translated and telescoped so that others can acquire with greater rapidity and fewer mistakes the capacity to perform well in this area. A conscious program to develop science affairs competence is both possible and desirable. And it should be accompanied by a staffing policy to place those properly trained in appropriate positions with suitable Departmental recognition. Both of these requirements can be met only if there is a strong partisan for them within the Department.[23] This task ought to be the direct concern and interest of the Director of International Scientific and Technological Affairs. For the development of this competence throughout the Department is essential to supplement the necessarily small staff resources of SCI.

THE SCIENCE ATTACHÉ PROGRAM

One of the major recommendations of the Berkner Report in 1950 called for the establishment of what amounted to a scientific foreign service to be located at American embassies overseas, integrated into the Foreign Service structure of the mission, and supported by the Office of the Science Adviser in Washington. A

[23] An experimental course to develop science affairs competence was offered by the Foreign Service Institute twice in January and November 1965 and repeated again in 1966.

variety of functions was outlined in the report for what have since come to be called science attachés. In essence, these functions were (1) reporting on trends of science and technology abroad, (2) facilitating the flow of scientific information and the international activities of American scientists, (3) representing American science abroad, and (4) advising the ambassador and embassy staff on scientific and technological matters. In line with the rest of the Berkner Report the emphasis was intended to fall largely on those duties that would assist the international scientific activities of American scientists and the free flow of scientific information. The report in fact stated: "The range of activity of such staffs will be the basic science and technology in foreign countries."[24]

Accordingly, the recruiting practices for science attachés in the early 1950's, and again after 1958, have tended to emphasize the search for well-known scientists, highly competent in their own fields. This was essential, given the definition of the task, for the attaché had to have easy access to the scientific community of the foreign country; a scientific reputation greatly facilitates that access. But there is no necessary correlation between a good scientific reputation and understanding of foreign affairs or of the making of foreign policy. How important is it that the attaché "understand" foreign affairs? What exactly is he expected to do and where do his most important responsibilities lie?

The exposition of Parts II and III of this book provide a guide to determine the priorities of the science attaché's mission. In Chapter 7, for example, it was shown how the rapidly growing volume of public and private

[24] *Berkner Report,* p. 103.

scientific relations between the United States and other nations, as well as the importance of the subject matter of these relations to national power and influence, has given them a new significance in U.S. bilateral foreign relations. Embassies abroad and the Department in Washington must be cognizant of the extent of these contacts, of their nature, of the ways they can serve or hinder American policy objectives, and of the levers they may offer for exerting American influence.

The point was also made that U.S. Government missions in many countries today need to be in touch with the local government's policy-making machinery in highly technical fields, just as the missions expect as a matter of course to be in touch with local government policy machinery in traditional political and economic areas. This contact is necessary in order to keep abreast of general scientific and technological developments of political interest (for example, in the German nuclear power program), and to be able to anticipate future trends that are likely to affect American relations with a country (for example in the implications for U.S./French relations of a move for an independent French or European communication satellite system). Technical contact with the local government is also necessary in order to know who are the key individuals in policy formulation in technically oriented areas, such as space or atomic energy, and, as a result, who are the individuals with the greatest influence on those issues.

Of course, in a more general sense, an embassy is constantly carrying out policies or dealing with the local government on matters that have important scientific or technological aspects. Even if the technical inputs have been adequate in policy making in Washington, there will often be a need at hand in the field for technical understanding, for immediate advice, and for an ability to discuss issues with the scientific advisers and officials of the local government.

The enormous scale of international scientific activities of the U.S. Government itself, discussed in Chapter 3, and the importance of knowing the effects of these activities on the countries in which they are carried out also bear directly on a science attaché's main job. Sensing and evaluation of the impact of U.S. operations must be done in the field, and much of the coordination of American government agencies must be the concern of the overseas missions.

Thus, the attaché's task is primarily a political one not at all dissimilar to the functions of other officers at an embassy. In effect, he must become an expert on the local government with good entree at the right places, must be cognizant of American policy interests in that country and how scientific and technological considerations relate and can contribute to those interests, must gain a feeling for the extent of American private as well as governmental relations with the country, and must know about technical plans and programs of other U.S. agencies within the nation. At the same time, he must know how to obtain scientific and technical advice when he himself needs it, must be able to relate that advice to policy issues, must be able to work with the nonscientists in the mission and must be reasonably conversant with the situation in Washington and in the scientific communities in the United States and the local country. And through it all, he must be a decent ambassador of American science without, however, having to spend much of his time on reporting scientific developments that are best transmitted through normal scientific channels in any case.

A tall order it is, and one that obviously cannot be satisfied perfectly for the twenty-three attachés and deputy attachés now (in 1966) authorized for sixteen countries.[25] Until recently, the Department has not been recruiting science attachés with these priority tasks in mind, although there have been a few resounding successes in the past such as Dr. Edgar L. Piret in Paris and Dr. Otto Laporte in Tokyo. As a result, the program has not generally been held in high esteem within or outside the Department. Now, SCI has begun to change its concept of the purposes of the attaché program, and recent directives have indicated a major shift is under way that roughly coincides with the description of the attaché's task presented here.[26]

Two caveats must be entered in this evaluation of what should be the priority functions of science attachés. One is the implied assumption in the discussion that all U.S. missions overseas represent similar assignments for science attachés. This is manifestly not the case.

Clearly, one major division is between the advanced and the less-developed countries. In the latter, contact with the technical elements of the local government is likely to be much less significant, but ideas for ap-

[25] Information from Arthur E. Pardee, Jr., Executive Director, Office of International Scientific and Technological Affairs, Department of State, Mar. 31, 1966.

[26] "Functions of Science Attachés," SCI Directive, March 2, 1965.

plying science and technology to local development problems will be much more so. The fact that there are important differences between missions does not, however, change the basic priorities of the attaché's job. It is simply that the key function, serving American foreign policy interests and objectives directly, calls for somewhat different emphasis in different missions. Another distinction would be between advanced countries that figure prominently in U.S. foreign relations like France and Britain, and others that are on the periphery, like the Scandinavian countries. Involvement with current U.S. foreign policy issues is likely to be much less in the latter countries, and correspondingly more attention can be given to purely scientific matters. However, wherever purely scientific matters are a primary focus, the State Department probably has no business providing the attaché. It would be much more appropriate and useful for an attaché program concerned exclusively with scientific activities to be mounted by the NSF rather than by the State Department.

A second caveat is that the interest and attitude of the Chief of Mission, and to a lesser extent the rest of the embassy staff, toward the attaché are critical. The best choice for science attaché will not get far if he rarely has access to the ambassador and is not kept conversant with the current political concerns facing the embassy. The success of Dr. Piret and Dr. Laporte were in no small measure due to the interest of Ambassadors Gavin, Bohlen, and Reischauer.

The Office of International Scientific and Technological Affairs in Washington also has a major role to play in the over-all performance of the attachés, going well beyond the responsibility for their recruitment. Although the heart of the work of the attaché is in his own embassy, he relies heavily on the backup he receives from Washington and on the effectiveness and influence of SCI in taking action on his information and advice.

The attaché is first of all dependent on Washington for scientific and technological information not available to him abroad and for advance warning of impending U.S. agency activities at home or abroad that will influence his work.

Second, the extent to which he can effectively coordinate and influence U.S. agency activities in his country is determined largely by what kinds of pressures he can generate in Washington. Therefore, if an attaché does not, for example, believe the military should start a research grant program in Japan or if he wants to delay a NASA site survey team, the impact of his views will be determined not only by the position his ambassador takes but also by how much influence SCI can exert in Washington.

Third, the use SCI makes of an attaché's information, whether it be a suggestion for a new scientific/political initiative the attaché believes to be ripe or the need for Washington coordination of several agencies' activities in his country, will obviously have an important bearing on how effective he is in his post.

These observations about the attachés' priority roles lead to the obvious question: Do they have to be scientists? Again, as for the Director of SCI, the answer in principle is that they need not necessarily be scientists, but in practice that is the only course possible for the next few years at least. Even to perform their priority tasks, and clearly so for the representation function, it is important that the attachés be accepted by their scientific colleagues in the local community and local government as competent scientists. Entree to scientific and engineering circles in government is necessary, and a scientific reputation helps. In addition, an attaché's prestige and influence among his American State Department colleagues depend at least initially on his scientific stature.

The deputy science attachés, on the other hand, do not require this scientific stature, and in time, as they become known, they may be able to take over the senior posts and be fully accepted.

For the immediate future, however, even if scientists of high reputation continue to be sought, some kind of special training is needed to provide attachés with adequate background for the policy aspects of their job before they take up residence. A competent scientist with little understanding of the Department or of political issues is not likely to be of much value as an attaché, nor of much value elsewhere in the Department. For the attaché program, as for the Office of International Scientific and Technological Affairs, the "new breed" of professionals who combine scientific and political competence is desperately needed.

ACDA, USIA, AID

There are three agencies of government closely allied with, or formally a part of, the Department of State that share many of the same needs in the interaction of science and foreign policy as the Department proper. These are the Agency for International Development

(AID), the Arms Control and Disarmament Agency (ACDA), and the U.S. Information Agency (USIA). Each is concerned primarily with one major issue of foreign affairs, although, quite naturally, no issue can be wholly isolated from other policy matters. The existing means for tying scientific and technological factors to other aspects of the issues with which these foreign affairs agencies are concerned warrant brief discussion here in the context of the State Department analysis.

Arms Control and Disarmament Agency. In the arms control area, the need for including scientific elements fully in policy formulation has long been recognized. As noted earlier in this chapter, from the close of World War II to the period after Sputnik, this need was met on an ad hoc basis, largely through the Office of the Special Assistant for Atomic Energy in the State Department. Scientists were brought in as consultants, or on temporary tours of duty as needed by that office or by other parts of the Department. The technical agencies of the government, however, were called on to serve as the continuing source of most of the needed technical inputs.

After Sputnik, the Office of the Special Assistant for Science and Technology in the White House became, in effect, the science advisers to State as well as to the President on all disarmament matters, with special emphasis on the test ban issue. This was a reasonable arrangement on an emergency basis but not for the long term. To develop disarmament policy adequately requires a more intimate and permanent relationship. There has to be sufficient full-time capability to explore the many policy alternatives that are possible, to weigh the significance of future developments in science and technology, to understand how technological changes affect underlying political factors, and to conduct research and development on inspection and control techniques. These functions must be performed within the agency charged with primary policy responsibility, not through an advisory office housed in a separate part of the government.

In addition, the White House science office had to be careful not to become permanently tabbed as an arm of one of the protagonists in disarmament policy debate within the government. If it did, its evaluations for the President of the views of other agencies could not remain as objective and independent of agency opinions as the President requires.

Accordingly, the Special Assistant and PSAC supported the move for the creation of a semi-independent disarmament agency that would have a scientific component within it. This was accomplished in 1961 with the creation of the Arms Control and Disarmament Agency. From the start, a Science and Technology Bureau was established in the new organization, on an equal footing with other divisions. It has been an arrangement that has worked well in practice, in large measure due to the excellent leadership first of Dr. Franklin Long of Cornell University, and then of Dr. H. P. Scoville. At present, the Bureau remains relatively small, with approximately twenty professional staff (one-third are Ph.D.'s) and an annual budget near $2.0 million.[27]

[27] Personal Communication from Herbert P. Scoville, Jr., Assistant Director, Science and Technology, Arms Control and Disarmament Agency, May 10, 1966.

The Special Assistant for Science and Technology in the White House and members of his staff still are involved in disarmament matters and often work closely with ACDA. But the latter now has the means to involve scientific elements in policy making more directly on its own.

U.S. Information Agency. The situation in USIA is quite different. That agency has never been able to build up a staff of any size in science in its policy planning. In operations, it has used scientists and engineers primarily on an ad hoc or consultant basis when necessary to help produce science fairs, science films, or other projects involving science and technology.

In the years after Sputnik, the White House science office attempted to work with USIA to help introduce new ideas for exploiting America's scientific strength but found that a continuing relationship was not feasible or productive. The Agency was not unreceptive to suggestions and did much more on its own than as a result of White House suggestions, but its efforts tended always to be low keyed. In practice, USIA relies heavily on the technical agencies of government, many of which carry out international "image" projects on their own authority and initiative. AEC, for example, has its own exhibits staff.

At present, USIA has one person, Mr. Simon Bourgin, who is responsible for integrating scientific considerations into policy planning for the Agency. Mr. Bourgin is not a scientist but is given a relatively free hand and considerable support by the senior officials of the Agency in his efforts. He has been effective, but whether a one-man operation of this kind is adequate for more than a low-keyed operation is doubtful. However, USIA is not one of the more favored agencies of government in terms of funds or political support, and it is unlikely that it is in a position at present to do more in science and technology than it does now.

Agency for International Development. AID is a more complicated matter. Technical elements are pertinent to so many of that Agency's activities that scientific and engineering competence has had to be built into the organization at many different levels.

In AID operations, technical industry, universities, nonprofit scientifically based companies, and individual scientists are utilized extensively. For planning and guidance of the Agency's technical activities, each of the four regional bureaus (the major operating divisions: Latin America, Near East and South Asia, Africa, and Far East) has a technical staff that oversees the technical assistance programs for that region and assists the overseas missions and the Washington headquarters of the regional bureau.

The size of these staffs varies between thirty professionals in the African bureau to fifty-five in the Latin American bureau.[28] Some of the larger missions have technical people on regular tours of duty. In addition, one regional bureau — Latin America — has had a contract with the National Academy of Sciences/National Research Council (NAS/NRC) for the support of a Science Board to advise the bureau on scientific programs and policies under the Alliance for Progress.[29]

[28] Personal communication from Dr. A. H. Moseman, Assistant Administrator for Technical Cooperation and Research, Agency for International Development, May 20, 1966.
[29] Harrison Brown, "Office of the Foreign Secretary," *News Report*, National Academy of Sciences/National Research Council, Vol. XIII, No. 2 (Mar.–Apr.), 1963, p. 20.

This relationship with the Academy has now been extended to AID as a whole by tying the Academy in an advisory relation to the Technical Cooperation and Research (TCR) office in the central administration of AID.

TCR has a good-sized technical staff with some seventy professional positions led by an Assistant Administrator of AID, at present Dr. Albert Moseman.[30] The staff is intended to provide the general technical guidance for the operating bureaus, to set over-all technical policy, and to facilitate communication and effective relations of AID as a whole with the American scientific community — inside and outside of government. In addition, this division of AID conducts the agency's research program, and has high-level advisory committees made up of natural and social scientists from universities and industry.

Thus AID has in principle the staff, organization, and external relations required to provide adequate consideration of the scientific elements in foreign economic assistance. In practice, it does not work as well as it should for a variety of reasons.

1. The first problem is, as always, one of relevant competence. AID has many on the staff or as advisers who are first class in their own field. The competence referred to here, however, is the competence to understand the very complex interactions between the technical factors and the political, economic, and social factors of economic development, as discussed in Chapter 9. AID has fewer on the staff with

[30] A. H. Moseman, *op. cit.*

this kind of competence, although the situation is improving. These interactions are not well understood in theory, and apparently hard to learn through exposure. Further, the body of experience that has been accumulated has not been sufficiently analyzed to draw the lessons that could serve as guides to policy and action.

2. Related to the first problem is the general lack of knowledge or agreement in AID about the role of science in development, and, for that matter, lack of sufficient understanding of science itself and how the scientific community operates.

3. The concept underlying the AID policy-making process itself often tends to impede effective integration of technical elements. To oversimplify, the policy process in this case is largely the program planning conducted for each country. In this process an attempt is made to insist that nations that wish to receive aid must produce their own development plan, with American or other help. This country plan is then submitted to AID, where it is evaluated by American experts prior to a decision as to which parts of it the United States will support. The concept is excellent: to produce a balanced plan for development in order to avoid uncoordinated efforts that dissipate resources, and at the same time to throw the burden of planning on the country itself so that it is fully aware of the steps it must take

and so that it develops the planning machinery and competence to carry development forward on its own momentum in the future.

The major flaw with regard to science and technology is that the competence and information often do not exist to allow those fields to be taken account of adequately in the plan. The competence does not usually exist in the countries and only rarely in the U.S. missions to those countries. Unfortunately, the previous system in the predecessor agencies to AID, in which there was little attention to country planning and too much attention to individual technical assistance projects was also inadequate. In that period, the problem tended to be the reverse: technological innovations were formulated and approved with little concern for the broader problems inherent in attempting to innovate in traditional societies.

The country planning approach is the preferable one — as long as it does not become a fetish — but if it is going to include scientific and technological aspects properly, a more effective mobilization and training at least of American talent will be required.[31] There are indications now that the Johnson Administration is moving to a middle position, retaining the country programming approach but at the

[31] There is a built-in barrier in this approach to seizing upon targets of scientific opportunity that may not have gone through, or *may not be able* to go through, the full panoply of the planning machinery. Somehow these should not be completely excluded.

same time focusing independently on a few major technical areas such as agriculture, health, and education.[32]

4. The relationship established with the National Academy of Sciences has not taken advantage of the potential contributions of that unique scientific body, for the Latin American Science Board had not been brought into sufficiently close contact with Agency operations to be able to render consistently useful and pertinent advice. Problems existed on both sides here, for scientists as a group do not yet have sophisticated understanding of development problems. Only a very close and detailed relationship between the Academy and AID could serve to acquaint the scientists with the hard substance of the formidable problems of development so that they could bring to bear realistic and valuable scientific advice. The new arrangement in which the Academy works with the Technical Cooperation and Research division of AID will hopefully make it possible to attack this deficiency.

5. Bureaucratic and Congressional problems also loom large. AID does not have great stability or popularity; one result has been close Congressional scrutiny, and resulting timidity on the Agency's part with regard to rules and procedures. This has caused grave difficulties, for example, in contracting relations with univer-

[32] "Facts About the Foreign Aid Program for FY1967, New Initiatives in Agriculture, Education, Health", Agency for International Development, Mar. 1966.

sities and has made it difficult to work with the nation's intellectual community.

Beyond that, bureaucratic problems and instability within the Agency have made it difficult for scientific staff to exert appreciable influence over the operating bureaus.

6. The research program of AID has suffered because of early management and leadership failures, and still experiences difficulty in recruiting an able staff of sufficient size to be able to mount the kind and caliber of program required. In addition, the response of the academic community to the opportunities for research on economic development problems the government faces has not been as good as was hoped. Many of the proposals reaching AID are not of the quality the importance of the subject warrants.

These, in summary, are a few of the difficulties encountered in attempting to inject scientific and technological elements effectively into policy making for foreign economic assistance. The most recent administrator, David Bell, understood these problems well and worked to improve the conditions wherever he could. His successor, William Gaud, will hopefully continue along the same lines. The process is slow.

One other point, with relevance beyond AID, must also be noted. That is the anomalous situation with regard to the technical assistance program as AID phases out of countries that reach economic self-sufficiency though still at low per capita income, Taiwan is a good example. In some ways, it is just when countries are able to advance without outside financial help that American technical assistance would be most useful to them. Yet it is just at that point that AID must step out as the country no longer requires outside economic aid. And the U.S. Government has at present no other organizational means for continuing technical assistance outside the foreign aid program.

This is another example of the "gray area" support problem discussed in Chapter 3 that requires some kind of organizational innovation in the Federal Government. A separate technical assistance agency that can support overseas technical aid on a modest scale in countries in which AID is able to phase out is one possible solution. An alternative solution is to give existing departments of government an operating role overseas in developing countries and to give NSF greater resources for international activities. This latter appears to be the trend President Johnson is introducing now in argriculture, health, and education, although at present funding must still come through AID. As long as the AID budget must bear the cost, however, the need to provide technical assistance for countries no longer requiring massive economic aid cannot be met. Another mechanism is required.

PART V

Science and Future Patterns of International Affairs

13

New Imperatives

The discussion in Parts II and III leaves little question about the extent of the involvement of science and technology with major current issues of foreign policy, or about the opportunities science and technology offer as instruments of policy. Foreign policy for many of the central areas of national interest simply cannot be made effectively today without integration of scientific and technological elements. But beyond that, a broader view of the interaction of science and foreign affairs leaves a nagging sense that not all the questions have been asked, that the forward rush of science and technology carries with it new imperatives for foreign affairs that will be of increasing concern in the future, and therefore should be of concern today.

What are these new imperatives? What implications do they have for international relations and for the Federal Government's direction and support of science and technology? Some of these have been alluded to briefly before, but they and other fundamental implications of science deserve discussion in a broader context than the immediate policy-making process.

GLOBAL TECHNOLOGY

Reference has already been made in Chapter 5 to one of the characteristics of many new technologies — their global nature. That is, with increasing frequency, new technologies emerge that require the participation or cooperation of many countries or that have effects that cannot be contained within the boundaries of single states. Many examples of such global technology are at hand or can be confidently predicted for the future. Communications satellites, or other applications of space vehicles, are typical illustrations. So, too, is the likely development of technology for controlling the weather and the promising technology for discovery and exploitation of mineral resources under the oceans. All of these will (or already do) require international cooperation and regulation if their benefits are to be realized. Fallout from atomic tests and the globe-girdling effects of Projects Westford and Starfish (discussed in Chapter 5) offer examples of the other kind — of technologies with effects that are not containable within national borders.

It is not only new technologies that are pertinent. Often it is the enlarged scale or intensity of application of well-known technologies that result in world-wide effects. The danger of carbon dioxide accretion in the atmosphere that may alter the planet's surface temperature, the potentially poisonous effects on plants and fish and ultimately on man of increased spread of pesticides and herbicides, and the threat to fish resources in the growing efficiency of fishing technology are typical examples.

A related phenomenon, but one with quite different implications, is the improving technical ability to inject ideas and information across borders into other societies, even when attempts are made to prevent such intrusion. The advent of a satellite able to broadcast radio or television directly to home receivers will give a strong boost to this capability.

The increasing prevalence of technology with such global implications represents a trend in current technological development, a trend that can confidently be predicted to intensify in the future. Such a trend has important long-term implications for this country's foreign policy, implications that deserve explicit recognition and extended analysis.

The steady diminution of a nation's freedom of action to apply science and technology as it sees fit even at times within its own borders, is one such implication. This restriction of action is not basically different from the better-recognized restrictions nations encounter because of the growing interdependence of national economies and societies. But the restrictions on action that flow from technology introduce a physical element that adds a new and compelling dimension to interdependence. The physical aspect makes it more tangible, and to the extent that some of the worldwide effects of technology may be irreversible, can provide a formidable rallying point for public opinion.

This gradual loss of national independence of action is paralleled by a requirement for international means to operate and to regulate global technology, and to provide a forum for airing disputes. Global technology thus tends to force decision making away from the decentralized national government level toward centralized international policy machinery.

In addition, there is the growing mismatch between the requirements of technology and the size and resources of nation-states. Today, most of the smaller countries of the world are unable to utilize all or even many modern technologies because of their limited national resources. The larger and richer states of Western Europe now find it impossible acting alone to mount meaningful programs in all prominent new technical fields. And even the United States and the Soviet Union find their resources strained in an attempt to compete in large systems fields.

There are already examples of amalgamations or consortia of nations brought together because of the imperatives of new technology: the Common Market efforts in atomic energy, and the broader European cooperation in space provide illustrations. Undoubtedly this tendency for joint action, too, will accelerate in the future as it is realized that cooperative undertakings are essential if the benefits as well as the dangers of global technologies are to be met.

The advent of modern technologies with global implications may have a powerful effect in quite a different direction: on the ability of a government to exclude potentially explosive ideas and unsettling cultural forces from a society. The political effects of increased contacts between people, which resulted in large part from revolutions in international communication and transportation, are readily evident today in modernizing societies that have not attempted to exclude external influences. In the Soviet Union and Eastern Europe, regions that tried for an extended period to limit foreign contacts, the effects are also dramatic. What can be predicted about Communist China? Can it continue effectively to exclude outside influences in an era in which technology tends to force contact with and dependence on outside nations, and makes possible unauthorized intrusion through radio and television? The implications of that question for policy toward China and toward nations that are or may fall under China's influence are obvious. The extreme attempts to remove bourgeois (Western) influences in China would seem to indicate that China's leaders are also concerned about this question.

Last is the more general observation that technological developments are likely to be even more dramatic in the future than they have been in the recent past. Man's environment almost surely will continue to be altered by conscious design, and too often accidentally, in the years to come as the desire to make "improvements" is matched by readily available power to do so. And "improvements" undertaken for local objectives may have far broader effects beyond national borders, not always to the approval of other nations.

Thus, science and technology are presenting this nation, and all nations, with a trend toward physical internationalization that, whether consciously appreciated now or not, is likely to force far-reaching changes in the structure of the international political system in the years to come. At the very least, the trend is certain to set up major new political stresses and pressures that are likely to force the pace of political change.

One lesson is obvious: to recognize the political imperatives of the developing technological situation and begin now to plan for and take preliminary steps on the international scene so as to guide political changes in directions consistent with American long-range foreign policy objectives. There is another lesson as well: the direction of future developments in science and technology, because of the resources they require, is likely to be increasingly determined in the *political* arena rather than independently; therefore, it is not amiss for responsible foreign policy officials to work with scientists and engineers *now* to explore international political initiatives that might provide a means of controlling the development of global technology. This latter point, a somewhat heretical one, deserves further elaboration.

CONTROL AND SUPPRESSION OF TECHNOLOGY

After World War II, the great German physicist Heisenberg was quoted as saying: "In the summer of 1939 twelve people might still have been able, by coming to mutual agreement, to prevent the construction of atom bombs."[1] Is this judgment valid? With the knowledge of the Hahn and Strassman fission experiments widely spread throughout the scientific community, is it conceivable that effective agreement could have been reached to forgo all further experiments on

[1] Robert Jungk, *Brighter Than a Thousand Suns* (New York: Grove Press, Inc., 1958), p. 81.

atomic fission? What guarantee could there have been that knowledge about the possibilities of a controlled chain reaction would not have been gained, perhaps accidentally, through research in quite different areas of physics or chemistry? In any case, would such a ban on research have been desirable on cultural, intellectual, and utilitarian grounds, even if feasible?

Attempts to suppress basic science are surely unwise and futile. They are unwise because of the penalties paid in the imposition of intellectual control that would be required; unwise because the agreements necessary with other countries to avoid the danger of scientific surprise would be unenforceable except under conditions of extreme and unrealistic intellectual control and hence dangerous on security grounds; and unwise because such a ban would mean forgoing highly desirable technological applications that arise from scientific discoveries. Attempts to suppress basic science would be futile, for there would be no way of knowing confidently in advance which fields to ban in order to prevent developments in a supposedly undesirable direction. Once launched on such a course of suppression of science, there would be no logical end to the degree and breadth of control that would be required.

But why is this even raised as a question? The answer, of course, is that the accretion of scientific knowledge continues to put ever more power under man's control, power with the potential of actual destruction of the human species or of alteration of the species and the environment in ways incommensurate with present values. The motivation can also be stated in more modest terms: scientific advances often lead to developments that increase the instability of power. Or, more precisely: the unpredictability of scientific advance implies that it is always a potentially destabilizing factor in international relations. The possibility of sudden developments that would make a new weapons system feasible, such as an effective missile defense or a discovery that reduces the cost and complexity of powerful weapons, thereby making them available to smaller countries, are cases in point.

It is a platitude to observe that it is not science itself that is destabilizing and it is not science that is the direct agent for evil. It is, instead, man's technological application of scientific knowledge that should be the focus of attention. But the layman has the right to ask not only whether technology can be controlled but also whether the underlying science that made the technology possible can be controlled.

Scientists have been derelict in refusing to take this question of suppression of science seriously, for the answers are not obvious to nonscientists. Especially are the answers unclear in an era in which many fields of science require massive resources supplied from public funds for their continued progress. A modest prediction may be made that in the future there will be many more challenges to the continued public support of science, especially expensive fields of science, when the beneficial results are not obvious and the potentially harmful effects, though unknown in detail, are feared.

High-energy physics could be one such field, for already there is speculation about new reactions (matter/antimatter) with fantastic releases of energy that are at least theoretically possible.[2] If, in fact, gigantic new

[2] Art Buchwald satirized this situation most effectively in his column February 8, 1966 (*Boston Globe*), when he pointed out that a

particle accelerators may make it possible to obtain the knowledge that would make such a reaction suitable for military use, the layman is asking a legitimate question when he wonders whether he wants his government to spend the money to bring that possibility about. What beneficial gains are likely to be realized that could offset the dangers? Would it not be better to cut off high-energy physics now, especially as the ability to suppress the field appears simple: refuse to build new accelerators? (And an international agreement not to build any large new accelerators ought to be easy to enforce.)

The major flaw in that argument, leaving entirely aside questions of whether it is wise on other grounds, is that it is impossible to predict not only what beneficial results would be obtained from continued research in high-energy physics but also whether the knowledge that is feared might not be obtained anyway through lower cost research in related fields. Attempting to stifle a science by refusing to provide expensive research equipment is not a certain way to prevent its advance.

Refusal to provide all or some research facilities may, however, serve to slow down the development of a field of science. A shortage of research facilities with little prospect for more may very quickly discourage first-class students from moving into a field and rather rapidly make it unpopular. From the very broadest view of public policy, the question of whether to impede the advance of a particular field of science be-

G-bomb was possible, many times more powerful than an H-bomb. But no one should worry for it would take at least ten years before an enemy could have one, and by that time the United States would have the much more powerful F-bomb.

cause of concern about its undesirable applications ought to be a legitimate question for political and scientific debate. However, the tools with which that debate would have to be conducted are so primitive and the dangers of wrong decisions so great that it can only be concluded that it is preferable to avoid confusing decisions about the support of science with these more controversial and speculative issues.

Although the conclusion that it is unwise and impractical to interfere with the progress of basic science is easy to arrive at, there may be other measures possible that will make more feasible the control of any subsequent undesirable applications growing from the science.

One of the major concerns in the development of a powerful new technology is the possibility of its uncontrolled use for narrow national ends. Might it be useful, therefore, to begin to support some sciences — or perhaps all — through international as well as national mechanisms? International sponsorship of science will not remove the danger of use of the resulting knowledge by individual nations, but it may serve to create a presumption that international means are appropriate to its control. Moreover, international sponsorship may help to reduce the fear of scientific or technological surprise because the same scientific information would be known to all. At a minimum, the existence of channels of communication and a habit of cooperation in a given field may make it easier to contemplate some kind of international agreement for the control of a dangerous technology that develops from the work in that field.

In principle, of course, suppression or retardation of

the applications of science in technology is much easier to accomplish. Such control is in effect exercised every day in R & D decisions in government and private industry, though rarely on the grounds that the technology is dangerous. Establishing confidence that a given technology is not being developed clandestinely in this or another country is another matter, determined by the nature of the technology, its potential usefulness in relation to its cost, the ability to detect such development, and the provisions of international control agreements if any exist. The limited test ban treaty is one of those rare examples of an international agreement that has the effect of retarding technological development by slowing R & D in weapons and at least impeding the development of certain kinds of weapons — nuclear weapons in this case — in signatory countries that do not have them. (It also has the ancillary effect of slowing the development of the peaceful technology of nuclear explosives.) The agreement at the United Nations not to station weapons of mass destruction in outer space, which both the United States and the U.S.S.R. supported, has somewhat similar effects with regard to outer space weapons systems.[3]

The history of the nuclear proliferation issues discussed in Chapter 2 demonstrates vividly the clash of a desire to control the spread of a dangerous technology with attempts to reap the peaceful and political benefits of the technology. Although considerable time

[3] "U.N. Resolution Against Orbiting of Nuclear Weapons," General Assembly Resolution #1884 (XVIII), Adopted Oct. 17, 1963. It should be noted that the willingness of both the United States and U.S.S.R. to support this resolution was heavily conditioned by the fact that they had little military interest in stationing nuclear weapons in outer space.

and attention, and some political capital, were devoted by this country to the development of bilateral and international mechanisms to prevent the diversion of fissionable material from peaceful to military uses by nonnuclear countries, these mechanisms remain weak and uncertain. The United States was so anxious to see the technology applied in useful ways and, for political purposes, applied with American help, that it conscientiously contributed to diffusion without according equal priority to the question of control. Now, even though this country has inaugurated more strenuous control measures, it is quite likely too late to stop a determined effort by any one of several nations to proceed with nuclear weapons development.

Without doubt, the world will face the question of control or suppression of technology increasingly in the future, perhaps with regard to developments even more frightening than nuclear weapons in their power to influence the global environment or human heredity. The issue deserves more concentrated attention and discussion if the history of nuclear proliferation is not to be repeated. And it may well be time to consider more seriously the internationalization of science support as a means of improving the prospects for control of dangerous technology.

THE DISAPPEARANCE OF TECHNICAL BARRIERS

An entirely different aspect of the scientific revolution is becoming more evident and more perplexing in its implications for international affairs. For the first time in history it is possible to say that the lack of technical knowledge is no longer a major barrier to solving man's material problems.

This does not mean that the physical knowledge is already in hand for all problems of agriculture, energy, exploitation of water and mineral resources, pollution, overpopulation, or any of the other problems that affect man's welfare. It does mean that man now has the tools to seek and find solutions to such problems and has already demonstrated in each category that solutions are possible.

The limitations on the development and application of technological solutions for material problems do not lie in science and technology. Rather, the limitations stem from the cost of the research; the scarcity of scientists and engineers; the cost, relative to other uses for scarce resources, of applying scientific knowledge; the cultural, social, and political barriers to new technology within a society; the political disinterest of the scientific "haves" for the "have-nots"; and the difficulty of making the essential judgments of priority because of the uncertainty of the benefits that will result from each choice.

Recognizing these and other limitations, however, still leaves the conviction that a situation in which science and technology can be applied successfully to solve almost any physical problem is a fundamentally new situation with potentially far-reaching implications. This has been recognized oratorically, perhaps, but too rarely in practice. Does this condition carry with it the imperative for the scientifically advanced nations to devote more of their scientific resources to the problems of mankind in other countries? Or, to remove the question from the moral plane, can science and technology more fully and successfully be harnessed to solve the physical problems that contribute to or are the causes of international tension?

There is a substantial amount of such direction of science and technology today. In particular, President Johnson has acted in the fields of health, education, and agriculture quite apparently from the conviction that more could be done on an international level in these fields through directed research and development. There is serious doubt, however, that the full significance of the new situation has been realized sufficiently so that public officials are prepared to tackle in strength the very real problems that are associated with attempting to direct large-scale scientific and technological resources to the improvement of man's physical condition.

SUMMATION

The continuing trend to technology with global effects, the need to face the question of control or suppression of technology, and the inherent promise lying in science and technology for the solution of man's material problems represent three general implications of the pace of scientific and technological advance that are creating a drastically changed environment for foreign affairs. To these must be added others, such as the gradual development — discussed in Chapter 7 — of a major scientific and technological gap between this country and others or the growing technical feasibility for an advanced nation to be completely self-sufficient in material resources.

These new trends and forces do more than simply alter the general environment within which policy must operate. They also raise questions about some of the cherished traditions of nationhood, about the assumptions associated with the present organization of the international political system, and about the principles and beliefs surrounding science and technology themselves. In an important sense it can be said that the underlying forces and relationships on which international politics rest have already been altered in basic ways from nineteenth-century concepts by the scientific revolution. Yet, foreign and domestic policies proceed about as always, with only sporadic recognition that control of territory has become an uncertain and ambiguous concept, that freedom of national action and inviolability of borders have long since lost so much of their traditional meaning, that the size of the resources of most nation-states are incommensurate with the requirements of modern technology, and that international organizations must fill a more important role than simply amplify big power goals.

And it must not be forgotten that the rapid advances of science and technology until now are but the prelude to even more rapid remaking of man's environment in the future. Technology will spread, will increase the dependence of one country on another, will create wholly new international relationships, will force new degrees of cooperation and dispute, will result in new threats to international stability, and will raise more problems of overpopulation and environmental pollution.

These developments cannot be predicted in detail, but neither are they impenetrable. Moreover, they are likely to force or call for additional, significant, and perhaps fundamental shifts in national attitudes toward both domestic and international affairs. Accordingly, a much greater effort is warranted in attempting to understand the nature of future developments and, most important, to understand their full meaning for international relations and for American foreign policy.

The preoccupation within the government with immediate issues is inevitable and makes it difficult to gain the attention of the most competent people for intensive study of underlying trends and likely future developments. Especially is it difficult when these trends and likely developments put in question traditional assumptions that are the basis for current policy. And it is made doubly hard when science and technology are directly involved and require the integration of sophisticated scientific and technological judgments with equally sophisticated judgments about international politics.

The difficulty of the task leads to only one conclusion: the need to understand the underlying and future significance of scientific and technological developments and their relation to basic patterns of international affairs warrants immediate attention.

Index

Acheson, Dean, 15, 224, 256
Act for International Development, 205
Advisory Group for Aeronautical R & D, 179
African Bureau, AID, 292
Agency for International Development, bureaucratic problems, 297; congressional problems, 296–297; foreign economic assistance, 187–207; international science programs, 51, 61; involvement of universities, 207; Latin American Science Board, 292, 296; motives for foreign aid, 185n; organization for integration of science and technology, 292–298; phasing out technical assistance, 297–298; program planning process, 294–295; relations with NAS/NRC, 292–293, 296; Research Advisory Committee, 206; research program, 201, 203–207, 297; Technical Cooperation and Research Office, 293–296; technical staffs in bureaus, 292; UNCSAT conference, 168–173

Agriculture Department, advisory study on science, 235; Argentine beef, 153–155; FAO, 162–163; FCST member, 245; PSAC review of research, 234; restricted to U.S.-related problems, 62; support of research in Europe, 56–57
Alliance for Progress, 234; Latin American Science Board, 292
Alteration in political forces and relationships due to science and technology, 315
American Association for the Advancement of Science, international ties, 76
American University, 57
Antiballistic missile systems, 107
Argentina, brain drain, 92; importation of beef, 153–154
Arms control and disarmament, effect on weapons systems design, 276; large-scale scientific experimentation, 89; policy making, 107–117; Pugwash, 143–147; role of international organizations, 164; scientists and arms policy, 109n

317